T0219866

Lecture Notes in Computer Science 11146

Commenced Publication in 1973
Founding and Former Series Editors:
Gerhard Goos, Juris Hartmanis, and Jan van Leeuwen

Editorial Board

David Hutchison
Lancaster University, Lancaster, UK
Takeo Kanade
Carnegie Mellon University, Pittsburgh, PA, USA
Josef Kittler
University of Surrey, Guildford, UK
Jon M. Kleinberg
Cornell University, Ithaca, NY, USA
Friedemann Mattern
ETH Zurich, Zurich, Switzerland
John C. Mitchell
Stanford University, Stanford, CA, USA
Moni Naor
Weizmann Institute of Science, Rehovot, Israel
C. Pandu Rangan
Indian Institute of Technology Madras, Chennai, India
Bernhard Steffen
TU Dortmund University, Dortmund, Germany
Demetri Terzopoulos
University of California, Los Angeles, CA, USA
Doug Tygar
University of California, Berkeley, CA, USA
Gerhard Weikum
Max Planck Institute for Informatics, Saarbrücken, Germany

More information about this series at http://www.springer.com/series/7408

Inmaculada Medina-Bulo · Mercedes G. Merayo
Robert Hierons (Eds.)

Testing Software and Systems

30th IFIP WG 6.1 International Conference, ICTSS 2018
Cádiz, Spain, October 1–3, 2018
Proceedings

Editors
Inmaculada Medina-Bulo
University of Cádiz
Cadiz, Spain

Robert Hierons
Brunel University London
Uxbridge, UK

Mercedes G. Merayo
Complutense University of Madrid
Madrid, Spain

ISSN 0302-9743 ISSN 1611-3349 (electronic)
Lecture Notes in Computer Science
ISBN 978-3-319-99926-5 ISBN 978-3-319-99927-2 (eBook)
https://doi.org/10.1007/978-3-319-99927-2

Library of Congress Control Number: 2018952568

LNCS Sublibrary: SL2 – Programming and Software Engineering

This Springer imprint is published by the registered company Springer Nature Switzerland AG
The registered company address is: Gewerbestrasse 11, 6330 Cham, Switzerland

Preface

This volume contains the proceedings of the 30th IFIP International Conference on Testing Software and Systems, ICTSS 2018. The conference was held in Cádiz, Spain, during October 1–3, 2018. The purpose of the ICTSS conference is to bring together researchers, developers, testers, and users from industry to review, discuss, and learn about new approaches, concepts, theories, methodologies, tools, and experiences in the field of testing of software and systems.

We received 29 submissions. After a careful reviewing process, the Program Committee accepted eight regular papers and six short papers. Therefore, the acceptance rate of the conference stayed close to 48%. The conference program was enriched by the keynote of Alexander Pretschner, on "Do We Care Enough About 'Good' Test Cases?"

Several people contributed to the success of ICTSS 2018. We are grateful to the Steering Committee for its support. We would like to thank the general chair, Francisco Palomo-Lozano, the Program Committee, and the additional reviewers, for their work in selecting the papers. The process of reviewing and selecting papers was significantly simplified through using EasyChair. Finally, the proceedings are published by Springer and we are grateful for the assistance provided by Alfred Hofmann and Anna Kramer.

On behalf of the ICTSS organizers, we hope that you find the proceedings useful, interesting, and challenging.

October 2018

Inmaculada Medina-Bulo
Mercedes G. Merayo
Robert Hierons

Organization

Program Committee

Rui Abreu	Universidade de Lisboa, Portugal
Bernhard K. Aichernig	TU Graz, Austria
Harald Altinger	Audi Electronics Venture GmbH, Germany
Gregor Bochmann	University of Ottawa, Canada
Mario Bravetti	University of Bologna, Italy
Ana Cavalli	Institut Mines-Telecom/Telecom SudParis, France
David Clark	University College London, UK
Pedro Delgado-Pérez	Universidad de Cádiz, Spain
Khaled El-Fakih	American University of Sharjah, UAE
Angelo Gargantini	University of Bergamo, Italy
Christophe Gaston	CEA, France
Arnaud Gotlieb	Simula Research Laboratory, Norway
Juergen Grossmann	Fraunhofer, Germany
Klaus Havelund	Jet Propulsion Laboratory, USA
Rob Hierons	Brunel University, UK
Teruo Higashino	Osaka University, Japan
Dieter Hogrefe	University of Göttingen, Germany
Jie-Hong Roland Jiang	National Taiwan University, Taiwan
Thierry Jéron	Inria, France
Ferhat Khendek	Concordia University, Canada
Moez Krichen	REDCAD Research Unit, Tunisia
Natalia Kushik	Tomsk State University, Russia
Pascale Le Gall	CentraleSupelec, France
Luis Llana	Universidad Complutense de Madrid, Spain
Radu Mateescu	Inria, France
Inmaculada Medina-Bulo	University of Cadiz, Spain
Mercedes Merayo	Universidad Complutense de Madrid, Spain
Edgardo Montes de Oca	Montimage, France
Manuel Núñez	Universidad Complutense de Madrid, Spain
Mike Papadakis	University of Luxembourg, Luxembourg
Jan Peleska	TZI, Universitat Bremen, Germany
Alexandre Petrenko	CRIM, Canada
Antoine Rollet	LaBRI, Bordeaux INP, University of Bordeaux, CNRS, France
Sébastien Salva	limos, Université de Clermont-Ferrand, France
Sergio Segura	University of Seville, Spain
Hasan Sozer	Ozyegin University, Turkey
Daniel Sundmark	Mälardalen University, Sweden

Kenji Suzuki	Kennisbron Co., Ltd., Japan
Masaki Suzuki	KDDI Research, Inc., Japan
Andreas Ulrich	Siemens AG, Germany
Hasan Ural	University of Ottawa, Canada
Tiziano Villa	Università di Verona, Italy
Burkhart Wolff	Université Paris-Sud, France
Hüsnü Yenigün	Sabanci University, Turkey
Nina Yevtushenko	Tomsk State University, Russia
Fang Yu	National Chengchi University, Taiwan

Additional Reviewers

Avellaneda, Florent
Carvallo, Pamela
Demiroz, Gulsen
Lopez, Jorge
Nguena Timo, Omer
Nguyen, Huu Nghia
Salva, Regainia

Do We Care Enough About "Good" Test Cases? (Invited Talk)

Alexander Pretschner

Technische Universität München, Germany

What is a good test case? While test automation certainly is a necessity, I believe that this question really is at the core of what we struggle with when testing systems. Structural and random tests have undoubted merits and, good news for academics, lend themselves to automating the generation of tests. Yet, are these really the tests we want to rely on when testing, say, advanced driver assistance systems? In this talk, I will revisit the idea of defect-based testing, argue why only tests based on defect hypotheses can be "good", and present a framework and several examples of how to render defect hypotheses operational.

Contents

Interactive Testing and Repairing of Regular Expressions. 1
   Paolo Arcaini, Angelo Gargantini, and Elvinia Riccobene

Validation of Transformation from Abstract State Machine Models
to C++ Code 17
   Silvia Bonfanti, Angelo Gargantini, and Atif Mashkoor

Security Testing for Chatbots 33
   Josip Bozic and Franz Wotawa

JMCTEST: Automatically Testing Inter-Method Contracts in Java 39
   Paul Börding, Jan Haltermann, Marie-Christine Jakobs,
   and Heike Wehrheim

Testing Ambient Assisted Living Solutions with Simulations 56
   Marlon Cárdenas, Jorge Gómez Sanz, and Juan Pavón

Generating OCL Constraints from Test Case Schemas For Testing
Model Behavior 62
   Nisha Desai and Martin Gogolla

Test Derivation for SDN-Enabled Switches: A Logic Circuit
Based Approach 69
   Jorge López, Natalia Kushik, Asma Berriri, Nina Yevtushenko,
   and Djamal Zeghlache

An Energy Aware Testing Framework for Smart-Spaces 85
   Teruhiro Mizumoto, Khaled El-Fakih, Keiichi Yasumoto,
   and Teruo Higashino

C++11/14 Mutation Operators Based on Common Fault Patterns 102
   Ali Parsai, Serge Demeyer, and Seph De Busser

Conformance Testing and Inference of Embedded Components. 119
   Alexandre Petrenko and Florent Avellaneda

Neural Networks as Artificial Specifications 135
   I. S. Wishnu B. Prasetya and Minh An Tran

Combining Model Learning and Data Analysis to Generate Models
of Component-Based Systems. 142
   Sébastien Salva, Elliott Blot, and Patrice Laurencot

Deriving Tests with Guaranteed Fault Coverage for Finite State Machines
with Timeouts   149
    Aleksandr Tvardovskii, Khaled El-Fakih, and Nina Yevtushenko

From Ontologies to Input Models for Combinatorial Testing   155
    Franz Wotawa and Yihao Li

Author Index   171

Interactive Testing and Repairing of Regular Expressions

Paolo Arcaini[1]([⊠]) [ID], Angelo Gargantini[2] [ID], and Elvinia Riccobene[3] [ID]

[1] National Institute of Informatics, Tokyo, Japan
arcaini@nii.ac.jp
[2] University of Bergamo, Bergamo, Italy
angelo.gargantini@unibg.it
[3] Dipartimento di Informatica, Università degli Studi di Milano, Milan, Italy
elvinia.riccobene@unimi.it

Abstract. Writing a regular expression that exactly captures a set of desired strings is difficult, since regular expressions provide a compact syntax that makes it difficult to easily understand their meaning. Testing is widely used to validate regular expressions. Indeed, although a developer could have problems in writing the correct regular expression, (s)he can easily assess whether a string should be accepted or not. Starting from this observation, we propose an iterative mutation-based process that is able to *test* and *repair* a faulty regular expression. The approach consists in generating strings S that *distinguish* a regular expression r from its mutants, asking the user to assess the correct evaluation of S, and possibly substituting r with a mutant r' that evaluates S more correctly than r; we propose four variants of the approach which differ in the policy they employ to judge whether r' is better than r. Experiments show that the proposed approach is able to actually repair faulty regular expressions with a reasonable user's effort.

1 Introduction

Regular expressions (*regexp*) are used in different contexts [4] (e.g., MySQL injection prevention, DNA sequencing alignment, etc.) to validate data, perform lexical analysis, or do string matching in texts. A regexp characterizes a set of strings (i.e., a *language*). Several studies [6,12] show that regexps often contain *conformance faults*, i.e., they do not exactly describe the intended language: they either accept strings that should be refused, or refuse strings that should be accepted, or both. Indeed, specifying a *correct* regexp is usually difficult, since regexps provide a compact syntax that makes the understanding of their exact meaning difficult.

P. Arcaini—The author is supported by ERATO HASUO Metamathematics for Systems Design Project (No. JPMJER1603), JST. Funding Reference number: 10.13039/501100009024 ERATO.

I. Medina-Bulo et al. (Eds.): ICTSS 2018, LNCS 11146, pp. 1–16, 2018.
https://doi.org/10.1007/978-3-319-99927-2_1

Due to their tolerant syntax, most regexps are free of syntax errors and it is unlikely to find conformance faults by syntax checking or static analysis [12]. For this reason, the most used form of regexp validation is *testing*, i.e., generating a set of strings S and comparing the behavior of the regexp under test r over S w.r.t. an oracle. Often, the oracle is the tester, who has to check whether r correctly evaluates the strings in S. A common assumption done by many validation and testing techniques is that for a human evaluating if a given string should belong to the desired language $\mathcal{L}$ is much easier than writing the regexp that characterizes $\mathcal{L}$. Based on this assumption, several programs and web services allow to validate regexps by generating a set of strings [6] or allowing the user to enter strings and check whether they are correctly rejected or accepted by the regexp under test. However, two issues arise: (i) As checking all possible strings is not feasible, which strings are more critical to validate a regexp? (ii) Once a wrongly evaluated string is found, can a *repair* be suggested to the user?

In this paper, we address both issues. We start with the assumption that syntactical faults usually done by developers are those described by a set of fault classes identified in literature [2]. Based on this assumption, we can restrict the testing activity to the strings able to distinguish a regexp from its mutants, i.e., the strings demonstrating the presence of particular syntactic faults. Regarding what to do when a fault has been discovered (i.e., a string s which is rejected but it should be accepted or vice versa), we propose to repair the regexp under test by substituting it with its mutant which instead correctly evaluates s.

We devised an iterative process which starts with a developer who has written a regexp r and (s)he wants to check if r is *correct*, i.e., if it correctly evaluates the intended language. Then, the process proceeds through a sequence of steps in which each iteration consists in: (i) generating some mutants of the regexp r under test, (ii) computing a set S of *distinguishing strings* that permit to distinguish r from its mutants, (iii) checking the *quality* of the mutated regexps and the original regexp over S by asking the user to assess the correctness of the strings evaluation, (iv) and choosing the *best* regexp r' (i.e., the one evaluating correctly the majority of generated strings), and updating r with r'. The process iterates until no r' better than r is found. We propose four versions of the previous general process. The *greedy* one changes the regexp as soon as it finds a better candidate among the mutants. The *multiDSs* mitigates the greediness by evaluating several strings before changing the candidate. The *breadth* approach, before changing the candidate, evaluates all the mutants. The *collecting* approach aims at distinguishing multiple mutants at the same time. Experiments show that the approach is able to repair 85% of faulty regexps; on average, the user must evaluate around 40 strings and the whole process (also considering the user's effort) lasts, at most, 4.5 min.

Paper Structure. Section 2 gives background on regexps and mutation operators for them. Section 3 introduces the notions of conformance and mutation fault. Section 4 presents our approach for repairing a (possibly faulty) regexp. Section 5 describes the experiments we performed, Sect. 6 reviews related work, and Sect. 7 concludes the paper.

2   Background

In our context, regular expressions are intended as valid regular expressions from formal automata theory, i.e., only regular expressions that describe regular languages. The proposed approach is indeed based on the use of the finite automata accepting the language described by the regular expressions.

Definition 1 (Regular expression). *A regular expression (*regexp*) r is a sequence of* constants, *defined over an alphabet Σ, and* operator *symbols. The regexp r accepts a set of* words $\mathcal{L}(r) \subseteq \Sigma^*$ *(i.e., a language).*

We also use r as predicate: $r(s) = true$ if $s \in \mathcal{L}(r)$, and $r(s) = false$ otherwise.

As Σ we support the Unicode alphabet (UTF-16); the supported operators are union, intersection, concatenation, complement, character class, character range, and wildcards.

Normally, acceptance is computed by converting r into an automaton $\mathcal{R}$, and then checking whether $\mathcal{R}$ accepts the string. In this paper, we use the library dk.brics.automaton[1] to transform a regexp r into an automaton $\mathcal{R}$ (by means of function toAutomaton(r)) and perform standard operations (complement, intersection, and union) on it. Moreover, we use the operator pickAword($\mathcal{R}$) that returns a string s accepted by $\mathcal{R}$, i.e., $s \in \mathcal{L}(\mathcal{R})$.

For our purposes, we give the notion of a string distinguishing two languages.

Definition 2 (Distinguishing string). *Given two languages $\mathcal{L}_1$ and $\mathcal{L}_2$, we say that a string s is* distinguishing *if it is a word of the symmetric difference $\mathcal{L}_1 \oplus \mathcal{L}_2 = \mathcal{L}_1 \setminus \mathcal{L}_2 \cup \mathcal{L}_2 \setminus \mathcal{L}_1$ between $\mathcal{L}_1$ and $\mathcal{L}_2$.*

Fault Classes and Mutation Operators. Our approach is based on the idea that conformance faults (see Definition 4) can be discovered by means of mutation analysis. In mutation analysis for regexps, a *fault class* represents a possible kind of mistake done by a developer when writing a regexp; a *mutation operator* for a fault class is a function that given a regexp r, returns a list of regexps (called *mutants*) obtained by mutating r (possibly removing the fault); a mutation *slightly* modifies the regexp r under the assumption that the programmer has defined r close to the correct version (competent programmer hypothesis [10]).

We use the fault classes and the related mutation operators proposed in [2]. In the following, given a regexp r, we identify with mut(r) its set of mutants.

3   Conformance Faults and Mutation Faults

In this section, we describe how to compare the language characterized by a developed regexp with the intended language. Given a regexp r, we suppose to have a reference *oracle* that represents the intended meaning of r. Formally:

---

[1] http://www.brics.dk/automaton/.

Definition 3 (Oracle). *An oracle o_r is a predicate saying whether a string must be accepted or not by a regexp r, i.e., $o_r(s) = true$ if s must be accepted by a correct regexp. We identify with $\mathcal{L}(o_r)$ the set of strings accepted by o_r.*

The oracle (a program or a human) can be queried and it must say whether a string belongs to $\mathcal{L}(o_r)$ or not, i.e., whether it must be rejected or accepted by r. Usually, the oracle is the developer who can correctly assess whether a string should be accepted or not (but (s)he may be not able to correctly write the correct regexp). A correct regexp is indistinguishable from its oracle (i.e., they share the same language) while a faulty one wrongly accepts or rejects some strings. We here define such strings.

Definition 4 (Conformance Fault). *A regexp r (supposed to behave as specified by o_r) contains a* conformance fault *if*

$$\exists s \in \Sigma^* \colon distStr(s, r, o_r)$$

where $distStr(s, r, o_r)$ indicates that s is a distinguishing string between the languages of r and o_r, i.e., $s \in \mathcal{L}(r) \wedge s \notin \mathcal{L}(o_r)$ or $s \notin \mathcal{L}(r) \wedge s \in \mathcal{L}(o_r)$. We name the first case as inclusion fault, *and the second case as* exclusion fault.

A fault shows that the user specified the regexp wrongly, possibly misunderstanding the semantics of the regexp notation. Finding all conformance faults would require to compute $\mathcal{L}(r) \oplus \mathcal{L}(o_r)$; however, we do not know $\mathcal{L}(o_r)$ in advance, and we can only invoke the oracle o_r to check whether a string belongs to $\mathcal{L}(o_r)$ or not. Therefore, proving the absence of conformance faults in r would require to evaluate, for all the strings $s \in \Sigma^*$, $distStr(s, r, o_r)$ by checking whether s belongs to $\mathcal{L}(r)$ and not to $\mathcal{L}(o_r)$, or vice versa. Such exhaustive testing is infeasible and so we aim at finding a subset of strings of Σ^* that are more likely faulty. Following a fault-based approach, we claim that the syntactic faults that are more likely done by developers are those described by the fault classes we introduced in [2]. If such assumption holds, most conformance faults should be those strings that are evaluated differently by the regexp and its mutants. For this reason, we introduce a stronger type of fault defined in terms of mutations.

Definition 5 (Mutation Fault). *A regexp r (that is supposed to behave as specified by o_r) contains a* mutation fault *if*

$$\exists r' \in \mathtt{mut}(r), \exists s \in (\mathcal{L}(r) \oplus \mathcal{L}(r')) \colon distStr(s, r, o_r)$$

We call (r',s) failure couple.

A regexp r contains a mutation fault if, given a mutant r', a distinguishing string s between r and r' shows that r is faulty. To find a mutation fault, we do not need to consider all the strings in Σ^*, since we know how to compute $\mathcal{L}(r) \oplus \mathcal{L}(r')$. Targeting mutation faults is beneficial thanks to this theorem.

Theorem 1. *Given a regexp r, if it contains a mutation fault with failure couple (r',s), then $\neg distStr(s, r', o_r)$, i.e., r' correctly evaluates s.*

Algorithm 1. Meta-algorithm for testing and repairing regular expressions

---

Require: r: initial regexp, o_r: oracle
Ensure: *result*: r' repaired regexp
1: $A \leftarrow \emptyset \quad R \leftarrow \emptyset$ ▷ strings **A**ccepted and **R**ejected by the oracle
2: **loop**
3:    $muts \leftarrow \mathtt{mutate}(r)$
4:    $r' \leftarrow \textsc{TestAndRep}(r, o_r, muts, A, R)$
5:    **if** $r \neq r'$ **then** $r \leftarrow r'$
6:    **else return** r'
7:    **end if**
8: **end loop**

Proof. Let us assume that $s \in \mathcal{L}(r) \oplus \mathcal{L}(r')$ and it is distinguishing w.r.t. the oracle, i.e., $distStr(s, r, o_r)$. This also means $s \in \mathcal{L}(r) \oplus \mathcal{L}(o_r)$. We can identify two cases. (1) s is accepted by r, i.e., $s \in \mathcal{L}(r)$, then s is rejected by both r' and o_r. (2) s is rejected by r, i.e., $s \notin \mathcal{L}(r)$, then s is accepted by both r' and o_r. In both cases, s is equally evaluated by r' and o_r, so $s \notin \mathcal{L}(r') \oplus \mathcal{L}(o_r)$.   □

Theorem 1 is central in our approach that combines testing and repairing: if we *test* a regexp r with strings distinguishing r from one of its mutants r' (instead of other strings, like random ones), then in case of failure (the test distinguishes r from its oracle) we also know how to *repair* r to remove that particular fault, by taking r' as new regexp. However, note that r' may still contain other faults.

4 Testing and Repairing Regular Expressions

Our repairing approach exploits Theorem 1 in order to test and repair a regexp in an interactive way. It is based on the assumption that the mistakes done by a developer are those described by the fault classes proposed in [2]. However, if we showed to the developer a mutated regexp, (s)he could still have problems in understanding whether that is the correct regexp. On the other hand, if we showed her/him a string s, (s)he would have no difficulty in assessing the correct evaluation. We therefore propose an approach that generates strings distinguishing a regexp r from its mutants and that selects one of the mutants in case of mutation fault. The approach is formalized by the meta-algorithm presented in Algorithm 1. The algorithm takes in input the regexp r we want to repair, and an oracle o_r (usually the oracle is the user able to assess the correct evaluation of all the strings). Two sets A and R are created for memorizing the strings that are known to be accepted and rejected by the oracle. Then, the following instructions are repeatedly executed:

- r is mutated with the operators defined in [2] (mutants are stored in *muts*);
- function TESTANDREP checks whether in *muts* there exists a regexp r' *better* than r, asking the user to evaluate some distinguishing strings;
- if a better regexp is found, the process is iterated again using r' as new regexp under test (line 5), otherwise r' is returned as final regexp (line 6).

Algorithm 2. TESTANDREP – Greedy approach

1: **function** TESTANDREP(r, o_r, $muts$, A, R)

2:   **for all** $m \in muts$ **do**

3:     $(ds, oEv) \leftarrow$ EvMUT($m, r, o_r, muts, A, R$)

4:     **if** $ds \neq null \wedge m(ds) = oEv$ **then**

5:       **return** m

6:     **end if**

7:   **end for**

8:   **return** r

9: **end function**

10: **function** EvMUT(m, r, o_r, $muts$, A, R)

11:   **if** $(\exists s \in A\colon s \notin \mathcal{L}(m)) \vee (\exists s \in R\colon s \in \mathcal{L}(m))$ **then return** $(null, null)$

12:   **end if**

13:   $ds \leftarrow$ genDs(r, m)

14:   **if** $ds = null$ **then return** $(null, null)$

15:   **end if**

16:   $oEv \leftarrow o_r(ds)$

17:   MARKDS(ds, oEv, A, R)

18:   **return** (ds, oEv)

19: **end function**

20: **procedure** MARKDS(ds, oEv, A, R)

21:   **if** oEv **then** $A \leftarrow A \cup \{ds\}$

22:   **else** $R \leftarrow R \cup \{ds\}$

23:   **end if**

24: **end procedure**

We identify four possible ways to select the new repaired regexp (function TESTANDREP), described in the following sections. Note that Algorithm 1 does not guarantee to always terminate with any approach and, in any case, it could iterate through several regexps (asking the user to evaluate several distinguishing strings) before terminating. For this reason, the user should specify a maximum number of evaluations *MaxEval*, after which the process is interrupted[2].

4.1 Greedy Approach

Algorithm 2 shows the greedy version of TESTANDREP. The function, for each mutant m in *muts*, performs the following instructions:

- m is evaluated by function EvMUT (line 3), working as follows:
  - if m evaluates wrongly a string in A or R, it returns ($null$, $null$), meaning that m must not be considered (line 11);
  - it generates a distinguishing string ds between r and m, using function genDs (line 13); see [2] for the implementation of genDs;
  - if no string is generated, r and m are equivalent; in this case, it returns ($null$, $null$), meaning that m must not be considered (line 14);
  - if a ds is generated, it stores the oracle evaluation of ds in oEv (line 16);
  - depending on the oracle evaluation, it adds ds either to A or R, using procedure MARKDS (line 17);
  - it returns the ds and its evaluation oEv (line 18);
- if a ds is returned, it checks whether the mutant m and the oracle assess the validity of ds in the same way (line 4). If this is the case, a mutation fault in r has been found, and m is returned as the new repaired regexp (line 5).

If no better mutant is found, r is returned (line 8). The approach guarantees to return a regexp that correctly accepts all strings in A and refuses those in R, while each of its mutants wrongly evaluates at least one of these strings.

---

[2] For the sake of simplicity, MaxEval is not shown in Algorithms 2, 3, 4, and 5.

Algorithm 3. TESTANDREP – `MultiDSs` approach (diff w.r.t. Alg. 2)

Require: N: number of strings to generate	12: ...
2: ...	13: $DSs \leftarrow$ genDs(r, m, N)
3: $DSsEvs \leftarrow$ EvMuT$(m, r, o_r, muts, A, R)$	14: **if** $DSs = \emptyset$ **then return** $\emptyset$
4: $numOK \leftarrow |\{(ds, oEv) \in DSsEvs : m(ds) = oEv\}|$	15: **end if**
5: $numNO \leftarrow |\{(ds, oEv) \in DSsEvs : r(ds) = oEv\}|$	16: $DSsEvs \leftarrow \emptyset$
6: **if** $numOK > numNO$ **then**	17: **for all** $ds \in DSs$ **do**
7: **return** m	18: $oEv \leftarrow o_r(ds)$
8: **end if**	19: $DSsEvs \leftarrow DSsEvs \cup \{(ds, oEv)\}$
9: ...	20: MARKDs(ds, oEv, A, R)
	21: **end for**
	22: **return** $DSsEvs$

4.2   MultiDSs Approach

The greedy approach returns the mutant m (line 5 of Algorithm 2) as new repaired regexp if it evaluates the generated string as the oracle. However, m may be distinguished by other strings and, so, changing the regexp could be a *too greedy* choice. To mitigate this problem, the `MultiDSs` approach (see Algorithm 3) generates N distinguishing strings (with $N \geq 2$) at line 13 (difference w.r.t. line 13 of Algorithm 2) and, at lines 6–7, takes m as the new repaired regexp only if it evaluates correctly more strings than r (difference w.r.t. lines 4–5 in Algorithm 2).

4.3   Breadth Approach

The approach in Sect. 4.1 and its extension in Sect. 4.2 are both greedy as they change the regexp under test as soon as a better regexp is found (it correctly evaluates the majority of generated strings). We here present a less greedy approach; Algorithm 4 shows the breadth search version of TESTANDREP. The algorithm evaluates all the mutants of a regexp under test and selects the *best* one (by function BESTCAND). If a better regexp is found, it is returned, otherwise r is returned.

In TESTANDREP, after the generation of the ds by EvMuT (line 4), if the mutant m correctly evaluates ds, it is stored in a set of possible candidates *cands* (line 6). Then, all the previously generated candidates that do not correctly evaluate ds are removed from *cands* (line 8). When all the mutants have been evaluated, if there is no candidate, then the algorithm terminates and r is returned as final regexp (line 10). Otherwise, a candidate is selected by function BESTCAND as follows. As long as there is more than one candidate:

- two candidates c_1 and c_2 are randomly selected (line 18);
- a ds is generated for c_1 and c_2 (line 19);
- if ds is *null* (i.e., c_1 and c_2 are equivalent), c_1 is removed from *cands* (line 25); otherwise, the following instructions are executed;
- the candidates not evaluating ds correctly are removed from *cands* (line 22);
- ds is added either to A or R using procedure MARKDs (line 23).

Algorithm 4. TESTANDREP – Breadth approach

1: **function** TESTANDREP(r, o_r, $muts$, A, R)	16: **function** BESTCAND($cands$, A, R)
2: $cands \leftarrow \emptyset$	17: **while** $\lvert cands \rvert > 1$ **do**
3: **for all** $m \in muts$ **do**	18: $(c_1,c_2) \leftarrow$ pick2Cands($cands$)
4: $(ds, oEv) \leftarrow$ EVMUT($m,r,o_r,muts,A,R$)	19: $ds \leftarrow$ genDs(c_1, c_2)
5: **if** $ds \neq null \wedge m(ds) = oEv$ **then**	20: **if** $ds \neq null$ **then**
6: $cands \leftarrow cands \cup \{m\}$	21: $oEv \leftarrow o_r(ds)$
7: **end if**	22: $cands \leftarrow \{c \in cands \mid c(ds)=oEv\}$
8: $cands \leftarrow \{c \in cands \mid c(ds) = oEv\}$	23: MARKDS(ds, oEv, A, R)
9: **end for**	24: **else**
10: **if** $\lvert cands \rvert = 0$ **then return** r	25: $cands \leftarrow cands \setminus \{c_1\}$
11: **else**	26: **end if**
12: **return** BESTCAND($cands$, A, R)	27: **end while**
13: **end if**	28: **return** $cands[0]$
14: **end function**	29: **end function**

At the end of the while loop, the only survived candidate (it is guaranteed to exist) is selected as best candidate and returned as new repaired regexp (line 28).

4.4   Collecting Approach

The previous approaches always generate a string ds for distinguishing a regexp r from one of its mutants m; often ds does not distinguish r from other mutants and other strings must be generated for distinguishing them, so requiring more effort from the user who must evaluate more strings. The aim of the collecting approach is to generate strings that distinguish as many mutants as possible. A string ds distinguishes r from a set of mutants $M = \{m_1, \ldots, m_n\}$ if ds is accepted by r and not accepted by any mutant in M, or if ds is not accepted by r and accepted by all the mutants in M; the distinguishing string is a word of one of these two automata:

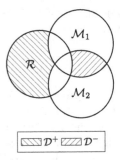

Fig. 1. Distinguishing automata

$$\mathcal{D}^+ = \mathcal{R} \cap \bigcap_{i=1}^{n} \mathcal{M}_i^{\complement} \qquad \mathcal{D}^- = \mathcal{R}^{\complement} \cap \bigcap_{i=1}^{n} \mathcal{M}_i$$

being $\mathcal{R}$, $\mathcal{M}_1$, ..., $\mathcal{M}_n$ the automata of r, m_1, ..., m_n. We name $\mathcal{D}^+$ and $\mathcal{D}^-$ as *positive* and *negative distinguishing automata*. Figure 1 shows a positive and a negative distinguishing automaton for two mutants m_1 and m_2 of a regexp r[3].

Algorithm 5 shows the collecting approach that exploits the definition of distinguishing automaton. It initially selects all the mutants $muts$ as candidates in $cands$ (line 2). Then, it performs the following actions as long as $cands$ contains at least one regexp:

---

[3] In this case, they can be collected both in a positive and negative automaton; in some cases, only one kind of automaton is suitable for collecting them, or also none.

Algorithm 5. TESTANDREP – Collecting approach

Require: *CollTh*: collection limit	17: **function** COLLECT(r, *cands*)
1: **function** TESTANDREP(r, o_r,	18: $\mathcal{R} \leftarrow$ toAutomaton(r)
muts, A, R)	19: **for** $\mathcal{D} \in \{\mathcal{R}, \mathcal{R}^{\complement}\}$ **do**
2: *cands* $\leftarrow$ *muts*	20: **for** $m \in$ *cands* **do**
3: **while** $\lvert cands \rvert > 0$ **do**	21: $\mathcal{M} \leftarrow$ toAutomaton(m)
4: $\mathcal{D} \leftarrow$ COLLECT(r, *cands*)	22: **if** $isPos(\mathcal{D})$ **then** $\mathcal{D}' \leftarrow \mathcal{D} \cap \mathcal{M}^{\complement}$
5: **if** $\mathcal{D} = \emptyset$ **then**	23: **else** $\mathcal{D}' \leftarrow \mathcal{D} \cap \mathcal{M}$
6: **return** r	24: **end if**
7: **end if**	25: **if** $\mathcal{D}' \neq \emptyset$ **then**
8: $ds \leftarrow$ pickAword($\mathcal{D}$)	26: $\mathcal{D} \leftarrow \mathcal{D}'$
9: $oEv \leftarrow o(ds)$	27: **if** numColl($\mathcal{D}$) $= CollTh$ **then return** $\mathcal{D}$
10: *cands* $\leftarrow$	28: **end if**
$\{m \in cands \lvert m(ds) = oEv\}$	29: **end if**
11: **if** $oEv \neq r(ds)$ **then**	30: **end for**
12: $r \leftarrow$ pickAregexp($\mathcal{D}$)	31: **if** $\mathcal{D} \neq \emptyset$ **then return** $\mathcal{D}$
13: **end if**	32: **end if**
14: **end while**	33: **end for**
15: **return** r	34: **return** $\emptyset$
16: **end function**	35: **end function**

- it collects as many regexp as possible using function COLLECT:
  - it randomly initializes a positive or a negative distinguishing automaton $\mathcal{D}$ (line 19);
  - for each mutant m, it tries to add it to $\mathcal{D}$ considering the polarity (lines 21–23); $\mathcal{D}$ is modified only if the addition does not produce an empty automaton (lines 25–26); if the addition has been performed and *CollTh* regexps have been collected (being *CollTh* a parameter of the approach), it returns $\mathcal{D}$ (line 27).
  - if after trying all the candidates, at least one regexp has been collected, it returns $\mathcal{D}$ (line 31); otherwise, it tries the distinguishing automaton with the opposite polarity (if any);
  - if no regexp can be collected in any distinguishing automaton of any polarity, the empty automaton is returned (line 34).
- if the returned automaton $\mathcal{D}$ is empty (meaning that all the candidates are equivalent to r), r is returned as selected regexp (line 6); otherwise, a word is randomly selected from $\mathcal{D}$ (line 8) and *cands* is updated with only the regexps that evaluate ds correctly (lines 9–10);
- if r does not evaluate ds correctly, it is changed with one mutant randomly selected among those collected in $\mathcal{D}$ (lines 11–12).

When there are no more candidates, r is returned as selected regexp (line 15).

TearRex. We implemented the approach in the tool TEARREX (TEst And Repair Regular EXpressions)[4]. Figure 2 shows an interaction with the tool. At the beginning, the user inserts the regexp [a-z]* for accepting all the strings

---

[4] The tool and all benchmarks are available at http://foselab.unibg.it/tearrex/.

1	Insert regexp: [a-z]*
2	Do you accept "a"? Y for yes, N for no **Y**
3	Do you accept "A"? Y for yes, N for no **Y**
4	The mutant is the new regexp: [A−z]*
5	Do you accept "0"? Y for yes, N for no **N**

6	Do you accept "z"? Y for yes, N for no **Y**
7	Do you accept "AA"? Y for yes, N for no **Y**
8	Do you accept ""? Y for yes, N for no **N**
9	The mutant is the new regexp: [A−z]+
10	The mutant is the final regexp: [A−z]+

Fig. 2. TEARREX– Testing and repairing of [a-z]* with oracle [a-zA-Z]+

containing only Latin letters; however, since (s)he misunderstood the semantics of operator * and of character classes, the developed regexp also accepts the empty string and does not accept upper-case Latin letters. The tool asks her/him to evaluate two strings, "a" and "A", and (s)he assesses that both strings should be accepted. Since the developed regexp does not accept "A", the tool modifies the regexp in [A-z]* that also accepts "A". The process continues by evaluating strings "0", "z", and "AA", that are all correctly evaluated. The empty string "", instead, is wrongly evaluated and the tool changes the regexp in the more correct version [A-z]+ that does not accept it. Since no possible mutation fault exists between [A-z]+ and its mutants, it is returned as final regexp.

5 Experiments

Websites http://www.regular-expressions.info/ and http://www.regexlib.com report, for different matching tasks (e.g., email addresses, credit cards, social security numbers, etc.), some regexps implementing them. To build the benchmark set `Bench`, we considered⋅20 tasks and, for each task, we selected two regexps, one acting as initial (possibly faulty) regexp and the other one as oracle; for 19 couples the initial regexp is indeed faulty, while in one couple the initial regexp is correct[5]. The initial regexps are between 17 and 279 chars long (60 on average) and have between 7 and 112 operators (24.45 on average).

Note that, in our approach, the oracle should be the user able to assess the evaluation of strings; in the experiments, we use another regexp as oracle for the sake of automation. However, in RQ2 we estimate which is the burden required to the user in evaluating the generated strings during the repair process.

We run the approaches `Greedy`, `MultiDSs3` (MultiDSs with $N = 3$), `Breadth`, and `Coll5` (collecting with *CollTh* = 5) on the selected regexps and fixing the maximum number of evaluations MaxEval to 10, 30, 100, and 200 strings.

Experiments have been executed on a Linux machine, Intel(R) Core(TM) i7, 4 GB RAM. All the reported data are the averages of 10 runs of the experiments.

Tables 1a and b report experimental results aggregated by type of repair *process* and maximum number of evaluations *MaxEval*. They both report the average number of strings generated and shown to the user for *evaluation* E, the average process *time* T, the percentage R of regexps that have been *repaired* (i.e., the final regexp has lower failure index than the initial one), and the percentage

---

[5] Note that the process guarantees to not worsen correct regexps; we introduced this correct regexp to double-check that this is indeed the case.

Table 1. Experiment results for `Bench` (E: avg # evaluations, T: avg time (secs), R: repaired (%), CR: completely repaired (%), R′: avg # r')

Process	E	R′	T	R	CR
`Greedy`	47.82	19.60	0.50	77.5	3.75
`MultiDSs3`	53.39	7.63	1.04	72.5	2.92
`Breadth`	41.41	3.33	1.74	85.0	3.75
`Coll5`	42.27	4.57	2.79	76.67	4.58

(a) Process type results

MaxEval	E	T	R	CR
10	9.95	0.29	76.67	0.42
30	27.55	0.57	75.83	3.75
100	61.6	2.21	78.75	4.58
200	85.44	2.99	80.42	6.25

(b) MaxEval results

CR of regexps that have been *completely repaired* (i.e., all the faults have been removed). Table 1a also reports the average number R′ of regexps r' that are changed during the process. The cells in gray highlight the best results. We evaluate our approach with a series of research questions.

RQ1. How many distinguishing strings are generated?

Since the correct evaluation of the generated strings must be assessed by the user, we want to keep their number low. Table 1a (column E) shows that the four approaches generate, on average, between 41 and 53 strings; the limited number of strings allows the manual evaluation by the user. `MultiDSs3` generates more strings than `Greedy` as three strings are generated for each mutant (if possible). `Breadth` generates slightly fewer strings than `Greedy` because, on average, the third changed regexp is the final expression (see column R′); `Greedy` changes on average 20 regexps, so producing more strings. `Coll5` also produces few strings, as it directly generates strings for set of mutants.

Table 1b (column E) shows that a higher maximum number of evaluations allows to generate more strings. However, with MaxEval equal to 10 and 30, the number of generated strings is close to MaxEval itself, while with MaxEval equal to 100 and 200 the number of strings is much lower than the limit: this means that, on average, the process requires less than 100 strings to terminate.

RQ2. How long does the repair process take and how much is the estimated user's effort?

Table 1a (column T) shows that `MultiDSs3` is twice slower than `Greedy`, as it generates more strings. `Breadth` is more than three times slower than `Greedy`; a possible reason is that although `Greedy` generates more strings than `Breadth`, it creates much fewer mutants (that is a costly operation). `Coll5` is the slowest one, as automata intersection (see lines 22 and 23 in Algorithm 5) is a costly operation. Table 1b shows that increasing the limit of evaluated strings also increments the time (as the process can continue the search).

All the experiments show that, regardless of the process configuration, the process is rather fast. However, the final time should be computed as $pTime + |A \cup R| \times eTime$, being $pTime$ the time of the generation and repair process (the one we measured), and *eTime* the time taken by a user to evaluate a string[6]. For example, considering 5 s per string as *eTime*, the average times would be: 4 min for `Greedy`, 4.5 min for `MultiDSs3`, 3.5 min for `Breadth`, and 3.6 min for `Col15`. This means that the whole process involving the user's evaluations is feasible. Note that `Greedy` and `MultiDSs3` would be equivalent from the time point of view (break-even) to `Breadth` and `Col15` if the user could evaluate the strings in less than 0.2 s, which seems impossible; so, `Breadth` and `Col15` are always advantageous in terms of time if the user's effort is taken into account.

RQ3. Is the proposed process able to repair regular expressions?

We are here interested in assessing whether the proposed approach is actually able to repair faulty regexps. We are able to assess whether a starting regexp r has been completely repaired by checking the equivalence between the final regexp r' and the oracle o_r. For not completely repaired regexps, we introduce the measure F_x counting the number of strings that a regexp x wrongly accepts or rejects, i.e., that are misclassified. As the number of misclassified strings is possibly infinite, we need to restrict the length of the considered strings to n. Being $\mathcal{L}^n(x) = \mathcal{L}(x) \cap \Sigma^n$, F_x^n is defined as follows:

$$F_x^n = |\mathcal{L}^n(x) \oplus \mathcal{L}^n(o_x)|$$

In order to know if the repaired regexp r' is better than r, we can compute $\Delta F = F_{r'}^n - F_r^n$ with a fixed n. In the experiments, we set n to 20, to count the strings of length n up to 20. If $\Delta F < 0$ or the final regexp is completely repaired, the regexp under test is considered *repaired*, otherwise, it means that the process did not remove any fault (or removed and introduced faults equally).

By Table 1a, we can see that the processes can repair (column R) between 72% and 85% of regexps, but they can completely repair (column CR) a small amount of them (between 2.92% and 4.58%). Thus, the proposed techniques are not reliable in finding the completely correct regexp, but they are very efficient in removing some faults. However, some regexps are not repaired. This can be due to two reasons. First, the new changed regexp r' behaves better than the original r on the strings that are generated and tested, but it fails to correctly accept/reject other strings that are not tested, so ΔF is actually greater than 0. Secondly, we are trying to repair a regexp r that is *too far* from the oracle, so each mutation of r is not better than it; indeed, when selecting the benchmarks, we did not assume the competent programmer hypothesis, so a regexp and its oracle may be very different. In RQ5, we will evaluate how the results change if the competent programmer hypothesis holds.

Table 1b (columns R and CR) shows that increasing the number of maximum number of evaluations permits to (completely) repair more regexps.

RQ4. Which is the best approach?

---

[6] Note that we could also specify two different evaluation times for accepted and rejected strings (supposing that one of the two tasks is easier).

Table 2. Experiment results for `MutBench` (E: avg # evaluations, T: avg time (secs), R: repaired (%), CR: completely repaired (%), R': avg # r')

Process	E	R'	T	R	CR
Greedy	37.05	10.07	0.40	87.5	8.75
MultiDSs3	48.33	7.36	2.03	92.08	7.5
Breadth	29.48	1.64	1.06	85.0	11.67
Coll5	27.24	2.01	5.11	85.83	12.92

MaxEval	E	T	R	CR
10	9.87	0.85	84.58	7.92
30	24.99	1.21	87.50	9.58
100	47.57	4.12	89.17	11.67
200	59.67	2.42	89.17	11.67

(a) Process type results   (b) MaxEval results

From Table 1a, we observe that `MultiDSs3` under-performs in all the measures. `Breadth` and `Coll5`, instead, are better approaches. `Breadth` repairs 7.5% more regexps than `Greedy` using fewer strings. Although `Breadth` is more than three times slower than `Greedy`, we saw in RQ2 that the program time (without string evaluation by the user) is negligible w.r.t. the evaluation time of the user: therefore, in order to contain the total time of the process, it makes sense to keep the number of generated strings limited. `Coll5` is the approach that completely repairs more regexps, although it does not behave so well in the repaired ones: this probably means that the strings generated over the collection are good to drive towards correct candidates, but also that `Coll5` is not incremental enough and it tends not to choose regexps that are only *slightly better*.

RQ5. How are the results if the competent programmer hypothesis hold?

When building `Bench`, we did not make any assumption and most of the selected couples of regexps are very different. However, the common assumption that is done in fault-based approaches is the *competent programmer hypothesis*, i.e., the programmer defined the regexp close to the correct one (only with one or few of the syntactic faults defined by the fault classes [2]). We here evaluate the approach performances when the competent programmer hypothesis holds. We built a second benchmark set, `MutBench`, as follows. We took the oracles of `Bench` and we randomly modified them introducing n faults (with $n = 1, \ldots, 3$), obtaining three faulty versions of the oracle; we therefore added to `MutBench` 60 couples of regexps. The regexps are between 43 and 302 characters long (108.15 on average) and contain between 11 and 63 operators (25.52 on average). We then applied our approach to `MutBench`. Table 2 reports the aggregated results for the experiments performed over the regexps in `MutBench`. Most of the observations we did for `Bench` are still valid for `MutBench`, although there are some interesting differences. First of all, by Table 2a, we observe that `Greedy` now behaves as good as `Breadth` in terms of repaired regexps (actually slightly better): this means that if the syntactic faults of the regexp under test are those identified by our fault classes, applying a greedy approach that changes the regexp as soon as a fault is found pays off. Moreover, for both approaches, the numbers of evaluated strings and of changed regexps are lower w.r.t. `Bench`: this means that the approaches converge faster to the final solution as they are able to apply the correct mutations to remove the syntactic faults. `MultiDSs3` is now the best approach in terms of repaired regexps: this probably means that generating more strings w.r.t. `Greedy` for reinforcing the decision makes sense only if there are few faults, otherwise additional strings are useless.

Remark. A threat to external validity is that the obtained results could be not generalizable to all regexps. In order to mitigate this threat, we tried to select the most diverse regexps performing different tasks; in order to evaluate the approach on the worst case scenario, we also did not assume the competent programmer hypothesis. We saw in RQ5 that, if the hypothesis holds (as it is assumed by fault-based approaches), the performance of the approach improves.

6   Related Work

As far as we know, no approach exists to repair regexps. The approaches proposed in literature mainly focus on regexps testing or on their synthesization.

Regarding test generation of labeled strings, MUTREX [2] is an open source tool able to generate fault-detecting strings. We exploit its mutation operators and its string generation facility (i.e., function `genDs`).

Another test generator is EGRET [6] that generates *evil* strings that should be able to expose errors commonly made by programmers. EGRET takes a regexp as input and generates both accepted and rejected strings. The user can estimate the regexp correctness by evaluating these strings and identifying those that are wrongly classified. As in our approach, the user is the oracle. Also EGRET applies mutation, but on the strings accepted by the regexp under test, and not on the regexp itself as in our case. The advantage of the strings we use in our approach is that, once we detect a failure, we also know how to remove the corresponding syntactic fault in the regexp; instead, using the strings generated by EGRET would leave open the problem to localize the syntactic fault.

Another tool that can be used for labeled string generation is Rex [13], a solver of regexps constraints. Rex translates a given regexp into a symbolic finite automaton; the Z3 SMT solver is used for satisfiability checking. Since Z3 is able to generate a *model* as witness of the satisfiability check, Rex can be used to build strings accepted by the regexp.

Reggae [7] is a tool based on dynamic symbolic execution that generates string inputs that are accepted by a regexp. Reggae aims at achieving branch coverage of programs containing complex string operations.

Several other tools for testing regexps exist, as EXREX, Generex, and regldg[7]. However, they are based on exhaustive or random generation of strings matching a given regexp, and the strings they generate are not useful for repairing regexps.

---

[7] https://github.com/asciimoo/exrex, https://github.com/mifmif/Generex, https://regldg.com/.

A different use of labeled strings is the synthesization of regexps. ReLIE [8] is a learning algorithm that, starting from an initial regexp and a set of labeled strings, tries to learn the correct regexp. It performs some regexp transformations (a kind of regexp mutation); however, no definition of fault class is given. Our approach could be adapted for regexps synthesis as well.

Our approach has some similarities with *automatic software repair*. The automatic repair of software requires an oracle: in our approach, the oracle is the user, while in software repair the oracle is usually specified using test suites [3,14], pre- and post-conditions [11], etc. Moreover, such approaches also identify techniques to repair the software when a fault is detected: in [9], for example, some *repair actions* are proposed, that are similar to our mutation operators.

Automatic repair has also been proposed for specifications, as, for example, automatic repair of feature models describing software product lines. The approach in [5] applies a cycle of *test-and-fix* to a feature model in order to remove its wrong constraints; the approach uses configurations derived both from the model and from the real system and checks whether these are correctly evaluated by the feature model. The approach has similarity with ours in alternating testing and fixing (similar to our repair phase); however, since the evaluation of configurations is done automatically on the system, the approach can produce several configurations, while in our approach we need to keep the number of generated labeled strings limited, as these must be assessed by the user.

The aim of our work is similar to that in [1] in which a *student* tries to learn an unknown regular set S by posing two types of queries to a *teacher*. In a *membership query*, the student gives a string t and the teacher tells whether it belongs to S or not. In a *conjecture query*, the student provides a regular set S' and the teacher answers *yes* if S' corresponds to S, or with a *wrong* string t (as our distinguishing string) otherwise. In our approach, the user plays the role of the teacher only for the first kind of query, but not for the second kind (if (s)he could, (s)he would also be able to write the correct regexp). Our tool, instead, plays the role of the student by providing membership queries.

7   Conclusions

The paper presents an approach able to detect and remove conformance faults in a regular expression, i.e., faults that make a regular expression to wrongly accept or reject some strings. The approach consists in an iterative process composed of a *testing* phase in which the user who wrote the regular expression is asked to assess the correct evaluation of some strings that are able to distinguish a regular expression from its mutants, and in a *repair* phase in which the mutant evaluating correctly all the generated strings is taken as new version of the regular expression. The approach terminates when it is no more possible to repair the regular expression under test. Experiments show that the approach is indeed able to remove conformance faults from regular expressions, in particular if the competent programmer hypothesis holds, i.e., the user did some small syntactical faults as those described by the fault classes proposed in literature.

In the experiments, we performed different evaluations regarding the effect of the process configuration on the final results, without assessing their statistical significance. As future work, we plan to perform experiments on a wider set of regular expressions and to conduct some statistical tests to assess the statistical significance of the drawn conclusions.

References

1. Angluin, D.: Learning regular sets from queries and counterexamples. Inf. Comput. **75**(2), 87–106 (1987)
2. Arcaini, P., Gargantini, A., Riccobene, E.: Fault-based test generation for regular expressions by mutation. Softw. Test. Verif. Reliab. e1664 (2018)
3. Arcuri, A.: Evolutionary repair of faulty software. Appl. Soft Comput. **11**(4), 3494–3514 (2011)
4. Chapman, C., Stolee, K. T.: Exploring regular expression usage and context in Python. In: Proceedings of the 25th International Symposium on Software Testing and Analysis, ISSTA 2016, pp. 282–293. ACM, New York (2016)
5. Henard, C., Papadakis, M., Perrouin, G., Klein, J., Le Traon, Y.: Towards automated testing and fixing of re-engineered feature models. In: Proceedings of the 2013 International Conference on Software Engineering, ICSE 2013, pp. 1245–1248. IEEE Press, Piscataway (2013)
6. Larson, E., Kirk, A.: Generating evil test strings for regular expressions. In: 2016 IEEE 9th International Conference on Software Testing, Verification and Validation (ICST), pp. 309–319, April 2016
7. Li, N., Xie, T., Tillmann, N., Halleux, J.D., Schulte, W.: Reggae: automated test generation for programs using complex regular expressions. In: Proceedings of the 2009 IEEE/ACM International Conference on Automated Software Engineering, pp. 515–519. IEEE Computer Society (2009)
8. Li, Y., Krishnamurthy, R., Raghavan, S., Vaithyanathan, S., Jagadish, H. V.: Regular expression learning for information extraction. In: Proceedings of EMNLP 2008, pp. 21–30. Association for Computational Linguistics (2008)
9. Martinez, M., Monperrus, M.: Mining software repair models for reasoning on the search space of automated program fixing. Empir. Softw. Eng. **20**(1), 176–205 (2015)
10. Papadakis, M., Kintis, M., Zhang, J., Jia, Y., Le Traon, Y., Harman, M.: Mutation testing advances: an analysis and survey. Adv. Comput. (2018). Elsevier
11. Pei, Y., Furia, C.A., Nordio, M., Wei, Y., Meyer, B., Zeller, A.: Automated fixing of programs with contracts. IEEE Trans. Softw. Eng. **40**(5), 427–449 (2014)
12. Spishak, E., Dietl, W., Ernst. M.D.: A type system for regular expressions. In: Proceedings of the 14th Workshop on Formal Techniques for Java-like Programs, FTfJP 2012, pp. 20–26. ACM, New York (2012)
13. Veanes, M., Halleux, P.D., Tillmann, N.: Rex: symbolic regular expression explorer. In: Proceedings of the 3rd International Conference on Software Testing, Verification and Validation, ICST 2010, pp. 498–507. IEEE Computer Society (2010)
14. Weimer, W., Forrest, S., Le Goues, C., Nguyen, T.: Automatic program repair with evolutionary computation. Commun. ACM **53**(5), 109–116 (2010)

Validation of Transformation
from Abstract State Machine Models
to C++ Code

Silvia Bonfanti[1]([⊠]), Angelo Gargantini[1], and Atif Mashkoor[2,3]

[1] Università degli Studi di Bergamo, Bergamo, Italy
{silvia.bonfanti,angelo.gargantini}@unibg.it
[2] Software Competence Center Hagenberg GmbH, Hagenberg, Austria
atif.mashkoor@scch.at
[3] Johannes Kepler University, Linz, Austria
atif.mashkoor@jku.at

Abstract. The automatic transformation of models to code is one of the most important cornerstones in the model-driven engineering paradigm. Starting from system models, users are able to automatically generate machine code in a seamless manner with an assurance of potential bug freeness of the generated code. Asm2C++ [4] is the tool that transforms Abstract State Machine models to C++ code. However, no validation activities have been performed in the past to guarantee the correctness of the transformation process. In this paper, we define a mechanism to test the correctness of the model-to-code transformation with respect to two main criteria: syntactical correctness and semantic correctness, which is based on the definition of conformance between the specification and the code. Using this approach, we have devised a process able to test the generated code by reusing unit tests. Coverage measures give a user the confidence that the generated code has the same behavior as specified by the ASM model.

1 Introduction

The Abstract State Machines (ASM) method [6] is a formalism that is used to guide the rigorous development of software and systems. The ASM-inspired development starts with an abstract specification of a system and then continues until all details of the system have been captured through a sequence of refinements. During this process, the specifier can apply classical validation and verification (V&V) techniques like simulation, scenarios validation, and model checking. The last step of the development process is the transformation of models into code. If not performed carefully, this step can be critical and error-prone.

The writing of this article is supported by the Austrian Ministry for Transport, Innovation and Technology, the Federal Ministry of Science, Research and Economy, and the Province of Upper Austria in the frame of the COMET center SCCH.

© IFIP International Federation for Information Processing 2018
Published by Springer Nature Switzerland AG 2018. All Rights Reserved
I. Medina-Bulo et al. (Eds.): ICTSS 2018, LNCS 11146, pp. 17–32, 2018.
https://doi.org/10.1007/978-3-319-99927-2_2

The automatic transformation of models into code is an important cornerstone of model-driven engineering [12]. This is also a common practice in industry. For example, Airbus uses automatic code synthesis from SCADE models to generate the code for embedded controllers in the Airbus A380 [3]. Following this paradigm, we have built the tool Asm2C++ [4], which is able to generate C++ code from formal specifications given in terms of ASMs. Furthermore, it is able to produce unit test cases [5], which can be used, for example, for regression testing.

The code generation activity, however, may introduce new issues in the development process, e.g., an error in model transformation may introduce faults in the code that jeopardize all the V&V activities performed during the modeling phase. Therefore, it is very critical that the generated code is syntactically well formed and, mostly, it faithfully transforms the specification into code. This also means that the code transformation process must also be analyzed, validated, and verified, which at times can become a difficult task [3].

There exist several techniques for the validation of a transformation, including the use of theorem proving or model checking [1]. In this paper, we propose an approach based on testing. In principle, testing a generated code could be a useless activity if the transformation could be formally proven correct. In practice, however, specifiers want to test code transformations in order to gain confidence that errors are not inadvertently introduced at any step (including code compiling, for example)[1]. In order to address such issues, in this paper, we tackle the problem of validation of model-to-code transformation τ by contributing in the following directions:

1. we formally define when the generated code is correct both syntactically and semantically w.r.t. the original specification,
2. we show that generated tests can detect possible errors in τ and help the designer to fix them in the implementation of τ,
3. we setup a methodology that uses a combination of code compiling and execution in order to validate τ, and
4. we provide a user with a measure (coverage) that helps in building the confidence that τ is correct.

The rest of the paper is organized as follows. We present ASMs in Sect. 2. In Sect. 3, we present the process applied to transform ASMs into C++ code. The validation of the transformation is presented in Sect. 4 and corresponding results are presented in Sect. 5. The related work is presented in Sect. 6. The paper is concluded in Sect. 7.

2   Abstract State Machines and Asmeta Framework

Abstract State Machines (ASMs) [6] are an extension of Finite State Machines (FSMs), where unstructured control states are replaced by states with arbitrarily

---

[1] Rephrasing what Ed Brinksma said in his 2009 keynote at the Testcom/FATES conference: "Who would want to fly in an airplane with software automatically generated with a code generator that has never been tested?".

complex data. ASM *states* are mathematical structures, i.e., domains of objects with functions and predicates defined on them. An ASM *location* - defined as the pair (*function-name*, *list-of-parameter-values*) - represents the abstract ASM concept of basic object containers. The ordered pair (*location*, *value*) represents a machine memory unit.

Location values are changed by firing *transition rules*. They express the modification of functions interpretation from one state to the next one. Note that the algebra signature is fixed and that functions are total (by interpreting undefined locations $f(x)$ with value *undef*). Location *updates* are given as assignments of the form $loc := v$, where loc is a location and v is its new value. They are the basic units of rule construction. There is a limited but powerful set of *rule constructors* to express: guarded actions, simultaneous parallel actions, sequential actions, nondeterminism, and unrestricted synchronous parallelism.

An ASM *computation* or *run* is, therefore, defined as a finite or infinite sequence of states $s_1, s_2, \ldots, s_n, \ldots$ of the machine. s_1 is an initial state and each s_{i+1} is obtained from s_i by firing the unique *main rule*, which could fire other transitions rules (see Fig. 1).

Fig. 1. An ASM run with a sequences of states and state-transitions (steps)

During a machine computation, not all the locations can be updated. Functions are classified as *static* (never change during any run of the machine) or *dynamic* (may change as a consequence of agent actions or *updates*). Dynamic functions are distinguished between *monitored* (only read by the machine and modified by the environment) and *controlled* (read in the current state and updated by the machine in the next state). A further classification is between *basic* and *derived* functions, i.e., those coming with a specification or computation mechanism given in terms of other functions.

An ASM can be *nondeterministic* due to the presence of monitored functions (*external* nondeterminism) and of choose rules (*internal* nondeterminism). Our code translation supports both types of nondeterminism, however, testing the generated code in the presence of internal nondeterminism is challenging as explained in Sect. 4.4.

Asmeta Framework. The ASM method can facilitate the entire life cycle of software development, i.e., from modeling to code generation. Figure 2 shows the development process based on ASMs. The process is supported by the `Asmeta` (ASM mETAmodeling) framework[2] [2] which provides a set of tools to help the developer in various activities:

---

[2] http://asmeta.sourceforge.net/.

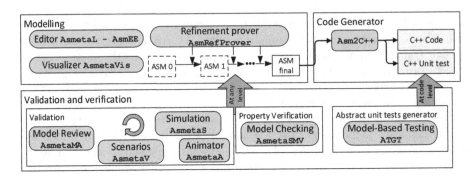

Fig. 2. The ASM development process powered by the `Asmeta` framework

- **modeling:** the system is modeled using the language `AsmetaL`. The user is supported by the editor `AsmEE` and by `AsmetaVis`, the ASMs visualizer which transforms the textual model into a graphical representation. The user can directly define the last ASM model or s/he can reach it through refinement. The refinement process is adopted in case the model is complex. In this case, the designer can start from the first model (also called the ground model) and can refine it through the refinement steps by adding details to the behavior of the ASM. The `AsmRefProver` tool ensures whether the current ASM model is a correct refinement of the previous ASM model.

- **validation:** the process is supported by the model simulator `AsmetaS`, the scenarios `AsmetaV`, and the model reviewer `AsmetaMA`. The simulator `AsmetaS` allows to perform two types of simulation: interactive simulation and random simulation. The difference between the two types of simulation is the way in which the monitored functions are chosen. During interactive simulation the user inserts the value of functions, while in random simulation the tool randomly chooses the value of functions among those available. `AsmetaS` executes scenarios written using the `Avalla` language. Each scenario contains the expected system behavior and the tool checks whether the machine runs correctly. The model reviewer `AsmetaMA` performs static analysis. It determines whether a model has sufficient quality attributes (e.g., minimality - the specification does not contain elements defined or declared in the model but never used, completeness - requires that every behavior of the system is explicitly modeled, and consistency - guarantees that locations are never simultaneously updated to different values).

- **verification:** the properties derived from the requirements document are verified to check whether the behavior of the model complies with the intended behavior. The `AsmetaSMV` tool supports this process.

- **testing:** the tool `ATGT` generates abstract unit tests starting from the ASM specification by exploiting the counter example generation of a model checker.

- **code generation:** given the final ASM specification, the `Asm2C++` automatically translates it into C++ code. Moreover, the abstract tests, generated by the `ATGT` tool, are translated to C++ unit tests.

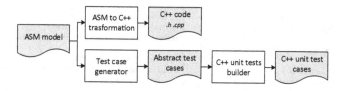

Fig. 3. `Asm2C++` tool

3   Code Generation

The `Asm2C++` tool implements the model-to-code transformation. The tool is divided into two activities: transformation of the ASMs specifications into C++ code and generation of C++ unit tests starting from the ASMs specifications (see Fig. 3). `Asm2C++` is based on Xtext[3], a framework for the development of domain-specific languages, which provides facilities for parsing and code generation and is fully compatible with the Eclipse Modeling Framework. The code generator has been developed as a model-to-text (M2T) transformation. The transformation code is written mainly in Xtend - a Java dialect provided by the Xtext framework with features for code generation and text transformation.

3.1   C++ Code Generation

The `Asm2C++` tool transforms an ASM to a C++ class [4]. The generated C++ class is split into a header (*.h*) and a source (*.cpp*) file. The header file (see Code 1) contains the translation of the ASM signature: domains declaration, domains definition, functions declaration and rules declaration. The rules implementation, the functions/domains initialization and the functions definitions are contained in the source file (see Code 2). The simulation of an ASM step, has been implemented using the step() method which calls sequentially the main method and the fireUpdateSet() method. The main method corresponds to the translation of the main rule into C++ code, while the fireUpdateSet method updates the locations to the next state values.

3.2   C++ Unit Tests Generation

The `Asm2C++` tool is also able to produce unit tests from ASM specifications [5]. It generates abstract tests starting from the ASM specification and then the tests are translated into C++ unit tests using the Boost Test C++ library.[4] The abstract tests are generated in two different ways. The first is based on the `Asmeta` simulator while the second exploits the `ATGT` tool. Once the unit tests and the C++ code of the ASM specification are compiled, they are linked together and the tests are run on the code.

---

[3] https://www.eclipse.org/Xtext/.
[4] https://www.boost.org/.

```
#ifndef asmSpecification_H
#define asmSpecification_H

#include ... /* include libraries */

/* Domain declaration */
namespace asmSpecificationnamespace{
/* enumerative domain */
enum domainName {value0, value1, ...};
/* concrete domain */
typedef domainType domainName;
}
using namespace asmSpecificationnamespace;
class asmSpecification{
/* Domain containers declaration:
concrete domain and enumerative domain */
const std::set<domainName>
              domainName_elems;
public:
/* Function declaration */
domainName functionName[2];
/* controlled function */
domainName functionName;
/* monitored function */
/* Rule declaration */
void ruleName (parameters);
asmSpecification();
void mainRule();
void fireUpdateSet();
void step();
};

#endif
```

Code 1. .h code

```
//asmSpecification.cpp automatically generated
#include "asmSpecification.h"
using namespace asmSpecificationnamespace;

// Conversion of ASM rules in C++ methods
void asmSpecification::ruleName (parameters){
    /* implementation */
}

void asmSpecification::mainRule(){
    /* implementation */
}

// Function and domain initialization
asmSpecification::asmSpecification():

// Static domain initialization
domainName_elems(value0,value1,...),
{
    //Function initialization
    functionName[0] = functionName[1]
                            = value;
}

// Apply the update set
void asmSpecification::fireUpdateSet(){
    functionName[0] = functionName[1];
}

void asmSpecification::step(){
    mainRule();
    fireUpdateSet();
}
```

Code 2. .cpp code

The translation from abstract tests to concrete tests is done by following the rules reported in Table 1. A test suite TS is defined by using the macro *BOOST_AUTO_TEST_SUITE(testSuiteName)*, it automatically registers a test suite named *testSuiteName*. A test suite is ended using *BOOST_AUTO_TEST_END()*. Each test suite can contain one or more test cases. A test case is declared using the macro *BOOST_AUTO_TEST_CASE(testCaseName)*. The content of a test case is enclosed by the symbols {} and the name is unique. Each test case contains an instance *sut* of the class which the ASM is translated to. Then, for each state transition in the abstract test, the test performs in order three tasks:

1. It sets the values of monitored functions (using the assignment operator).
2. It checks the value of controlled functions by using the macro BOOST_CHECK.
3. It performs an ASM step by calling the step method in the C++ class.

After each step, the monitored locations will be changed and the controlled location will be checked again, till the end of the abstract test sequence.

3.3   Code Generation Correctness

First, we want to introduce the notion of *conformity* of the target C++ code to the source ASM. Formally, we can define the model-to-code transformation

Table 1. Translation of abstract tests to concrete tests

Abstract Test		Concrete Test
Test suite TS		BOOST_AUTO_TEST_SUITE(testSuiteName) *translation of each test case in TS* BOOST_AUTO_TEST_SUITE_END( )

Test case $t: s_0, s_1 \ldots s_n$		BOOST_AUTO_TEST_CASE(testCaseName) {
		  SUTClass sut;
		  translation of each state transition in t
		}

ASM step $s_i \rightarrow s_{i+1}$		*set monitored locations in s_i* *check controlled locations in s_i* sut.step();
State	Monitored location $m = val$	sut.m = val;
	Controlled location $c = val$	BOOST_CHECK(sut.c[0] == val);

as a function τ that takes an ASM A and returns a C++ class $\tau(A)$ with the corresponding fields and methods. Each location l of the ASM A is transformed to a member (field or method) of the class $\tau(A)$ (as explained in [4]).

Definition 1 (State conformance). *Given an ASM A, we say that the state of an object O of the class $\tau(A)$ conforms to a state s of A if the value of every location l in s is equal to the value of $\tau(l)$ in the target object O.*

Informally, to compare ASM states and C++ states we look at the values of the ASM functions that are translated to C++ members. To compare values, we use the equality but in the future we may extend the concept of conformity between locations in order to introduce some tolerance, e.g., by allowing a small difference between two values. We can refer to *controlled conformity*, if we restrict to only controlled locations.

Additionally, we want to introduce the notion of behavioral conformance. In our approach, we want that the target C++ class C preserves the behavior of the ASM. Since ASMs are executable, we require that every execution of the class C has a corresponding behavior in the abstract specification.

Definition 2 (Behavioral conformance). *We say that a class $C = \tau(A)$ behaviorally conforms to the ASM A, if starting from any reachable state r of any object O of C such that r is conforming to the state s of A, by executing O.step() we obtain a state r' that is controlled conforming to the next state s' of A.*

Informally, our C++ code behaves like the original ASM, if starting from a conforming state (with the same monitored and controlled locations) and executing a step, then the code will arrive to a next state that has the same controlled locations.

We now introduce the concept of *correctness* of model-to-code transformation. We deal with the correctness from two distinct points of view: first *syntactic* or *type-correctness* and second *semantic* or *behavioral* conformity.

Definition 3 (Transformation correctness). *We say that the transformation* $\tau(A)$ *is correct if the C++ class is syntactically correct and behaviorally conforms to A.*

Verifying the correctness of the translation τ would require the use of formal techniques like model checking or theorem proving. As shown in [1], several attempts already exist in this direction. In our case, this would require, at least, to formalize the target language C++ and this would be a great overhead. Moreover, proving the correctness of the transformation may still not be enough in case of critical systems. For such systems, the transformation should also be tested in any case (recall the statement of Ed Brinksma). As observed in [8], a translation validation approach, that is based on testing, seems to be a better solution in an engineering context. Therefore, we have concentrated our efforts in validating the transformation by testing. This activity exploits the generated unit tests, as explained in Sect. 3.2, and is based on the following theorem.

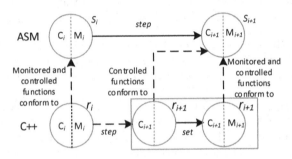

Fig. 4. ASM/C++ Conformance

Theorem 1 (Correctness by testing). *Given a C++ test* t *obtained by translating any run* $s_1, \ldots, s_n$ *of* A, *if* $\tau(A)$ *is correct, then, when executing* t, *each C++ state before the i-th* `O.step()` *will conform to* s_i, *all controlled locations will be checked by* t, *and* t *will pass with no errors.*

Proof. The evolution and the relations between t and the abstract states are depicted in Fig. 4. If τ is correct, then the C++ code is correct and it can be executed. Let's consider the pair of states s_i and s_{i+1} and assume that r_i in C++ conforms to s_i in the abstract run both in the controlled part C_i and the monitored part M_i. The controlled conformity of r_{i+1} is guaranteed, thanks to Definition 2, by executing immediately before each state the instruction $O.step()$ (see Table 1). Then, the unit test sets the monitored variables in C++ to the values in s_{i+1} (see Table 1). At the end, the state in C++ immediately before the $(i + 1)$-th step conforms again to s_{i+1}. The test will check the controlled part, and due to the assumption that τ is correct, it will find the expected values for the controlled part. By induction on i, we can prove the theorem. □

Thanks to Theorem 1, we are sure that every test will check the conformance of the states in it with the original sequence of the ASM, and that if a test fails, then there is a fault in the translation. Of course, testing cannot prove the correctness of the transformation but can help us in gaining confidence in the translation correctness. In the following section, we explain the process we have devised to put in practice the proposed methodology.

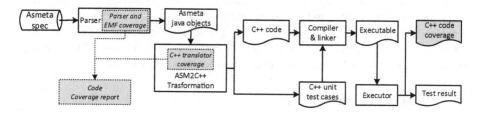

Fig. 5. Validation process

4   Validation of the Transformation

In this section, we explain how we have devised a process able to validate our transformation by testing. In principle, to validate the transformation τ, we would need a set of inputs (a set of ASMs) or a way to generate inputs according to some criteria and an oracle that tells whether the output of τ (C++ code) is what is intended (for example, the user could write by hand the expected C++ code for each ASM in the test set). We follow a different path since we use the unit tests to validate the transformations. In our approach, to check whether the resulting code is what is intended, we first check the well-formedness of the code and then we test its behavior in order to check whether it conforms to the original ASM. This is consistent with our definition of correctness given in Definition 3 and is based on Theorem 1. This is a sort of *indirect* testing [1], in which we do not test directly the transformation rules but the results of such transformations. We exploit the fact that both the ASM and its translation to C++ are executable.

The validation process is depicted in Fig. 5 and is explained as follows. Given an Asmeta textual specification A, A is parsed by the Asmeta parser that builds the corresponding Java objects. For the specification A, we apply our Asm2C++ tool that implements the code transformation τ in order to obtain the C++ code. Besides, we apply the test generator component [5] and generate a set of abstract test cases that can be translated to C++ unit tests. Then, we perform the following validation activities: testing the transformation correctness and coverage computation.

4.1   Testing the Transformation Correctness

Syntactic Correctness. Using the C++ compiler, we first check the syntactical correctness of the generated code. We use the -Wall option and quit the process in case of an error. This first phase captures translation faults that produce invalid source code. Also the tests are compiled in order to obtain the corresponding obj files. The objs for the `Asmeta` specification and for the tests are linked together.

Semantic Correctness. The obtained executable is executed in order to check that the behavior as specified by the tests corresponds to the behavior of the generated code. The tests will set the suitable monitored values and check the conformance of the controlled parts. In this way, we test the semantic correctness of the code according to Theorem 1. A failing test means that the C++ code does not conform to its specification and since the code has been obtained by applying the transformation, a fault in the transformation has been found.

4.2   Coverage Computation

Although it suffers from well-known shortcomings, the measure of the coverage of software artifacts during testing can give a good feedback about the depth of the testing activity itself. For this reason, we propose to measure the coverage of the following aspects.

1. First, the *coverage of the source language*, `AsmetaL` in our case, gives a good indication on how many constructs are tackled by the transformation under test τ. The more constructs τ is able to deal with during testing, the higher the applicability of τ is. A request of a good level of coverage avoids the problem of transformations that are well tested but only on a limited set of source specifications. In our approach, we instrument the `Asmeta` parser in order to collect the information during parsing. This represents the coverage of the *inputs* of the transformation.
2. Second, the *coverage of the transformation code*, the `Asm2C++` code that implements the transformation written in Xtend and Java in our case, gives a good indication on how much the transformation code itself is tested. If some parts of the transformation are never covered, there is the risk that some critical conditions are actually not tested, or that some code is useless and never used therefore. This represents the pure coverage of the transformation.
3. Third, the *coverage of the produced code*, the C++ code including the unit tests in our case, gives an indication on how much the tests are able to exercise the generated C++ code. Although among the three coverage measures this is less significant as it depends also on the technique used to generate the tests, it is important to check whether there are parts of the produced code that are never covered and this may be a signal that the transformation produces some meaningless code. This represents the coverage of the *outputs* of the transformation.

4.3   Tools Used

To support the validation process, we have used several tools. Ant[5] is a tool that supports users while developing software across multiple platforms. The configuration files are written using XML where each file contains one project

---

[5] https://ant.apache.org/.

and one or more targets. A target is composed of one or more tasks - pieces of code that can be executed. Moreover, the configuration file contains properties to support the user in customizing the build process.

To compute the java code coverage we use JaCoCo[6], which is a free code coverage library for Java. JaCoCo requires Ant tasks to compile and run Java programs and to create the coverage report of the executed code. We have written a project using Ant to automatically compile and run JUnit tests to test the Asm2C++ generator. Once the specifications are translated into C++ code, another task generates C++ unit tests and runs the tests on the generated C++ code. After C++ unit tests are executed, the Ant file invokes a task to run the JaCoCo tool, which provides the coverage of the selected code. To compute the coverage of C++ code, we use gcov that instruments the generated C++ source code and outputs coverage information when it is executed.

4.4 Dealing with Internal Nondeterminism

In ASMs, internal nondeterminism is represented by the following choose rule:

choose x **in** D **with** P **do** R

meaning to execute rule R with an arbitrary x chosen in D, which is a domain or a set of elements, and satisfying the property P. In C++, the choose rule is translated by randomly searching an element in D satisfying P and then executing the code obtained by the translation of R. In this way, however, the ASM and the C++ code may choose different values for x. The test obtained from the abstract test case may, therefore, fail only because of this reason. To tackle this problem, we have enabled the test case generator and the C++ translator to enforce a deterministic behavior that consists in taking the *first* element of D such that P is true and use that for the variable x. Substituting a known nondeterministic behavior with a deterministic alternative is adopted also in [14]. Although this approach cannot guarantee that the actual nondeterministic translation is correct, it allows us to test the translation of the choose rule and the specification containing it.

5   Results

We have taken 44 ASM models taken from the public repository of the Asmeta framework[7] and we apply the validation process to each of them. The validation activity has allowed us to find and fix several faults and the coverage has given us a good indication on how to extend and improve the Asm2C++ tool.

5.1 Discovered Faults

The validation process has allowed us to find faults in the transformation that have been classified into four categories:

---

[6] http://www.eclemma.org/jacoco/.
[7] Source code and examples are available at http://asmeta.sourceforge.net/.

1. *missing translation:* the translation of an ASM construct to C++ is missing;
2. *syntactically incorrect translation:* the translation to C++ is syntactically incorrect and the compiler finds the error;
3. *semantically incorrect translation:* the code is compiled by the C++ compiler, but the test cases fail because the behavior of the code does not conform to the behavior of the specification; and
4. *incorrect test case generation:* the generation of test cases is not correct.

The identification between the first two categories of errors is easy because in the first case the Asm2C++ generator throws an exception and in the second case the compiler fails to compile the C++ code and prints an error message. The classification of errors between the third and the fourth category requires a deep analysis, because in both cases the tests fail when a conformance fault is found without providing any other information.

Missing Translation. These errors are caused probably by forgetfulness or distraction of the programmer. In our case, for example, the first error reported by the Asm2C++ tool concerned the translation of natural numbers which was missing. We have now translated natural numbers as unsigned integers.

Another fault we have discovered is the missing translation of abstract domains. We have now added a translation rule that for each abstract domain A produces a C++ class C_A, while constants in A are translated as objects. A set that contains all the objects of type C_A is also added to C_A to keep track of the static constants of A.

Syntactically Incorrect Translation. These errors are due to a misunderstanding of the semantics of the source notation (ASMs) and how it is translated to the target notation (C++). It can be also caused by an incomplete knowledge of the target language, C++ in our case. For instance, the compiler has found an error in the translation of *case terms*. Each case is translated as nested if-else and the otherwise clause was translated using the "otherwise" keyword which does not exist in C++, and that caused an error during compilation. This error has been resolved by replacing "otherwise" with the "else" keyword.

Semantically Incorrect Translation. These errors are caused because ASMs and C++ are executed differently. ASMs runs are sequences of states (rules are executed and then the functions are updated) while C++ programs execute instructions sequentially. For example, we found an error regarding the semantics of seqRule. In ASM specifications, rules are executed in parallel, but sometimes it is allowed to model sequential execution by means of seqRule. In case of a sequential block, the value of controlled functions must be updated immediately in both current and next states. This behavior had not been taken into consideration and some test cases failed.

Incorrect Test Case Generation. These errors are caused when the test generation produces wrong test cases or when the translation from abstract test cases to concrete tests is incorrect. For example, we found an error that concerns invariants, which are constraints that must be satisfied during the ASMs execution. Sometimes the expression of an invariant contains monitored functions which are chosen automatically by the test generator in order to build test cases. Initially, they were chosen randomly, but some test cases failed because the corresponding invariants could not be satisfied. To overcome this problem, we have forced the test generator to continue choosing values for monitored functions until they satisfy the corresponding invariants.

5.2   Coverage

In Sect. 4.2, we have listed the measures of code coverage one should perform during the testing of the transformation: coverage of the source language, coverage of the transformation code, and coverage of the produced code. In this section, we present the results obtained for each coverage criteria.

Figure 6 shows the coverage of source language in terms of number of Asmeta constructs covered during parsing. The coverage increases with the number of specifications, until most of the constructs are covered (80% of the total). We did not cover all of them, because there are some constructs that are not used in any Asmeta specification in the repository. We initially started to write ad hoc Asmeta specifications but then we realized that the language contains useless constructs and such language overspecification should be addressed before in order to simplify the language.

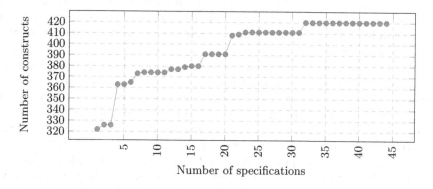

Fig. 6. Coverage of Asmeta parser

Coverage of the transformation code is shown in Fig. 7. The result obtained is satisfactory because most of the code is covered, despite not all the classes are 100% covered. This is because the code contains many redundant checks in case of critical situations that should never happen.

The third coverage is about the produced code. Initially, the value was low because the ASM rules were translated in two execution modes: the first was in the parallel mode (the standard ASM mode), while the second was in the sequential mode. The sequential mode is used rarely in ASM specifications and the unused code contributes to decrease the percentage of code coverage (the

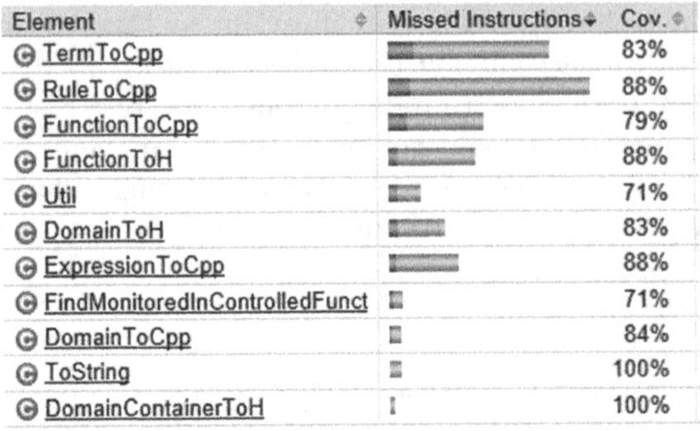

Element	Missed Instructions	Cov.
⊕ TermToCpp	▆▆▆▆▆▆▆▆▆▆▆▆	83%
⊕ RuleToCpp	▆▆▆▆▆▆▆▆▆▆▆▆	88%
⊕ FunctionToCpp	▆▆▆▆▆	79%
⊕ FunctionToH	▆▆▆▆▆	88%
⊕ Util	▆▆	71%
⊕ DomainToH	▆▆▆	83%
⊕ ExpressionToCpp	▆▆▆	88%
⊕ FindMonitoredInControlledFunct	▪	71%
⊕ DomainToCpp	▪	84%
⊕ ToString	▪	100%
⊕ DomainContainerToH	▪	100%

Fig. 7. Asm2C++ coverage

highest coverage was ≈70%). For this reason, we have improved the translator by producing the sequential version of rules only if they are actually called by seqBlock rules. The result of this improvement is a higher percentage of code coverage and in most cases it reaches 100% of the generated code.

6 Related Work

The challenging nature of model transformation creates the need for validation of this systematic process. This need and the associated challenges have been documented by several researchers, e.g., [3,9,15]. A comprehensive survey on the related state of the art can be found in [1,7].

Wimmer et al. [16] present a language-agnostic approach for testing model-to-text and text-to-model transformations. They extend the Object Constraint Language with additional String operations to specify contracts for practical examples and to evaluate the correctness of current UML-to-Java code generators offered by some UML tools. As compared to this work, our input models are verified and validated by both users and tools, i.e., they are well-formed, implement the specified requirements, and do not contain unintended behaviors.

Conrad [8] proposes a translation validation workflow for the generated code in the context of the IEC 61508 standard. The translation validation process is comprised of (a) numeric equivalence testing between the generated code and the corresponding model, and (b) additional measures to demonstrate that unintended functionality has not been introduced during the translation process. In a similar work [11], Sampath et al. present a technique for verifying and validating Stateflow[8] model translation to C code. However, both these works, i.e., [8,11], are based on the proprietary tool Simulink[9]. Our work, on the other hand, is based on the Asmeta framework, which is an open-source project and freely available.

---

[8] Stateflow is a hierarchical state-machine modeling language that is part of the Simulink/Stateflow tool-suite from The MathWorks Inc.

[9] www.mathworks.com/products/simulink.

In [10], Küster et al. present their initial experiences with a white box model-based approach for testing model transformations within the context of business process modeling. They propose multiple techniques for constructing test cases and show how to use them to locate errors in model transformations. As aforementioned, this work is performed within the context of business process modeling and uses a supported notation. Our work, in comparison, is generally applicable across multiple domains and uses ASMs, which is a scientifically well-founded method for systems engineering.

In [13], Stümer et al. present a general and systematic test approach for model-based code generation. This approach undertakes formal descriptions of the optimizations under test by using graph transformation rules. The proposed tool automatically creates test models (first-order test cases) from the classification tree, which is used to derive a formal description of the input space of an optimization rule. In a further step, test vectors (second-order test cases) are generated, which ensure structural coverage of the test model and the corresponding code. Model and generated code then undergo a back-to-back test using these test vectors. A signal comparison of the test outputs is used to determine functional equivalence between the model and the code. The main difference between this work and our approach is that, although many of their observations are general, they target Simulink and Stateflow programs. Moreover, we extend their use of coverage information to measure the quality of the testing activity by explicitly distinguishing between several types of coverage.

7   Conclusion

In this paper, we have presented a process to automatically validate the transformation correctness from Asmeta specifications to C++. The process is based on the notion of conformity between C++ code and Asmeta specifications, and on the definition of correctness (see Definition 3). It consists in parsing an Asmeta specification, and generating the C++ code and unit test cases. The source code is compiled, linked, and executed. During tests execution, possible faults can be found and code coverage information is collected. The coverage regards several artifacts involved in the transformation, namely the inputs (ASM specs), the transformation itself (Xtext code), and the outputs (the generated C++ code).

We have applied this process to a set of ASMs and we were able to discover several faults both within the transformation code and the test generator component. Such faults were sometimes due to the subtle misunderstanding of ASM semantics (like the SeqRule) that requires a peculiar translation to C++. Further, this activity has allowed us to increase the applicability of the transformation by extension to missing ASM constructs, and identification of parts of the Asmeta language, which are not used in practice.

References

1. Rahim, L.A., Whittle, J.: A survey of approaches for verifying model transformations. Softw. Syst. Model. **14**(2), 1003–1028 (2015)
2. Arcaini, P., Gargantini, A., Riccobene, E., Scandurra, P.: A model-driven process for engineering a toolset for a formal method. Softw.: Pract. Exp. **41**, 155–166 (2011)
3. Baudry, B., Ghosh, S., Fleurey, F., France, R., Le Traon, Y., Mottu, J.M.: Barriers to systematic model transformation testing. Commun. ACM **53**(6), 139–143 (2010)
4. Bonfanti, S., Carissoni, M., Gargantini, A., Mashkoor, A.: Asm2C++: a tool for code generation from abstract state machines to Arduino. In: Barrett, C., Davies, M., Kahsai, T. (eds.) NFM 2017. LNCS, vol. 10227, pp. 295–301. Springer, Cham (2017). https://doi.org/10.1007/978-3-319-57288-8_21
5. Bonfanti, S., Gargantini, A., Mashkoor, A.: Generation of C++ unit tests from abstract state machines specifications. In: 14th Workshop on Advances in Model Based Testing (A-MOST 2018) @ICST 2018, Västerås, Sweden (2018)
6. Börger, E., Stark, R.F.: Abstract State Machines: A Method for High-Level System Design and Analysis. Springer, Heidelberg (2003). https://doi.org/10.1007/978-3-642-18216-7
7. Calegari, D., Szasz, N.: Verification of model transformations: a survey of the state-of-the-art. Electron. Notes Theor. Comput. Sci. **292**, 5–25 (2013). Proceedings of the XXXVIII Latin American Conference in Informatics (CLEI)
8. Conrad, M.: Testing-based translation validation of generated code in the context of IEC 61508. Form. Methods Syst. Des. **35**(3), 389–401 (2009)
9. France, R., Rumpe, B.: Model-driven development of complex software: a research roadmap. In: 2007 Future of Software Engineering, FOSE 2007, pp. 37–54. IEEE Computer Society, Washington, DC, USA (2007)
10. Küster, J.M., Abd-El-Razik, M.: Validation of model transformations – first experiences using a white box approach. In: Kühne, T. (ed.) MODELS 2006. LNCS, vol. 4364, pp. 193–204. Springer, Heidelberg (2007). https://doi.org/10.1007/978-3-540-69489-2_24
11. Sampath, P., Rajeev, A.C., Ramesh, S.: Translation validation for stateflow to C. In: 2014 51st ACM/EDAC/IEEE Design Automation Conference (DAC), pp. 1–6, June 2014
12. Schmidt, D.C.: Model-driven engineering. IEEE Comput. **39**(2), 25–31 (2006)
13. Stuermer, I., Conrad, M., Doerr, H., Pepper, P.: Systematic testing of model-based code generators. IEEE Trans. Softw. Eng. **33**(9), 622–634 (2007)
14. Tillmann, N., de Halleux, J.: Pex–white box test generation for .NET. In: Beckert, B., Hähnle, R. (eds.) TAP 2008. LNCS, vol. 4966, pp. 134–153. Springer, Heidelberg (2008). https://doi.org/10.1007/978-3-540-79124-9_10
15. Van Der Straeten, R., Mens, T., Van Baelen, S.: Challenges in model-driven software engineering. In: Chaudron, M.R.V. (ed.) MODELS 2008. LNCS, vol. 5421, pp. 35–47. Springer, Heidelberg (2009). https://doi.org/10.1007/978-3-642-01648-6_4
16. Wimmer, M., Burgueño, L.: Testing M2T/T2M transformations. In: Moreira, A., Schätz, B., Gray, J., Vallecillo, A., Clarke, P. (eds.) MODELS 2013. LNCS, vol. 8107, pp. 203–219. Springer, Heidelberg (2013). https://doi.org/10.1007/978-3-642-41533-3_13

Security Testing for Chatbots

Josip Bozic[(✉)] [iD] and Franz Wotawa [iD]

Graz University of Technology, Institute for Software Technology, A-8010 Graz,
Austria
{jbozic,wotawa}@ist.tugraz.at
http://www.ist.tugraz.at

Abstract. Services like chatbots that provide information to customers
in real-time are of increasing importance for the online market. Chatbots offer an intuitive interface to answer user requests in an interactive
manner. The inquiries are of wide-range and include information about
specific goods and services but also financial issues and personal advices.
The notable advantages of these programs are the simplicity of use and
speed of the search process. In some cases, chatbots have even surpassed
classical web, mobile applications, and social networks. Chatbots might
have access to huge amount of data or personal information. Therefore,
they might be a valuable target for hackers, and known web application vulnerabilities might be a security issue for chatbots as well. In
this paper, we discuss the challenges of security testing for chatbots. We
provide an overview about an automated testing approach adapted to
chatbots, and first experimental results.

Keywords: Adaptive systems · security testing · chatbots

1 Introduction

Since Joseph Weizenbaum [27] introduced ELIZA, the first computer program
that interacts with users in a natural language, in 1966, humanlike communication with a machine has been of growing interest, leading to improvements,
e.g., see [14,26] and finally to chatbots, which rely on artificial intelligence for
emulating natural conversation with humans. Whereas some chatbots realize
conversation using pre-specified patterns, others make use of machine learning
techniques [19,23]. These intelligent chatbots provide the user a more personalized conversation by remembering and reusing specific information from previous conversations. Chatbots have also gained a lot of interest from industry.
The evolution of these systems over the years has been analyzed and there are
predictions about the rise of the chatbot market in the future [5,7].

Like any other technology also chatbots do not come without drawbacks.
Despite their intuitive novelty, chatbots are built upon existing technology.
They are often integrated into online websites. Therefore, they rely on HTTP(S)

I. Medina-Bulo et al. (Eds.): ICTSS 2018, LNCS 11146, pp. 33–38, 2018.
https://doi.org/10.1007/978-3-319-99927-2_3

and other existing communication protocols. Smart chatbots are connected to databases, thereby performing SQL queries. Data integrity and privacy, as well as user authentication and authorization must be ensured to the clients, especially by personalized chatbots. If a chatbot fails in this task, data leaks can compromise the user's privacy and may lead to financial losses. Because of these facts, it is very likely that even chatbots become a target for attackers, where known vulnerabilities and attacks, like cross-site scripting (XSS) and SQL injections (SQLI), can be exploited. Therefore, it is inevitable to cover security issues when testing chatbots as well.

In this paper, we discuss the issue of security testing for chatbots, where we describe an automated approach for the detection of intrinsic software leaks in order to prevent their exploitation. We do not test the chatbots' performance nor their functionality, e.g. natural language processing, or ask what the underlying machinery should be allowed to do [21]. We solely focus on security testing. The result is an offensive testing approach that targets two very common exploitations, namely XSS and SQLI, which has – to the best of our knowledge – not been considered before in the context of chatbots.

The paper is organized as follows. Section 2 gives an overview about the overall testing approach. Then, Section 3 explains a concrete example and discusses the outcome. Section 4 enumerates related work, whereas the paper is concluded in Section 5.

2   Overview of the approach

When designing chatbots, the primary focus lies on the processing of natural language. There the developers must take into consideration the correct understanding and answering of the user's inquiries. In addition, the system should be able to handle errors and unexpected inputs appropriately [6]. Existing tools [1,2,11] primarily target the system's functionality but do not guarantee security. The chatbot can fulfil its functional requirements but still remain vulnerable to malicious actions. The still open challenge is to test chatbots regarding their resistance to unintended and malicious user inputs. Figure 1 depicts an overall structure of an online system comprising a chatbot.

In this example, a chatbot is set up online and the communication proceeds accordingly to the standard HTTP(S) protocol. We further assume that the chatbot is connected to a database comprising client-related private information. A smart chatbot would be able to increase the amount of information about a user during communication. Therefore, user authentication must be guaranteed as well as the integrity of all stored information. [9,15,17] showed that several web vulnerabilities can be exploited due to security leaks in systems. For example, the vulnerabilities SQLI and XSS can be triggered because of insufficient input sanitization. The consequence can be unauthorized database access or malicious script execution on side of the client, which has to be avoided.

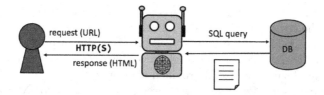

Fig. 1. Communication flow in the chatbot system

For our approach to chatbot security testing, we rely on an adapted execution framework and test oracles for both types of vulnerabilities from previous work [12]. This framework comprises two test sets for XSS and SQLI, respectively. Both test sets consist of a list of individual malicious inputs, called attack vectors. In case of XSS, the list encompasses JavaScript code, and for SQLI, a list of SQL statements is used in the tests. The test inputs are sent sequentially to the chatbot, i.e., the system under test (SUT). The resulting outputs from the chatbot are read and checked against the test oracles, and a test verdict is given back as a result. Figure 2 depicts the overall approach.

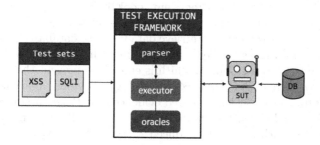

Fig. 2. Security testing approach for chatbots

The framework is implemented in Java and comprises several elements. Both test sets are attached to an executor. Then, every attack vector is put into generated HTTP requests individually and sent against the SUT. A HTML parser [8] reads the corresponding output in search for critical content that is needed by the test oracle. Finally, the testing procedure terminates when both test sets have been exhausted. Section 3 will describe the test scenario in more detail on an example.

3   Case Study

In this case study, we used the described approach for security testing a chatbot. Although several chatbots are developed and used by private companies, some of them are publicly available, e.g., [3,4]. For this case study, we selected *Program*

O, which is written in PHP and comprises a MySQL database [10], because it
perfectly fits the structure provided in Figure 2. *Program O* makes use of conversational patterns that have to be specified in the Artificial Intelligence Markup
Language (AIML) [25]. According to given patterns, the chatbot formulates its
responses by analyzing the user's provided keywords.

For security testing *Program O* we developed test suites for XSS and SQLI.
Scripts for XSS have the following form:

```
<script>alert(document.cookie)</script>">
```

For SQLI, we add SQL queries containing for example the following code:

```
' OR 1=1 #
```

When testing the chatbot, we make use of the provided input field used to
communicate with humans. According to the mentioned test oracles from [12],
we draw the conclusions for the obtained test verdicts.

When testing with the test suite for XSS, the parsed response from the SUT
indicates that the script was not triggered. Unfortunately (for the attacker),
critical parts, namely the `<script>` elements, were filtered out from the input
string thus preventing its execution. The response HTML contains only a fraction
of the original script, e.g. `alert(document.cookie)">`.

We obtained a similar result for SQLI attack related test input where the
depicted attack vector is meant to retrieve data from the database. The chatbot's
HTTP response body shows evidence that this input has been filtered out as well
(by escaping out the apostrophe ', which is enough to prevent the execution).

Although, we were not able to successfully trigger a vulnerability for *Program
O*, the testing framework at least showed evidence that *Program O* has no trivial
security bugs. In addition, we showed that, the overall challenge of security
testing of online chatbots can be reduced to general security testing for web
applications. In both cases, the same challenges exist, namely how to define
attack vectors and how to construct efficient detection mechanisms.

4   Related Work

To the best of our knowledge, there are no papers dealing with security testing of
chatbots. There are papers describing methods and tools for testing functionality
and usability (e.g. [24]), and also other papers considering testing of AI systems
in general [18,22]. In the general context of security testing there has been some
publication dealing with testing against certain attacks like XSS and SQLI.

In [20] the authors present QED, a system that is based on goal-directed
model checking for testing against XSS and SQLI. It uses a definition of the
vulnerability to be tested and a set of input values for test case generation. QED
targets on automated testing of Java web applications. There a model checker
is used to generate attack vectors for the SUT via searching for candidates that
are likely to detect a vulnerability.

Duchene et al. [15] present a testing tool for XSS that relies on fuzzing and model inference. The underlying method is a black-box fuzzer and makes us of a genetic algorithm with the help of an attack grammar. The work sets focus on the input generation of XSS attack vectors by applying mutation and crossover operators. A fitness function guides the choice of inputs for test case generation, which attack vectors are then executed against web applications.

In our previous work [12], we use visual depictions of attacks against web applications. There we specified attack patterns for XSS and SQLI that guide test execution. The result is an abstract state machine that offers a high degree of configurability and extendibility for black-box security testing purposes.

Other works that cover XSS and SQLI include [16] and [13].

5   Conclusion and Future Work

In this paper, we introduced a first version of a security testing approach to be applied to chatbots. We claim that the topic covers a challenge of growing interest and importance. This is due to growing interest of chatbots from industry (see [7]). Most interestingly, the scientific literature lacks solutions for the challenge of testing chatbots for vulnerabilities. In this paper, we briefly introduced a testing framework for security testing chatbots and discuss first results we obtained using an available chatbot implementation.

Although, we were not able to trigger vulnerabilities, we could show that the framework fits well its purpose. In addition, the tests raise evidence that the used chatbot is resistant to some common attack vectors. It is worth noting that the current test execution framework is not limited to XSS and SQLI attacks. In the future, we will extend testing chatbots against other vulnerabilities [9]. In addition, we want to further investigate on automated test case generation for security testing of chatbots.

Acknowledgments. The research presented in the paper has been funded in part by the Cooperation Programme Interreg V-A Slovenia-Austria under the project AS-IT-IC (Austrian-Slovenian Intelligent Tourist Information Center).

References

1. Botium - new generation testing. http://www.botium.at, accessed: 2018–05-07
2. BotMan - The PHP messaging and chatbot library. https://botman.io, accessed: 2018–05-20
3. BotMill.io - We Mill Bots and Create Bot Milling Tools! http://www.botmill.io, accessed: 2018–05-22
4. CharlieBot. https://sourceforge.net/projects/charliebot/, accessed: 2018–05-22
5. Chatbot Market Size And Share Analysis, Industry Report, 2014–2025. https://www.grandviewresearch.com/industry-analysis/chatbot-market, accessed: 2018–05-07
6. Chatbottest. http://chatbottest.com, accessed: 2018–05-07

7. Gartner Top Strategic Predictions for 2018 and Beyond. https://www.gartner.com/smarterwithgartner/gartner-top-strategic-predictions-for-2018-and-beyond/, accessed: 2018–05-07
8. jsoup: Java HTML Parser. https://jsoup.org/, accessed: 2018–02-02
9. OWASP Top Ten Project. https://www.owasp.org/index.php/Category:OWASP_Top_Ten_Project, accessed: 2018–01-31
10. Program O AI Chatbot - The Friendly Open Source PHP, MySQL, AIML Chatbot. https://www.program-o.com, accessed: 2018–02-04
11. QMetry BOT Tester. http://www.qmetry.com/qmetry-bot-tester/, accessed: 2018–05-07
12. Bozic, J., Wotawa, F.: Security Testing Based on Attack Patterns. In: Proceedings of the 5th International Workshop on Security Testing (SECTEST'14) (2014)
13. Clarke, J., Fowler, K., Oftedal, E., Alvarez, R.M., Hartley, D., Kornbrust, A., O'Leary-Steele, G., Revelli, A., Siddharth, S., Slaviero, M.: SQL Injection Attacks and Defense, 2nd edn. Syngress, (2012)
14. Colby, K.: Artificial Paranoia: A Computer Simulation of Paranoid Process. Pergamon Press, New York (1975)
15. Duchene, F., Rawat, S., Richier, J.L., Groz, R.: KameleonFuzz: Evolutionary Fuzzing for Black-Box XSS Detection. In: CODASPY. pp. 37–48. ACM (2014)
16. Fogie, S., Grossman, J., Hansen, R., Rager, A., Petkov, P.D.: XSS Attacks: Cross Site Scripting Exploits and Defense. Syngress, (2007)
17. Halfond, W.G.J., Viegas, J., Orso, A.: A Classification of SQL Injection Attacks and Countermeasures. In: Proceedings of the IEEE International Symposium on Secure Software Engineering. Arlington, VA, USA (2006)
18. Liu, G., Liu, Q., Zhang, W.: Model-Based Testing and Validation on Artificial Intelligence Systems. In: Second International Multisymposium on Computer and Computational Sciences (2007)
19. Lowe, R., Noseworthy, M., Serban, I.V., Angelard-Gontier, N., Bengio, Y., Pineau, J.: Towards an Automatic Turing Test: Learning to Evaluate Dialogue Responses. In: Proceedings of the 5th International Conference on Learning Representations (ICLR) Workshop. Toulon, France (2017)
20. Martin, M., Lam, M.S.: Automatic Generation of XSS and SQL Injection Attacks with Goal-Directed Model Checking. In: 17th USENIX Security Symposium (2008)
21. McCarthy, J., Hayes, P.J.: Some Philosophical Problems from the Standpoint of Artificial Intelligence. In: Meltzer, B., Michie, D. (eds.) Machine Intelligence 4, pp. 463–502. Edinburgh University Press (1969), reprinted in McC90
22. Rushby, J.: Quality Measures and Assurance for AI Software. In: NASA Contract Report 4187, Washington DC (1988)
23. Shawar, B.A., Atwell, E.: Using corpora in machine-learning chatbot systems. In: International Journal of Corpus Linguistics, vol. 10 (2005)
24. Vasconcelos, M., Candello, H., Pinhanez, C., dos Santos, T.: Bottester: Testing Conversational Systems with Simulated Users. In: IHC 2017: Proceedings of the XVI Brazilian Symposium on Human Factors in Computing Systems (2017)
25. Wallace, R.S.: The Elements of AIML Style. In: ALICE A.I. Foundation (2003)
26. Wallace, R.S.: The Anatomy of A.L.I.C.E. In: ALICE A.I. Foundation (2004)
27. Weizenbaum, J.: ELIZA-A Computer Program For the Study of Natural Language Communication Between Man and Machine. In: Communications of the ACM Volume 9, Number 1 (January 1966) (1966)

JMCTest: Automatically Testing Inter-Method Contracts in Java

Paul Börding[1], Jan Haltermann[1], Marie-Christine Jakobs[2]([✉]),
and Heike Wehrheim[1]

[1] Paderborn University, Paderborn, Germany
[2] LMU Munich, Munich, Germany
M.Jakobs@lmu.de

Abstract. Over the years, Design by Contract (DbC) has evolved as a powerful concept for program documentation, testing, and verification. Contracts formally specify assertions on (mostly) object-oriented programs: pre- and postconditions of methods, class invariants, allowed call orders, etc. Missing in the long list of properties specifiable by contracts are, however, *method correlations*: DbC languages fall short on stating assertions relating methods.

In this paper, we propose the novel concept of *inter-method contract*, allowing precisely for expressing method correlations. We present JMC as a *language* for specifying and JMCTest as a *tool* for dynamically checking inter-method contracts on Java programs. JMCTest fully automatically generates objects on which the contracted methods are called and the validity of the contract is checked. Using JMCTest, we detected that large Java code bases (e.g. JBoss, Java RT) frequently violate standard inter-method contracts. In comparison to other verification tools inspecting (some) inter-method contracts, JMCTest can find bugs that remain undetected by those tools.

1 Introduction

Design by Contract (DbC), first proposed by the Vienna definition language [35], has become a popular concept for documentation, testing, and verification of (mainly) object-oriented software. Today, DbC concepts exist for languages like Eiffel [28], Java (JML [26]), .Net (Code Contracts [19]), C (like used in VCC [17]) or Python [31]. Typically, contracts are directly written into the code and thus also document programs. Contracts are moreover the basis for test generation (e.g., [7,11,14,29,30] for JML) and runtime verification (e.g., [9,13] for JML).

Contracts can refer to different entities of object-oriented programs. Most DbC languages contain pre- and postconditions of methods on normal, i.e. nonexceptional, behavior and class invariants. More sophisticated languages allow to specify history constraints, behavioral subtypes, or type-state properties (call order of methods), incorporate the description of normal as well as exceptional behavior, and include so-called model variables as convenient way of specification. However, all these languages cannot explicitly state method *correlations*.

© IFIP International Federation for Information Processing 2018
Published by Springer Nature Switzerland AG 2018. All Rights Reserved
I. Medina-Bulo et al. (Eds.): ICTSS 2018, LNCS 11146, pp. 39–55, 2018.
https://doi.org/10.1007/978-3-319-99927-2_4

(1) Object o;
true → o.equals(o)

(2) Object o1, o2, o3;
o1.equals(o2) AND o2.equals(o3)
→ o1.equals(o3)

(3) Object o1, o2;
o1.equals(o2) →
o1.hashCode() == o2.hashCode()

(4) MyClass mc;
mc.incr() AND int v = mc.get() →
mc.decr() AND v == mc.get()

```java
public class MyClass {
    private int i;
    @Override
    public boolean equals(Object o){
        if (o == null) return false;
        if (o == this) return true;
        if (!(o instanceof MyClass))
            return false;
        return i == ((MyClass) o).i;
    }
    @Override
    public int hashCode(){
        return super.hashCode(); }
    public void incr() {i++;}
    public void decr() {i--;}
    public int get() {return i;}}
```

Fig. 1. Four contracts (left) on the Java method `equals` and the Java methods `incr` and `decr`, respectively, and an example class violating contract 3 (right).

Method correlations describe interactions between methods, i.e., the effects of a method execution on the results of other methods or the relation between method results. Such correlations often exist and constitute an integral part of the (intended) behavior of classes. Even the Java API documentation *informally* states such correlations and expects application classes extending predefined Java classes or implementing Java interfaces to satisfy these. The most prominent one is the contract on the methods `equals` and `hashCode` of class `Object`:

"If two objects are equal according to the `equals` method, then calling the `hashCode` method on each of the two objects must produce the same integer result."   (From: Java API documentation of class `Object`)

While this example concerns a general case (all classes must adhere to this behavior), correlations might also be application specific like one method having the inverse effect of another (e.g. an increment and a decrement). Today's DbC language, however, fall short on specifying method correlations.

In this paper, we rectify this situation by proposing a new type of contract, called *inter-method contract*, that allows to specify method correlations. We propose the language JMC (Java Method Contracts) for writing inter-method contracts for Java. JMC allows to state relations between arbitrary methods of (not necessarily the same) classes. In its syntax, JMC closely follows Java and is thus easy to use for Java programmers. As our running example consider the four contracts given in the left of Fig. 1. The first three contracts specify requirements on the `equals` method: contract (1) states reflexivity, contract (2) transitivity, and contract (3) the above mentioned interplay between `equals` and `hashCode`. Contract (4) specifies that a decrement is the inverse of an increment, a property not expressible in existing DbC languages. All contracts take the form of an implication (denoted by →): if the first part in the implication is "true", the second part should hold as well. Expressions and method calls in JMC follow standard Java syntax.

With JMCTEST we furthermore developed a tool that automatically tests JMC contracts on Java classes. JMCTEST is built on Java's reflection mechanism to retrieve constructors of classes under test and to call these as to fully automatically generate objects for test input. Using this input, JMCTEST carries out tests evaluating the validity of JMC contracts. Being a dynamic analysis tool, JMCTEST aims at finding violations of contracts, not at proving their correctness. For the example class of Fig. 1, JMCTEST easily finds a violation of the `equals-hashCode` contract (as the class specializes `equals` to the object variable of the class, but not `hashCode`).

To evaluate the effectiveness of JMCTEST, we applied it on real-world production software. Our experiments show that JMCTEST can find contract violations in large code bases and detect violations that static analyzers miss.

2   Inter-Method Contracts

Inter-method contracts describe correlations between methods. We next start with presenting the syntax and semantics of inter-method contracts.

Syntax. The BNF-style grammar shown in Fig. 2 sketches the syntax of inter-method contracts like the ones shown in Fig. 1. Terminal symbols are given in quotes, * denotes iteration (including 0 times) and + iteration at least once. To ease contract specification and test generation, we decided to rely on Java syntax for the four non-terminals VARDECLARATION, BOOLEXPR, METHODCALL, and VARDEFINITION (thus they are not explicitly specified in the grammar).

An inter-method contract specification consists of a set of inputs followed by the actual contract specification. The inputs of a contract state its *participants* and their types. During testing, different (Java) objects will be generated as concrete participants. The actual contract specification follows the concept of inference rules and consists of a *premise* (the part in front of the arrow) and a *conclusion*. Both, premise and conclusion, consist of a sequence of statement blocks which inspect, manipulate or derive information about objects or classes.[1] We distinguish two types of statement blocks: *predicate blocks* and *function blocks.*

Predicate Blocks. The predicate blocks of a contract determine its validity. More concretely, each predicate block describes a property on the participants of the contract and possible additionally declared entities. To avoid misunderstandings of contracts caused by mistakenly ignoring operator precedence, predicate blocks must not mix conjunction and disjunction.

Function Blocks. In contrast to a predicate block, the task of a function block is limited to changing the state, e.g., to properly initialize or configure objects, and to extract and store information for later usage.

---

[1] An empty sequence is an abbreviation for the one-element sequence `true`, see contract (1) in Fig. 1.

```
SPECIFICATION ::= INPUTS CONTRACT
INPUTS ::= VARDECLARATION+
CONTRACT := STATEMENTBLOCKS '->' STATEMENTBLOCKS
STATEMENTBLOCKS ::= STATEMENTBLOCK*
STATEMENTBLOCK ::= PREDICATEBLOCK | FUNCTIONBLOCK
PREDICATEBLOCK ::= DISJUNCTION | CONJUNCTION
DISJUNCTION ::= BOOLEXPR | BOOLEXPR 'OR' DISJUNCTION
CONJUNCTION ::= BOOLEXPR | BOOLEXPR 'AND' CONJUNCTION
FUNCTIONBLOCK ::= FUNCTIONAL+
FUNCTIONAL ::= METHODCALL | VARDEFINITION
```

Fig. 2. Grammar for inter-method contracts

As an example, consider contract (3) of Fig. 1. The contract declares two participants (objects o1 and o2). Its premise and conclusion consist of a single predicate
block. Also, contract (2) has just *one* predicate block in the premise. The AND
operator joins two boolean expressions (BOOLEXPRs), not predicate blocks.

Semantics. Our inter-method contracts use an execution-based semantics, which
builds upon the Java semantics. This has the advantage that the semantics is
well-known to the user and we avoid a semantic gap between contracts and tests.
To execute a contract, we require concrete values for the inputs (participants).

Definition 1. *A concrete input for a contract is a function that maps each
input variable (participant) of the contract to a value/object of a proper type.*

Given a concrete input for a contract, we can define the semantics of the
contract on that concrete input. To this end, we first of all need to define the
execution of the contract with the given input. Due to side-effects of e.g. method
calls in function blocks, the execution order of statements matters. Our semantics
uses a *sequential* execution order that starts with the first block of the premise
and ends with the last block of the conclusion. The statements in predicate and
function blocks are also executed from left to right. However, there is a difference
between the execution of predicate and function blocks. While function blocks
only need to be executed, for predicate blocks also the validity of the property
checked by that block must be recorded. During testing, the validity may be
stored directly in a (boolean) variable or encoded implicitly in the control-flow.
Furthermore, a predicate block will be executed lazily, i.e., as soon as its result
(boolean value) is fixed, the remaining expressions are not executed. Thus, we
use the Java operators && and || for conjunction and disjunction during testing.

Next to the execution, we must also define the validity of a contract on
that concrete input. Testing aims at finding contract violations. Thus, we define
when a contract is *violated*. Since thrown exceptions are ambiguous, they may be
thrown because a contract is violated or the contract is improper (e.g. violates
method preconditions), we exclude exceptions from our violation definition.

Definition 2. *A concrete input violates a contract if (1) all predicate blocks occurring in the premise evaluate to true, (2) at least one predicate block occurring in the conclusion evaluates to false, and (3) the execution terminates normally.*

Note again that ANDs and ORs are not used to join predicate blocks, just boolean expressions. This semantics of contracts is the basis for test generation.

3   Test Generation

The goal of test generation is to automatically build JUnit tests [23] that check whether a given set of classes adheres to a contract. The JUnit tests depend on two main building blocks: (1) checking whether concrete inputs violate contracts and (2) generating the concrete inputs for testing (test input data generation).

Generating Violation Checking Test Code. First of all, we need code that checks whether a concrete input violates the contract. To achieve modularity, we decided to generate a method `testContract` for that check and to provide the concrete input via parameters as e.g. done in parameterized JUnit tests. Input generation itself is done by the second building block. The `testContract` method has the following signature

```
int testContract(list_of_input_types)
```

where `list_of_input_types` is a placeholder for the list of parameters. The list of parameters will contain one parameter for each input variable of a contract.

We use an integer return value instead of a boolean one and no assert statements in the method `testContract` to be able to return some more information about the outcome of the check (0 = premise not fulfilled, 1 = premise and conclusion fulfilled, 2 = contract violated). More specifically, for each contract, we generate a violation check method of the following form. The generation of the parameter list, the premise and the conclusion is contract dependent and explained below.

```
public int testContract(<parameter list>) {
    <premise>
    <conclusion>
    return 1; }
```

Generating the *parameter list* is simple. Since in the INPUTS of a contract we use variable declarations without initialization to specify the input variables, we simply turn the INPUTS into a parameter list. For the premise code, we need to translate a sequence of statement blocks. The idea is to generate a sequence of Java statements by translating each statement block into a Java statement. Function blocks are easy (since this is already correct Java code): we just take them as they are. In contrast, a predicate block is translated into an if-statement as to capture the semantics of contracts, which crucially depends on the evaluation of predicate blocks. The if-statement takes the following form:

```
if ( !(< property >)) {
   return 0; }
```

The if-statement checks whether the property of the predicate block is not fulfilled. In this case, the value 0 is returned, i.e., the contract is not violated on the concrete test input because the premise is already not fulfilled. Note that this is correct since a violation (see Definition 2) requires all predicate blocks in the premise to evaluate to true. The property of a predicate block itself is either a disjunction or a conjunction, and thus translated either using || or &&.

Generating code for the *conclusion* (second STATEMENTBLOCKS element in a contract) is similar to the generation of the premise code. The only difference is the return value, which for the conclusion is 2 when a property is not fulfilled. Figure 3 shows the testContract method generated for the equals-hashCode.

```
public int testContract(Object o1, Object o2) {
   if (!(o1.equals(o2))) {
      return 0; }
   if (!(o1.hashCode() == o2.hashCode())) {
      return 2; }
   return 1; }
```

Fig. 3. Generated testContract method checking violation of equals-hashCode

Detecting a contract violation with a single concrete input is unlikely. A contract must be checked with many different concrete inputs. While we could have created one test case per concrete input, we decided to bundle all violation checks for a particular class into *one* JUnit test case and report violation details in a log. This improves the clarity of the test result. The method testContractImpl checks such a set of inputs, calling for each input the testContract method, and logs the following data.

Logging Test Inputs. For each observed contract violation or exception, the toString() representations of all input values is logged. For the first n^2 violations or exceptions, the input values are also serialized to a file associated with the respective violation or exception.

Logging Statistical Data. Besides test inputs, the testContractImpl method logs statistical data about the contract checks for the implementation (class). A list of this data can be found in Table 1.[3]

The method testContractImpl ends with the JUnit assertion
   assertTrue(failures == 0 && exceptions == 0);
referring to the collected statistical data, i.e., JUnit signals a successful test when no test input violates the contract nor causes an exception to be thrown.

---

[2] The number n is user-configurable.

[3] The ratio of PremiseFF to Runs is a metric indicating how many of the generated tests are relevant for contract checking.

Table 1. Logged statistics

Name	Description
Runs	Number of executions of method `testContract`
PremiseFF	Number of executions of method `testContract` with fulfilled premise
Failures	Number of executions of method `testContract` with violations
Exceptions	Number of executions of method `testContract` which threw exceptions
FailRate	Failures * 100/PremiseFF

Generating Test Input Data. To execute test cases, we need concrete inputs. We build the concrete inputs from input data given for each input variable. Hence, we need to generate input values for each type occurring in the INPUTS of a contract. Note that with respect to coverage, we need not achieve coverage of the `testContract` method, which existing white-box input generators would likely try, but rather of the contract and the methods involved in the contract. Thus, we decided to use an efficient, black box strategy that mainly generates input values randomly. In addition, we allow user guidance to steer or restrict the random generation. Table 2 summarizes the configuration options for test input generation. In our random generation, we distinguish between primitive types, Strings, and other object types.

Table 2. Configuration parameters for test input generation

Type	Options	Description
Int	Sampling	Values for `ints` chosen at random, range and number parameterizable
	Fixed	Values for `ints` user defined
Double	Sampling	Values for `doubles` chosen at random, range and number parameterizable
	Fixed	Values for `doubles` user defined
String	Sampling	Values for `Strings` chosen at random, pattern and number parameterizable
	Fixed	Values for `Strings` user defined
Object	Depth	Maximal nesting depth in constructor calls.
	AllowNull	Allow/Disallow `null` as parameter in constructor calls above Depth
	Creation	`Search` (all constructor combinations) or `Random` samples
	#Empty	Number of objects constructed with parameterless (empty) constructor
	#NonEmpty	Number of random objects constructed with other (non-empty) constructors (only if Creation is set to `Random`)

Primitive Data Types. We use a rather standard generation for primitive data types. For boolean types, the test generator uses both values `true` and `false`. In all other cases, the test generator relies on a predefined selection from the range of the data type. The selection depends on the configuration and consists of the fixed set and a number of random values from the sample range.

Strings. Whenever a String value is required, the test generator chooses the value from a predefined set of String literals. This predefined set consists of a set of user-provided Strings and a fixed number of randomly created Strings.

Objects. In contrast to the previous values, arbitrary objects cannot be represented by literals. To create objects, one must call *constructors*. Depending on the constructor, parameter values are also required. For primitive data types and Strings as parameters, the predefined value sets described above are used. All other objects have to be created, which again requires calling constructors and building objects for their parameters. The nesting depth of object creation is set by the user. Beyond that limit, only null values are used to avoid infinite object creation. By default, the test generator does a search, i.e., via Java's *reflection* mechanism it retrieves all available constructors of a class and calls these with all combinations of parameter values available, which is rather exhaustive. To speed up the test process, the user can fix the number of created objects for each input variable with an object type. In this case, the constructors are selected randomly for each object creation. Additionally, the user may add the `null` value and decide if the parameterless constructor should be used multiple times.

JUnit Test Generation. Knowing how to check contract violations and how to generate test input data, we have everything at hand to generate the actual tests. To easily identify the generated tests for a contract, we decided to generate one JUnit test class per contract. The class is named after the contract. The following code skeleton illustrates the structure of the generated JUnit test class.

```
// imports
public class <contract name> {
  // set-up
  // test cases
    // testContract and testContractImpl
    // testImplXXX methods   }
```

The import section ensures that the types, the classes under test, and the JUnit elements are known. The set-up section hard codes the test values for primitive data types and Strings, initializes the object generator, and ensures that for each test case the object generator creates test values for all input objects that are not under test. Furthermore, it sets up the loggers.

The third part adds the test cases. Next to the two methods `testContract` and `testContractImpl` described above, there exists one test case per implementation (class **XXX** under test).[4] Each test case tests whether the respective

---

[4] Note that we could have used one parameterized JUnit test instead, but we think our solution simplifies the detection of the contract violating implementations.

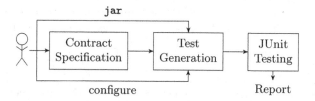

Fig. 4. JMCTEST workflow

class under test sticks to the contract. All test cases are defined by the same schema illustrated by the following piece of code.

```
@Test
public void testImplXXX() {
  XXX[] cut =
   (XXX[]) objectGenerator.createInput(XXX.class);
  testContractImpl(...,cut,...); }
```

A test case is described by a `testImplXXX` method. The method is annotated with the `@Test` tag to tell the JUnit framework that the method should be treated as a test case. During its execution, it generates the input values for those input variables that are under test[5]. To this end, it uses the creation method of the object generator. Thereafter, it calls the `testContractImpl` method to test the implementation against the contract. For the parameters, it uses the local array cut and the test values defined in the set-up part.

4 Implementation and Evaluation

We briefly explain our implementation of this testing framework (called JMCTEST) and report on the results of our experimental evaluations.

4.1 JMCTEST

JMCTEST is a research prototype written in Java that supports specification and automatic testing of inter-method contracts for Java.

Figure 4 describes the workflow of JMCTEST. The user starts with the contract definition using the graphical contract editor of JMCTEST. Thereafter, she configures and starts the test generation for that contract. In her configuration, she specifies how to generate input data. Additionally, she provides a `jar`-file that defines which class implementations to test. Based on the given configuration, JMCTEST automatically creates a set of JUnit tests, one for each class in the `jar`-file. After all tests are generated, they are executed with the JUnit 4 Framework [22]. Finally, the number of executed and failed test cases as well

---

[5] Currently, all input variables under test must have the same object type.

as the failed test cases together with their failure reason are reported. Detailed information about the executed and failed test cases are provided in the log files.

4.2 Evaluation

We carried out a number of experiments to evaluate the effectiveness and efficiency of JMCTEST. Since our JMC language contains a large part of Java's expression language, we easily expressed the informal Java API contracts as well as all contracts from our projects in JMC. Writing contracts in JMC is effective.

Comparison with Other Tools. For the evaluation, we wanted to compare JMCTEST with other analysis tools (for Java). As there have been no inter-method contracts before, the number of tools checking a comparable sort of properties is limited. Model checkers like Java PathFinder [34] are designed to check specific properties of programs and thus cannot directly be used for inter-method contracts. Nevertheless, we found two categories of tools that principally can check at least some form of inter-method contracts: (a) property-based testing tools (similar to QUICKCHECK [15]) and (b) bug pattern detection tools. To decide against which tools to compare JMCTEST, we took a closer look at some tools and evaluated them with respect to the following criteria:

- for testers only: the ability to automatically generate test input, for primitive data types as well as for objects,
- the ability to check arbitrary contracts, possibly via an encoding of them in a different form (e.g., property),
- the ability to work on a `jar`-file and test *all* classes in it,
- the ability to return all errors found (vs. stop with the first error found).

In the first category, we chose the property-based tester JCHECK[6] found at GitHub. There were more options available, but none seemed to be frequently used. For the second category, we chose three tools: EQUALSVERIFIER[7], which is specifically tailored to properties of the `equals`-method, FINDBUGS [2,22], a static analysis tool frequently employed today (e.g. also at Google) to find common bug patterns in Java programs, and RANDOOP [30], a feedback-directed random test generator. An alternative for FINDBUGS could have been PMD[8], but we decided not to have two tools using the same basic checking principle. Table 3 provides a summary of the evaluation. Due to their limitations e.g. on input generation, JCHECK and EQUALSVERIFIER are improper for automatic contract checking. Thus, we only compare JMCTEST with FINDBUGS and RANDOOP.

---

[6] http://www.jcheck.org/.

[7] https://github.com/jqno/equalsverifier.

[8] https://pmd.github.io/.

Table 3. Functionality of tools considered for the comparison

Tool	Input generation		Arb. contracts	`jar`	All errors
	Primitive data type	Object			
JCHECK	✓	×	✓	×	✓
EQUALSVERIFIER	✓	×	×	×	×
FINDBUGS	n.a.	n.a.	×	✓	✓
RANDOOP	✓	✓	×	✓	✓
JMCTEST	✓	✓	✓	✓	✓

Claims. Besides showing that it is feasible to use JMCTEST for testing inter-method contracts, our experiments aimed at evaluating the following claims.

Claim 1 JMCTEST can find real violations of inter-method contracts.
Claim 2 JMCTEST can find violations that other tools do not detect.
Claim 3 JMCTEST is fast enough to be integrated into the build process.

For the evaluation of these claims, we planned the following experiments.

Claim 1. We used JMCTEST to check the `equals-hashCode` contract on three real-world software projects: (1) CPACHECKER (a software analysis tool, [5]), (2) JBoss (a J2EE middleware framework) and (3) Java rt.jar (the Java system library). We restricted ourselves to the `equals-hashCode` contract since it is universally applicable to all Java source code and Java programmers are trained to follow this contract. Thus, violations of the contract constitute a bug.

Claim 2. To evaluate claim 2, we compare JMCTEST against FINDBUGS and RANDOOP. FINDBUGS checks for specific patterns, e.g., classes overriding either `equals` or `hashCode`, to detect violations of the `equals-hashCode` contract. RANDOOP generates random sequences of constructor and method calls and e.g. checks that the resulting objects meet the `equals-hashCode` contract.

Claim 3. For the evaluation of the last claim, we run JMCTEST on the three software projects with different configurations (in particular, differences in the number of objects constructed). In the experiments, we wanted to see the runtime and the number of objects to be constructed until bug finding converges, i.e., until no more bugs are found when the number of test cases is increased. This helps to see whether it is possible to run JMCTEST during a nightly build.

Results. We performed our experiments on a machine with an Intel i5-300HQ v6 CPU with a frequency of 2.3 GHz, 16 GB of memory, and a Windows 10 operating system. Execution times are reported in seconds. Note that a ground truth for the experiments, i.e., the real number of violations of the `equals-hashCode` contract in the three software projects, is not known.

Table 4. Overview of the JMCTEST analysis

Software	Tested classes	Reported errors	#NonEmpty objects	Depth
CPACHECKER	316	3	50	3
JBoss	214	9	50	3
Java rt.jar	1088	124	100	3

Claim 1. For all three software projects, Table 4 shows the number of classes[9] tested against the `equals-hashCode` contract, the number of contract violations found as well as the number of objects constructed during the test using *non-empty* constructors (i.e., not the parameterless constructor) and the nesting depth of object creation. We see that JMCTEST detects contract violations in all three projects, even in the Java runtime library (Java rt.jar). Violations in Java rt.jar were found in the package `com.sun.org.apache.bcel.internal.generic`.

Claim 2. We let FINDBUGS, RANDOOP, and JMCTEST analyze the same classes and compared the number of reported violations. Figure 5 shows the results of this comparison in two bar charts. Each bar chart shows for every analyzed software project[10] the number of violations reported by FINDBUGS (RANDOOP), by JMCTEST, by both (i.e., the intersection of bugs found), and by JMCTEST only (i.e., bugs found by JMCTEST, but not by the other tool). We see that JMCTEST always finds some violations that are not detected by the other tool (rightmost bars). FINDBUGS and RANDOOP always find more violations than JMCTEST. A manual inspection of some randomly chosen warnings revealed that many of FINDBUGS' violations are false warnings. Some real bugs are, however, missed by JMCTEST. Real bugs reported by FINDBUGS are missed because JMCTEST fails to construct objects of the classes under test due to (1) abstract classes (no object construction possible) and (2) missing access permissions, which disallowed object construction. As such problems are inherent to our technique (testing needs object creation and method execution), we see no way of circumventing them. For two bugs reported by RANDOOP, JMCTEST's random input generator did not build suitable inputs, although in principle it could. The other three are missed because JMCTEST cannot deal with generics and does not test the `equals-hashCode` contract with objects of different classes.

Claim 3. Finally, for claim 3 we were interested in runtimes of JMCTEST. To be practically usable, testing results should be obtained in a reasonable amount of time. Figure 6 shows the results for the three software projects. On the x-axis the number of non-empty constructor calls made during the tests is given. The y-axis gives the runtimes in seconds. For both CPACHECKER and Java rt.jar,

---

[9] We tested all public classes which did not use `Object.equals`.

[10] We compare RANDOOP and JMCTEST only on the CPACHECKER project because RANDOOP failed on `Java rt.jar` and got stuck on `JBoss`.

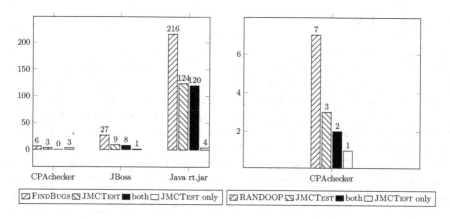

Fig. 5. Comparing JMCTEST with FINDBUGS (left) and RANDOOP (right)

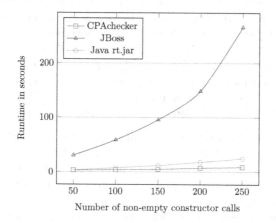

Fig. 6. Runtimes of JMCTEST

test results are obtained within some seconds. For JBoss, runtimes are higher. This is due to the complicated nature of constructors in JBoss, which for instance have to bind ports. We were also interested in finding out how many constructor calls are necessary to find all bugs: for CPACHECKER and JBoss the number of bugs remains stable after testing with 50 constructor calls, for Java rt.jar it is 100 constructor calls. More experiments are, however, needed to find out what a good value for the #NonEmpty configuration parameter is. Nevertheless, even if we set this configuration parameter to 150 or 200, JMCTEST finished after a few minutes. Thus, JMCTEST is fast enough to run as part of the build process.

In summary, the experiments show that JMCTEST can be practically applied, also on large code bases, and can detect contract violations, which other tools do not detect.

5   Related Work

Behavioral Contract Languages. One of the first contract language is the Eiffel language [28]. Nowadays, various contract languages exist. All of them are either embedded contracts or contracts defined by an additional language. Embedded contract languages like e.g. jContractor [24], TreatJS [25], the Spec# programming language [3] or the conditional properties used by QuickCheck [15] directly write contracts in the programming language itself. In contrast, contracts like Jass [4], the Java modeling language (JML) [26], Praspel [18], and the VCC annotated C [17] are defined in an additional language, whose sole purpose is to specify the respective contract. Nevertheless, the mentioned contracts are often embedded in the comments of the source code. We also developed a separate contract language. Instead of pre-, postconditions, invariants, protocols or refinement, our language tackles inter-method relations. The only other contract languages that can express inter-method relations are conditional properties [15] and parametrized unit tests [33], which express properties by arbitrary function code. In contrast to our approach, both mix specification and testing code, which impairs the developer's access to inter-method contracts.

A different type of contracts are algebraic specifications of abstract data types [21]. Algebraic specifications use algebraic equations, the contracts, to state relationships among operations of abstract data types. Our inter-method contracts cover these relations, but allows us to specify relations beyond abstract data types, e.g., relations between methods of different classes.

Checking Behavioral Contracts. Techniques like static analysis [1,3,8], runtime verification [3,4,18,20,26], or testing [7,11,14,16,27,29,30,32,36] are used to check behavioral contracts. Next, we focus on testing, the technique we apply.

Few test approaches [16,32] automatically test fixed contracts. JCrasher [16] creates tests to inspect the robustness of public methods. Pradel and Gross [32] test substitutability of subclasses. Both randomly sample primitive values. Constructors and methods with a proper return type are used to create objects. JMCTEST checks user-defined contracts, also uses random primitive values in addition to fixed values, but only uses constructors for object creation.

Like us, many test approaches, e.g., [7,11,12,27,29,30,36], use the contract specification to generate a test oracle, which decides if a test fails or passes. Those approaches, however, build the oracle from class invariants and a method's pre- and postconditions and differ in their input generation.

The JML-JUnit framework [11] is semi-automatic and generates tests based on user-specified inputs. Bouquet et al. [6] build tests that cover all parts of a (method's) specification. Often, test inputs are generated randomly. Jartege [29] randomly creates sequences of method calls to generate input objects. Similarly, JET [12] applies a random approach in which input objects are created by a constructor call followed by a sequence of method calls mutating the object. Both, Jartege and JET rely on JML specifications. In contrast, RANDOOP [30] and ARTGen [27] check contracts provided by classes implementing specific interfaces. RANDOOP [30] builds a test case concatenating randomly chosen existing sequences and extending them with a random method call. ARTGen [27] performs adaptive random testing [10], i.e., it selects the test case from a pool of test inputs that is farthest away from the already used test cases. The pool is modified randomly, calling methods on existing objects or adding new objects created from random method sequences. QuickCheck [15] tests properties defined by functions in the code. Test cases are created randomly with (user-defined) generators. Parametrized unit tests [33], unit test methods with parameters similar to our testContract method, check properties defined in the test method code. Often, test inputs are generated with symbolic execution to execute the parametrized unit tests and to achieve high code coverage.

In contrast to JMCTEST, Korat [7] and JMLAutoTest [36] systematically explore a bounded search space. Korat [7] uses a finitization code that describes the search space and a predicate checking if an input is valid. JMLAutoTest [36] also relies on finitization code. Provided with a finitization and a JML specification, it systematically generates all non-isomorphic test cases, excluding those which violate class invariants, and checks them against the JML specification

JMCTEST uses the inter-method contract as test oracle and generates inputs from random samples and fixed inputs. However, it is limited to constructor calls for object generation. While conditional properties [15] and parametrized unit tests [33] subsume our inter-method contracts, in contrast to QuickCheck and parametrized unit tests, JMCTEST is fully automatic.

6   Conclusion

For more than 20 years, languages and tools have been developed to support the idea of Design by Contract. Regardless, existing languages and tools mostly focus on pre-, postconditions, and invariants. This makes it difficult if not impossible to state and check contracts that focus on correlations between methods.

Our inter-method contract language offers a mechanism to formally describe method correlations and, thus, enables their automatic validation. Due to its similarity to Java, our language is easy to learn. Furthermore, we did not stop at the language level, but we carried on with tool support for specification and validation of inter-method contracts. Our prototype tool JMCTEST provides a user interface for inter-method contract specification. It can automatically test a set of implemented classes against a specified inter-method contract. Although JMCTEST is an academic prototype, it already detected real violations of the equals-hashCode contract in existing, well-maintained software projects. More impressively, some of these violations have not been found by other tools.

References

1. Ahrendt, W., et al.: The KeY platform for verification and analysis of Java programs. In: Giannakopoulou, D., Kroening, D. (eds.) VSTTE 2014. LNCS, vol. 8471, pp. 55–71. Springer, Cham (2014). https://doi.org/10.1007/978-3-319-12154-3_4
2. Ayewah, N., Hovemeyer, D., Morgenthaler, J.D., Penix, J., Pugh, W.: Using static analysis to find bugs. IEEE **25**(5), 22–29 (2008). https://doi.org/10.1109/MS.2008.130

3. Barnett, M., Leino, K.R.M., Schulte, W.: The Spec# programming system: an overview. In: Barthe, G., Burdy, L., Huisman, M., Lanet, J.-L., Muntean, T. (eds.) CASSIS 2004. LNCS, vol. 3362, pp. 49–69. Springer, Heidelberg (2005). https://doi.org/10.1007/978-3-540-30569-9_3

4. Bartetzko, D., Fischer, C., Möller, M., Wehrheim, H.: Jass - Java with assertions. Electr. Notes Theor. Comput. Sci. **55**(2), 103–117 (2001). https://doi.org/10.1016/S1571-0661(04)00247-6

5. Beyer, D., Keremoglu, M.E.: CPACHECKER: a tool for configurable software verification. In: Gopalakrishnan, G., Qadeer, S. (eds.) CAV 2011. LNCS, vol. 6806, pp. 184–190. Springer, Heidelberg (2011). https://doi.org/10.1007/978-3-642-22110-1_16

6. Bouquet, F., Dadeau, F., Legeard, B.: Automated boundary test generation from JML specifications. In: Misra, J., Nipkow, T., Sekerinski, E. (eds.) FM 2006. LNCS, vol. 4085, pp. 428–443. Springer, Heidelberg (2006). https://doi.org/10.1007/11813040_29

7. Boyapati, C., Khurshid, S., Marinov, D.: Korat: automated testing based on Java predicates. In: ISSTA, pp. 123–133. ACM (2002). http://doi.acm.org/10.1145/566172.566191

8. Chalin, P., Kiniry, J.R., Leavens, G.T., Poll, E.: Beyond assertions: advanced specification and verification with JML and ESC/Java2. In: de Boer, F.S., Bonsangue, M.M., Graf, S., de Roever, W.-P. (eds.) FMCO 2005. LNCS, vol. 4111, pp. 342–363. Springer, Heidelberg (2006). https://doi.org/10.1007/11804192_16

9. Chalin, P., Rioux, F.: JML runtime assertion checking: improved error reporting and efficiency using strong validity. In: Cuellar, J., Maibaum, T., Sere, K. (eds.) FM 2008. LNCS, vol. 5014, pp. 246–261. Springer, Heidelberg (2008). https://doi.org/10.1007/978-3-540-68237-0_18

10. Chen, T.Y., Leung, H., Mak, I.K.: Adaptive random testing. In: Maher, M.J. (ed.) ASIAN 2004. LNCS, vol. 3321, pp. 320–329. Springer, Heidelberg (2004). https://doi.org/10.1007/978-3-540-30502-6_23

11. Cheon, Y., Leavens, G.T.: A simple and practical approach to unit testing: the JML and JUnit way. In: Magnusson, B. (ed.) ECOOP 2002. LNCS, vol. 2374, pp. 231–255. Springer, Heidelberg (2002). https://doi.org/10.1007/3-540-47993-7_10

12. Cheon, Y.: Automated random testing to detect specification-code inconsistencies. In: Karras, D. (ed.) Conference on Software Engineering Theory and Practice, pp. 112–119. International Society for Research in Science and Technology (2007)

13. Cheon, Y., Leavens, G.T.: A runtime assertion checker for the Java Modeling Language (JML). In: Conference on Software Engineering Research and Practice, pp. 322–328. CSREA Press (2002)

14. Cheon, Y., Rubio-Medrano, C.E.: Random test data generation for Java classes annotated with JML specifications. In: Arabnia, H.R., Reza, H. (eds.) Conference on Software Engineering Research and Practice, pp. 385–391. CSREA Press (2007)

15. Claessen, K., Hughes, J.: QuickCheck: a lightweight tool for random testing of Haskell programs. In: ICFP, pp. 268–279. ACM (2000). http://doi.acm.org/10.1145/351240.351266

16. Csallner, C., Smaragdakis, Y.: JCrasher: an automatic robustness tester for Java. Softw. Pract. Exper. **34**(11), 1025–1050 (2004). https://doi.org/10.1002/spe.602

17. Dahlweid, M., Moskal, M., Santen, T., Tobies, S., Schulte, W.: VCC: contract-based modular verification of concurrent C. In: ICSE, pp. 429–430. IEEE (2009). https://doi.org/10.1109/ICSE-COMPANION.2009.5071046

18. Enderlin, I., Dadeau, F., Giorgetti, A., Ben Othman, A.: Praspel: a specification language for contract-based testing in PHP. In: Wolff, B., Zaïdi, F. (eds.) ICTSS 2011. LNCS, vol. 7019, pp. 64–79. Springer, Heidelberg (2011). https://doi.org/10.1007/978-3-642-24580-0_6

19. Fähndrich, M.: Static verification for code contracts. In: Cousot, R., Martel, M. (eds.) SAS 2010. LNCS, vol. 6337, pp. 2–5. Springer, Heidelberg (2010). https://doi.org/10.1007/978-3-642-15769-1_2

20. Fähndrich, M., Barnett, M., Logozzo, F.: Embedded contract languages. In: SAC, pp. 2103–2110. ACM (2010). http://doi.acm.org/10.1145/1774088.1774531

21. Guttag, J.V., Horning, J.J.: The algebraic specification of abstract data types. Acta Informatica 10(1), 27–52 (1978). https://doi.org/10.1007/BF00260922

22. Hovemeyer, D., Pugh, W.: Finding bugs is easy. SIGPLAN Not. 39(12), 92–106 (2004). http://doi.acm.org/10.1145/1052883.1052895

23. JUnit: Junit4 (2012–2017). http://junit.org/junit4/

24. Karaorman, M., Hölzle, U., Bruno, J.: jContractor: a reflective java library to support design by contract. In: Cointe, P. (ed.) Reflection 1999. LNCS, vol. 1616, pp. 175–196. Springer, Heidelberg (1999). https://doi.org/10.1007/3-540-48443-4_18

25. Keil, M., Thiemann, P.: TreatJS: higher-order contracts for JavaScripts. In: Boyland, J.T. (ed.) ECOOP. LIPIcs, vol. 37, pp. 28–51. Schloss Dagstuhl-Leibniz-Zentrum fuer Informatik (2015). https://doi.org/10.4230/LIPIcs.ECOOP.2015.28

26. Leavens, G.T., Baker, A.L., Ruby, C.: Preliminary design of JML: a behavioral interface specification language for Java. SIGSOFT Softw. Eng. Notes 31(3), 1–38 (2006). http://doi.acm.org/10.1145/1127878.1127884

27. Lin, Y., Tang, X., Chen, Y., Zhao, J.: A divergence-oriented approach to adaptive random testing of Java programs. In: ASE, pp. 221–232. IEEE (2009). https://doi.org/10.1109/ASE.2009.13

28. Meyer, B.: Design by contract: the Eiffel method. In: TOOLS, p. 446. IEEE (1998). https://doi.org/10.1109/TOOLS.1998.711043

29. Oriat, C.: Jartege: a tool for random generation of unit tests for Java classes. In: Reussner, R., Mayer, J., Stafford, J.A., Overhage, S., Becker, S., Schroeder, P.J. (eds.) QoSA/SOQUA -2005. LNCS, vol. 3712, pp. 242–256. Springer, Heidelberg (2005). https://doi.org/10.1007/11558569_18

30. Pacheco, C., Lahiri, S.K., Ernst, M.D., Ball, T.: Feedback-directed random test generation. In: ICSE, pp. 75–84. IEEE Computer Society (2007). http://doi.acm.org/10.1145/1297846.1297902

31. Ploesch, R.: Design by contract for Python. In: APSEC, pp. 213–219. IEEE (1997). https://doi.org/10.1109/APSEC.1997.640178

32. Pradel, M., Gross, T.R.: Automatic testing of sequential and concurrent substitutability. In: ICSE, pp. 282–291. IEEE (2013). https://doi.org/10.1109/ICSE.2013.6606574

33. Tillmann, N., Schulte, W.: Parameterized unit tests. In: FSE, pp. 253–262. ACM (2005). http://doi.acm.org/10.1145/1081706.1081749

34. Visser, W., Havelund, K., Brat, G.P., Park, S., Lerda, F.: Model checking programs. Autom. Softw. Eng. 10(2), 203–232 (2003). https://doi.org/10.1023/A:1022920129859

35. Wegner, P.: The Vienna definition language. ACM Comput. Surv. 4(1), 5–63 (1972). http://doi.acm.org/10.1145/356596.356598

36. Xu, G., Yang, Z.: JMLAutoTest: a novel automated testing framework based on JML and JUnit. In: Petrenko, A., Ulrich, A. (eds.) FATES 2003. LNCS, vol. 2931, pp. 70–85. Springer, Heidelberg (2004). https://doi.org/10.1007/978-3-540-24617-6_6

Testing Ambient Assisted Living Solutions with Simulations

Marlon Cárdenas$^{(\boxtimes)}$, Jorge Gómez Sanz$^{(\boxtimes)}$, and Juan Pavón$^{(\boxtimes)}$

Department of Software Engineering and Artificial Intelligence,
Complutense University of Madrid, Madrid, Spain
{marlonca,jjgomez,jpavon}@ucm.es

Abstract. The paper introduces a testing solution for evaluating Ambient Assisted Living systems by means of 3D simulations generated with a game engine, complex event processing, and classifiers. The solution aims to ensure that: (1) some key features of the problem appear in the simulation, and (2) the assistive solution interacts with the persons in the right way. A specific testing solution is needed because of the evolving nature of the simulation (each iteration of the requirements specification involves changes in the activities within the simulation) and the assistive solution (it operates in real time and evaluating its performance may require manually inspecting hours of simulation). The approach is illustrated with a proof-of-concept experiment.

Keywords: 3D simulation · Ambient Assisted Living (AAL)
Real-time simulation · Requirements gathering

1 Introduction

One of the main areas of application of Ambient Intelligence (AmI) is the support for improving the autonomy and quality of life of ageing population with Ambient Assisted Living (AAL) solutions [8]. They cover many needs of the daily life, such as facilitating the administration of medication, fall detection, and monitoring of chronic diseases or common activities, among others.

Although these tasks are usually performed by care-givers, AAL technologies are contributing to the assistance of older persons at home with new services, which can work 24 h a day and reach a larger population. The development of an assistive solution must take into account the participation of the end-users in its process, which has to be user-centered and co-creative [6], to prevent technology rejection situations. Co-creation happens usually in the context of expensive facilities, such as living labs.

Some recent tools [7] are translating the co-creation effort to the computer, addressing both the modeling of the problem and its corresponding assistive solution through computer 3D simulations [3]. 3D simulations are easier to understand than technical specifications, and do not require special skills by the users.

© IFIP International Federation for Information Processing 2018
Published by Springer Nature Switzerland AG 2018. All Rights Reserved
I. Medina-Bulo et al. (Eds.): ICTSS 2018, LNCS 11146, pp. 56–61, 2018.
https://doi.org/10.1007/978-3-319-99927-2_5

This facilitates communication in multidisciplinary teams. Though this is an advance, they have led to new problems: *how to ensure that each new iteration of the 3D simulations is consistent with previous iterations, and how to verify that the assistive solution and the simulated characters within are behaving as they should.* Since simulations are run in real time, validation requires some sort of time accounting while analyzing the events that are produced by the simulation. A way to do this is by using Complex Event Processing (CEP). This technique analyses incoming events from some user defined sources and applies user-defined rules to find patterns in them. We apply this feature to arrange unit tests to support the analysis of the 3D simulation progress.

The contributions of this work are an informal formulation of a unit test and the identification of the required elements for the validation of 3D simulations of AAL solutions. Section 2 presents an informal unit test definition. This is followed by a description of the deployment structure of the solution in Sect. 3. Section 4 presents a proof of concept, an example of memory loss scenario, which has been developed using simulations generated with the AIDE (*Ambient Intelligence Development Environment*) software framework [5], which is based on the use of model driven development techniques [4], and has been applied in different domains [2]. Finally, Sect. 5 summarizes the findings.

2   A Unit Test Definition

The unit test considers either the validation of simulation components (be it the behavior of its constituents, including the assistive solution) or the simulation as a whole. If the assistive solution is conceived within a use case of a certain technology in one or many scenarios, a single simulation represents one (preferably) of those scenarios. The developer expects to model a scenario that reflects some problem of a person (for instance, a person at home forgets to close a cupboard door because she initiates another activity), and an assistive solution (for instance, something detects the situation and reminds her that the door should be closed).

The testing goal is to generate validation instructions for each of these two issues (the description of the problem and the assistive solution), and both are assessed according to the progress of the simulation. The simulation consists of several elements, which imply specific validation issues:

Avatar. A character that performs actions within the simulation and interacts with the assistive solution. **Avatar validation** implies that (1) the character is in certain locations and that (2) it initiates, and (3) completes certain activities, successfully or not. The outcome of the activity, since it may involve an interplay with the assistive solution, needs to account the sensory input of the avatar (e.g., determining if anyone has talked to the character) or the status of some elements in the environment.

Activities. Activities in the simulation are presented as graphical animations of the gestures the character should make, such as running, walking, falling, water tap open, switch on light, to cite some. **Activities validation** implies that (1) they occur along the simulation in a particular sequence, and that (2), despite the animation being used, the character is showing certain gestures, such as bending the arm, even-though there is no explicit isolation animation for that and it is just a part of a bigger animation. The outcome of the activity is evaluated at the avatar level.

Environment. The place where activities take place: a house, a mall, an university building, etc. This includes *Actuators*, objects that allow avatars in the simulation to interact with the environment, such as power switches, TV remote control, water taps, etc. **Environment validation** implies that (1) the objects in the environment produce the expected stimulus at the expected order, such as a TV showing the expected TV program, and that (2) they perceive the avatar's or assistive solution's actions, such as a fridge door being closed by the avatar or a house alarm being activated by the assistive solution.

Sensors. They provide information on what is happening in the simulation, from an avatar, the environment, or the interaction among them. They intend to reproduce the expected output of a real sensor. **Sensors validation** implies (1) determining that the expected sensory input is present at the necessary moments as a consequence of some actions performed along the simulation by the character, other objects, or the assistive solution itself. Also, (2) that the sensor output matches in frequency and data quality those values obtained by real sensors. For instance, some sensors need to be modeled with noisy signals because of limitations of the current technology.

2.1   Validation Success Criteria

Evaluating the success of an assistive solution-simulation interplay requires taking into account two issues. First, that the simulation continuously produces **streams of events** that have to be processed on-line (if the simulation is a long one and the developer wants to identify failures sooner) or off-line (if the simulation is a short one). Second, that the interaction of the assistive solution and the simulation may be intermittently successful along the simulation.

The idea of **time window** is used to partially deal with these two issues. A **time window** classifies the events from the simulation into groups corresponding to those produced within two instants of time. The size of the time window will be defined by the developer depending on the domain.

The success of the simulation-solution will then be defined in terms of: *what situations should occur, or should not, within the time window; and whether what happened in some window, should or should not happen in some/any/all existing time windows along the execution.*

3   Testing Infrastructure

The software components that are necessary for this validation are run within three separated nodes, as shown in Fig. 1. **Simulations** are created and run with

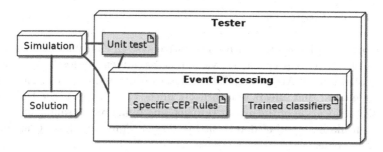

Fig. 1. UML deployment diagram showing nodes and artifacts involved in the testing

the AIDE tool. AIDE also enables communication between the **Solution** and the **Simulation**. The **Tester** is the one being introduced in this paper.

The **Solution** runs outside the **Simulation**, so as to reproduce real situations where delays in the decision making may lead to failures in assisting people. It can be made of emulators (e.g., Android emulators or IoT emulators) or plain processes enabled with communication facilities towards the simulation. It interacts with the **Simulation** through AIDE [5] middleware, obtaining information from the simulated sensors deployed within the simulation (e.g., movements of some limbs of the avatar) and triggering actions (e.g., speaking to the avatar). The **Simulation** uses the open source 3D game engine JMonkey to run the actions as defined in a custom visual language [1]. The simulation runs in real time, though it can be accelerated to some extent.

The **Tester** is the node performing the validation of the simulation and the interplay of simulation and the solution. It initializes and launches a Complex Event Processing (CEP) instance with the necessary files containing the **Specific CEP rules**, the **Trained classifiers**, and a particular **time window** (CEP is configured with one). The **Specific CEP rules** analyze the stream of events as produced by the simulation and generates success/failure states within each time window. The rules identify patterns in the generated events along the **time window** and generates new labeled events, such as *the avatar is in the living room* or *the avatar is running*. Other CEP rules combine the new labeled events with other pieces of information to implement the success criteria within a time window and across time windows.

Some low level information cannot be informed directly by the simulation, such as whether a door is open or closed, if there are people speaking, or if the character is raising a hand. Focusing on the later, if the situation to be reproduced is a character that cannot perform movements with an arm, this cannot be identified by just checking what animations are being run. The only way is by checking position and movement data associated to the hand component in the simulation. **Trained classifiers** allow to deal with such cases. They are connected directly with the **Simulation** and classify low level events, e.g., position of elements, into some predetermined categories, such as *the arm is being moved*. The classifiers have to be trained to the situations to be recognized, though, which may not be trivial for all developers.

4 Proof of Concept

This framework is illustrated with an assistive system that should detect when doors are left open. This case is relevant in cases of memory loss, which are frequent in patients with Alzheimer. Table 1 describes the sequence of validations to be performed and that affects both objects in the environment (the fridge door, the glass), the location of the avatar (kitchen and living room), and the activities (walking, drinking, opening doors, sitting down). Some low level evaluation is required to decide.

Table 1. Definition of the activities of the simulation and the corresponding validation steps

Order - Patient Activities	Test Case	sensors	Expected output
1-patient is in the living room of the house watching television	checkStop	s_1, s_2, s_3	true
2-patient walks to the refrigerator	checkMovements	s_2, s_3	'get up/get down'
3-patient opens the refrigerator door	checkMovement	s_2	'get up hand'
4-patient drinks water for 30 sec	checkMovement	s_2	'get glass'
5-patient closes the refrigerator door	checkMovement	s_2	'get down hand'
6-patient returns to the sofa	checkMovements	s_2, s_3	'get up/get down'
7-end simulation	checkStop	s_1, s_2, s_3	true

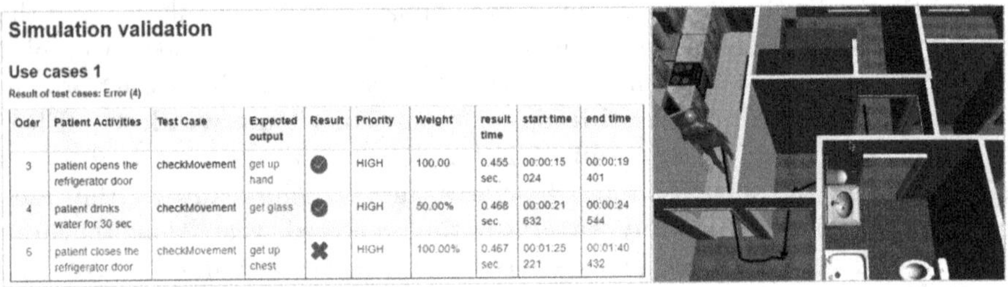
Simulation validation

Use cases 1

Result of test cases: Error (4)

Oder	Patient Activities	Test Case	Expected output	Result	Priority	Weight	result time	start time	end time
3	patient opens the refrigerator door	checkMovement	get up hand	✔	HIGH	100.00	0.455 sec.	00:00:15 024	00:00:19 401
4	patient drinks water for 30 sec	checkMovement	get glass	✔	HIGH	50.00%	0.468 sec.	00:00:21 632	00:00:24 544
5	patient closes the refrigerator door	checkMovement	get up chest	✖	HIGH	100.00%	0.467 sec.	00:01:25 221	00:01:40 432

Fig. 2. Result of all the tests after running the 3D simulation of the scenario

It is expected that step number 5 fails because the patient forgets to close the door. Only an assistive solution will change the situation and make the test complete successfully. The assistance could be as simple as reminding the avatar that the door was left open. To achieve so, the challenge is to determine the minimal amount of affordable sensors to be deployed in the simulation. The use case assumes the sensors are located over the avatar (chest - s_1, left hand - s_2, right hand - s_3). The generated sensor feed is processed by the assistive solution, or the validation component, the same way as a real sensor feed. With this information, it is possible to detect gestures with specific **trained classifiers**, such as *get up/get down hand*. The execution of the simulation with the analysis of the outputs made with the CEP infrastructure is presented in Fig. 2. The streams of events are analyzed and the success of each step decided. Each validation step is associated with a time window at the right hand part of the figure. To the left, an actual 3D simulation snapshot is presented. To the right, a sample report generated by the unit test is presented where step 5 fails. Now, it would be up to the co-creation team to determine what assistive solution can solve this issue.

5   Conclusion and Future Work

This paper has introduced elements necessary to validate 3D simulations that capture a daily living issue and permit to address the features required from an assistive solution. The paper has presented the elements to be validated and illustrated the general approach using complex event processing technology combined with classifiers to analyze low level raw data. The result is validated in a 3D scenario where one of the validation steps fails and can only succeed when the assistive solution is attached. This necessary failure could be maintained along the development to ensure the assistive solution is really making a difference.

Acknowledgments. We acknowledge support from the project "Collaborative Ambient Assisted Living Design (ColoSAAL)" (TIN2014-57028-R) funded by Spanish Ministry for Economy and Competitiveness; and MOSI-AGIL-CM (S2013/ICE-3019) co-funded by the Region of Madrid Government, EU Structural Funds FSE, and FEDER.

References

1. Campillo-Sanchez, P., Gomez-Sanz, J.J.: A framework for developing multi-agent systems in ambient intelligence scenarios. In: Proceedings of the 2015 AAMAS Conference, AAMAS 2015, pp. 1949–1950 (2015)
2. Fernández-Isabel, A., Fuentes-Fernández, R.: Analysis of intelligent transportation systems using model-driven simulations. Sensors **15**(6), 14116–14141 (2015)
3. Gomez-Sanz, J.J., Campillo-Sánchez, P.: Domain independent regulative norms for evaluating performance of assistive solutions. Pervasive Mob. Comput. **34**, 79–90 (2017)
4. Gómez-Sanz, J.J., Pavón, J.: Meta-modelling in agent oriented software engineering. In: Garijo, F.J., Riquelme, J.C., Toro, M. (eds.) IBERAMIA 2002. LNCS (LNAI), vol. 2527, pp. 606–615. Springer, Heidelberg (2002). https://doi.org/10.1007/3-540-36131-6_62
5. GRASIA: AIDE (2018). http://grasia.fdi.ucm.es/aide
6. Pallot, M., Trousse, B., Senach, B., Scapin, D.: Living lab research landscape: from user centred design and user experience towards user cocreation. In: First European Summer School "Living Labs" (2010)
7. Pax, R., Cárdenas Bonett, M., Gómez-Sanz, J.J., Pavón, J.: Virtual development of a presence sensor network using 3D simulations. In: Alba, E., Chicano, F., Luque, G. (eds.) Smart-CT 2017. LNCS, vol. 10268, pp. 154–163. Springer, Cham (2017). https://doi.org/10.1007/978-3-319-59513-9_16
8. Rashidi, P., Mihailidis, A.: A survey on ambient-assisted living tools for older adults. IEEE J. Biomed. Health Inf. **17**(3), 579–590 (2013)

Generating OCL Constraints from Test Case Schemas For Testing Model Behavior

Nisha Desai[✉] and Martin Gogolla

Department of Mathematics and Computer Science, University of Bremen,
28334 Bremen, Germany
{nisha,gogolla}@informatik.uni-bremen.de

Abstract. This contribution studies testing behavioral aspects of a given UML and OCL model. In our approach, a so-called model validator can automatically generate test cases (object models) by using configurations for the object models and manually formulated OCL invariants. But expressing OCL invariants can be complex and difficult, especially for novel or occasional modelers. In this contribution, we present an approach to automatically transform a diagrammatic test case schema into a corresponding OCL invariant. The schema is a visual representation of a behavioral test scenario constructed by the developer and which is instantiated by the model validator to achieve different concrete test cases. This approach enhances the underlying testing technique in making it developer-friendly and independent of OCL expertise.

1 Introduction

As the size and complexity of models grow, there is an increasing need for testing their correctness. Today, modeling languages such as the UML along with the OCL are used to describe structural and behavioral aspects of a system.

For checking such crucial properties of a UML and OCL model, the tool USE can be employed to transform a given application model into an equivalent so-called filmstrip model [5]. In USE, a model validator (MV) can automatically generate valid object diagrams based on given configurations (determining finite sets of objects, links and attribute values) and external OCL invariants. For the validation process, external OCL invariants are currently manually formulated. However, writing OCL expressions is a difficult and time-consuming task and often results in erroneous constraints. To address this problem, we propose an approach where developers can express a scenario by constructing a so-called *test case schema (TC schema)* which then can automatically be transformed into an OCL invariant. Furthermore, the MV is used to instantiate the abstract TC schema in order to generate multiple concrete test cases.

The rest of the paper is structured as follows. Section 2 provides the background and motivation of our work. Section 3 describes TC schemas with an

© IFIP International Federation for Information Processing 2018
Published by Springer Nature Switzerland AG 2018. All Rights Reserved
I. Medina-Bulo et al. (Eds.): ICTSS 2018, LNCS 11146, pp. 62–68, 2018.
https://doi.org/10.1007/978-3-319-99927-2_6

example and its transformation to an OCL invariant is explained in Sect. 4. In Sect. 5, we show test case generation using the MV. Section 6 presents related work and we conclude our paper with future work in Sect. 7.

2   Background

The MV in USE is specifically designed for structural analysis of models. Therefore, we use our filmstrip approach which transforms invariants (structural properties) and operation pre- and postconditions (behavioral properties) of an application model into a filmstrip model which possesses only invariants.

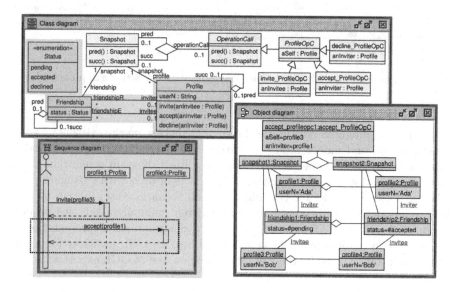

Fig. 1. Application model and filmstrip model.

The filmstripping approach can be explained best in terms of an example. A simple `SocialNetwork` model in which a user can invite, accept and reject a friendship request is chosen as an example. The upper part of Fig. 1 shows the class diagram of the filmstrip model. The original application model, consisting of the classes `Profile` and `Friendship` with the associations `Invite` and `Invitee`, is completely contained in the filmstrip model and indicated in a gray-shaded style. The small sequence diagram also represents elements of the application model. The application model is automatically transformed with a plug-in into the filmstrip model: the non-gray shaded classes and invariants (not shown) are added. In essence, the application model sequence diagram becomes a filmstrip model object diagram. `Snapshot` objects explicitly allow to capture single system states from the application model. Operation call objects (suffix OpC) describe operation calls from the application model. Basically, each operation is transformed into an `OperationCall` class with attributes for the `self` objects and for the operation parameters. Thus, for example, the call `profile3.accept(profile1)` (dotted box) from the sequence diagram is represented by the object `accept_profileopc1` in the filmstrip object diagram. The effect of the operation call is represented by the differences between the left and the right snapshot: The `accept` operation call changes the attribute `status`. The four `Profile` and the two `Friendship` objects represent different object states before and after the operation call. So one could say that the object `profile2` is a later incarnation of the object `profile1`.

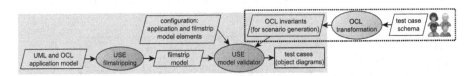

Fig. 2. Overview on filmstrip validation (gray box) with TC schema approach (dotted box).

The gray highlighted part in Fig. 2 gives an overview on the existing filmstrip transformation and model validation process. In the validation process, external OCL invariants are specified to guide the object diagram generation into a particular direction, e.g., for attesting that objects or links with particular properties exist (for example, for the initial or final scenario state) [5]. Up to now, these external OCL invariants had to be written manually. Thus, we propose an approach where a TC schema, which is a diagrammatic representation of a scenario, can automatically be transformed into an OCL invariant for model validation in order to make the validation process free of OCL expertise.

3   Test Case Schema Example

A TC schema is basically a partial filmstrip object diagram consisting of different snapshots which represent system states, and these snapshots can contain application model objects and links. The objects of different snapshots can be connected through filmstrip (pred,succ) links. We now show the construction of a TC schema for an example scenario of the `SocialNetwork` model.

The description of the user defined test scenario is as follows: There have to exist two user profiles. In the initial state, they are not linked with each other, and in the final state, they are linked with each other through a friendship request. Figure 3 shows the TC schema for this scenario. In `Snapshot1`, there exist two user profiles which are not linked with each other. In `Snapshot3`, the `Profile3` is linked to `Profile6` through `Invite` and `Invitee` links as well as a `Friendship` object. For each snapshot, developers have a choice between a so-called *open* snapshot and a *closed* snapshot, and the specification of snapshots will be according to the expected scenario generation. If a snapshot is classified

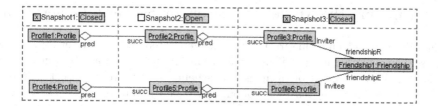

Fig. 3. TC schema of the test scenario.

as closed, only the stated links (if any) are allowed between the snapshot objects in a generated test case; if a snapshot is classified as open, other links are allowed between the snapshot objects in a generated test case. More details about the classification of snapshots and their OCL representations are discussed below.

4 Transformation of a TC Schema into an OCL Invariant

As previously stated, a TC schema is comprised of snapshots (application objects and links) and filmstrip links. So during the transformation from a TC schema to an OCL invariant, these elements must be transformed into OCL expressions. The OCL expressions for the filmstrip (pred,succ) links which connect different snapshot objects are directly generated using the succ role name. However, different OCL representations are possible for the snapshots, as they can be classified as an *open* or *closed*. In the *open* case, the mentioned objects and links are fixed by the generated OCL invariant, but it is possible that more links are present in generated test case. However, in the *closed* case, apart from the mentioned objects and links, other possible application links which are not explicitly mentioned, are excluded by the generated OCL invariant. To illustrate the generation of an OCL invariant, we continue with the TC schema shown in Sect. 3. The generated OCL invariant is as follows:

```
context Snapshot inv FirstLastClosedSnapshots:
 Profile.allInstances->exists(p1,p2,...,p6|Set{p1,p2,..,p6}->size()=6 and
  p1.succ=p2 and p2.succ=p3 and p4.succ=p5 and p5.succ=p6 and
  Friendship.allInstances->exists(f1|
   p1.friendshipR.invitee->excludes(p4) and // Snapshot1
   p1.friendshipE.inviter->excludes(p4) and
   p4.friendshipR.invitee->excludes(p1) and
   p4.friendshipE.inviter->excludes(p1) and
   p3.friendshipR->includes(f1) and f1.inviter = p3 and // Snapshot3
   p6.friendshipE->includes(f1) and f1.invitee = p6  ))
```

For the closed snapshots, OCL expressions are generated guaranteeing (a) the absence of links between Profile1 and Profile4 in Snapshot1 and (b) the presence of links between Profile3 and Profile6 in Snapshot3. In the open snapshot, OCL expressions are not generated, as there are no links.

5   Applying the Model Validator for Scenario Generation

The MV uses a given configuration and the generated OCL invariant for setting the sequence of operation calls by fixing (a) attribute values and (b) objects and links that have been left open in the TC schema in order to construct different test cases. We check the feasibility of our approach by transforming a TC schema into an OCL invariant and analyze the generated test cases.

From many generated test cases (filmstrip object diagrams), two are shown in Figs. 4 and 5: one test case is an invite; accept; the other one is an invite; invite. In the TC schema, one friendship is expected between two profiles. In

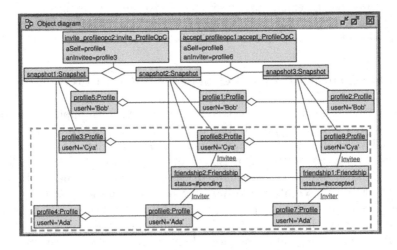

Fig. 4. Automatically generated test case 1

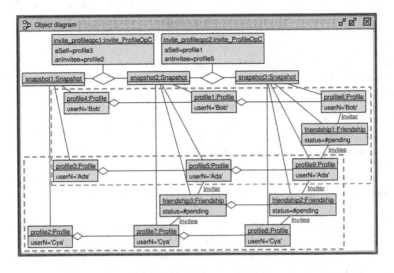

Fig. 5. Automatically generated test case 2

order to satisfy the scenario at least one `invite` operation call should exist, and another operation call could be an `accept`, `decline` or `invite` as the attribute `status` of the `friendship` object is not specified. In both test cases, the test schema is satisfied (highlighted with dashed rectangles). The objects and links in the open snapshots have been decided by the MV depending on the operation calls.

In both shown test cases, the expected test scenario is precisely generated. These show the successful transformation of an OCL invariant from a given TC schema, and validate that our concept of distinguishing between open and closed snapshots lead to the desired results. Various other larger models and larger test case schemas have been developed. Due to space limitations we stick to the small demonstration example.

6   Related Work

There are several contributions discussing techniques and approaches for OCL transformation and test case generation. In [1], the authors are using the Semantic Business Vocabulary and Rules (SBVR) to transform constraints written in natural language to OCL statements. In [6], the tool MoMuT::UML is presented to generate fault based test cases for UML state machine models. In [4], the authors describe symbolic scenarios as operation sequences to generate functional test cases. In [2], the authors propose a method to generate test data on a higher-order representation of OCL models. In [3], the tool UMLtoCSP allows a developer to perform verification and validation of a UML/OCL model based on Constraint Logic Programming. In contrast to all these works, our approach is the only one generating OCL constraints automatically from a developer-specified scenario to generate concrete test cases for behavior model validation.

7   Conclusion

This contribution proposed a transformation for automatically generating an OCL invariant from a TC schema. We showed scenario generation using a model validator which constructed valid behavioral scenarios with different sequences of operation calls based on the generated OCL invariant. Future work will consider more options for attribute specification in the transformation, as this should help developers to express a scenario more effectively. More and larger case studies must check the applicability of the approach.

References

1. Bajwa, I.S., Bordbar, B., Lee, M.G.: OCL constraints generation from natural language specification. In: Proceedings of the 14th IEEE International Enterprise Distributed Object Computing Conference, pp. 204–213. IEEE Computer Society (2010)

2. Brucker, A.D., Krieger, M.P., Longuet, D., Wolff, B.: A specification-based test case generation method for UML/OCL. In: Dingel, J., Solberg, A. (eds.) MODELS 2010. LNCS, vol. 6627, pp. 334–348. Springer, Heidelberg (2011). https://doi.org/10.1007/978-3-642-21210-9_33
3. Cabot, J., Clarisó, R., Riera, D.: UMLtoCSP: a tool for the formal verification of UML/OCL models using constraint programming. In: 22nd IEEE/ACM International Conference on Automated Software Engineering, pp. 547–548. ACM (2007)
4. Castillos, K.C., Dadeau, F., Julliand, J.: Scenario-based testing from UML/OCL behavioral models - application to POSIX compliance. STTT **13**(5), 431–448 (2011)
5. Gogolla, M., Hamann, L., Hilken, F., Kuhlmann, M., France, R.B.: From application models to filmstrip models: an approach to automatic validation of model dynamics. In: Proceedings of Modellierung. LNI, vol. 225, pp. 273–288. GI (2014)
6. Krenn, W., Schlick, R., Tiran, S., Aichernig, B.K., Jöbstl, E., Brandl, H.: MoMut: : UML model-based mutation testing for UML. In: 8th IEEE International Conference on Software Testing, Verification and Validation, pp. 1–8. IEEE Computer Society (2015)

Test Derivation for SDN-Enabled Switches: A Logic Circuit Based Approach

Jorge López[1(✉)], Natalia Kushik[1], Asma Berriri[1], Nina Yevtushenko[2], and Djamal Zeghlache[1]

[1] SAMOVAR, CNRS, Télécom SudParis/Université Paris-Saclay,
9 Rue Charles Fourier, 91000 Évry, France
{jorge.lopez,natalia.kushik,asma.berriri,
djamal.zeghlache}@telecom-sudparis.eu
[2] Ivannikov Institute for System Programming of the Russian Academy of Sciences,
25 Alexander Solzhenitsyn street, 109004 Moscow, Russia
evtushenko@ispras.ru

Abstract. The paper is devoted to testing critical Software Defined Networking (SDN) components and in particular, SDN-enabled switches. A switch can be seen as a forwarding device with a set of configured rules and thus, can be modelled and analyzed as a 'stateless' system. Correspondingly, in this paper we propose to use appropriate logic circuits or networks to model the switch behavior. Both active and passive testing modes can benefit from such representation. First, this allows applying well-known test generation strategies such as for example, test derivation techniques targeting Single Stuck-at Faults (SSFs). We also specify a number of mutation operators for switch rules and propose an algorithm for eliminating equivalent mutants via SAT solving. Logic circuits simulating the behavior of the switches can be effectively utilized for run-time verification, and such logic circuit based approach is also discussed in the paper. Preliminary experimental results with Open vSwitch, on one hand, demonstrate the necessity of considering new fault models for logic circuits (apart from, for example well established SSFs) and on the other hand, confirm the efficiency of the proposed test generation and verification techniques.

Keywords: Software Defined Networking (SDN)
SDN-enabled switches · Mutation testing · Run-time verification
Logic circuits

1 Introduction

As communication technologies progress rapidly, more attention is now paid to virtual networks and various 'softwarization' techniques. In fact, virtualization opens a large number of possibilities when the common resources can be

I. Medina-Bulo et al. (Eds.): ICTSS 2018, LNCS 11146, pp. 69–84, 2018.
https://doi.org/10.1007/978-3-319-99927-2_7

effectively shared and specific network services manage the policies for using these resources. Nevertheless, whenever a given virtual network is requested, it is necessary to assure that its implementation strictly corresponds to the submitted request. In order to guarantee this property, all the hardware and software components involved into the chaining and virtualization processes need to be thoroughly tested and verified.

Software Defined Networking [20] is known to be one of the fundamental building blocks for the creation of virtual networks and thus, SDN-enabled devices such as for example, switches and/or controllers need to be certified, guaranteeing the absence of (specific) bugs and misconfigurations.

We focus on testing SDN switches that act as forwarding devices receiving and sending network packets in accordance with a set of configured rules. Nowadays, such devices are predominantly implemented in software, and therefore different software bugs can induce different functional faults. For example, while using the ONOS controller [2] and Open vSwitch (OVS) [22] we have detected a potential overflow with respect to (w.r.t.) the switch port numbers. Namely, any request with an output port number which is greater than or equal to 2^{16} produces inconsistent results. Each of such requests gets the assigned port number modulus 2^{16}. The OpenFlow Switch Specification [18] states that the maximal physical and logical port number is 4294967040 (0xffffff00). Therefore, one can conclude there is a bug in the OVS implementation[1]. Such software bugs lead to the incorrect packet processing, i.e., the specification given as a set of rules for the switch is not respected. Thus, detecting such bugs is crucial for improving the functional correctness of the SDN infrastructure.

In this paper, we apply model based testing techniques for an SDN-enabled switch. In particular, we propose to model the switch behavior as a corresponding logic circuit in order to take advantage of various scalable manipulations over such circuits as well as to benefit from well-established techniques for their testing. Both, active (Sects. 4 and 5.1) and passive testing (Sects. 4.5 and 5.2), can take advantage of such representation. In particular, we estimate the usefulness of logic circuit based fault models such as for example Single Stuck-at Faults (SSFs) for detecting bugs and misconfigurations in the SDN-enabled switch implementations. Correspondingly, we introduce potential mutations over the switch rules and discover which of these mutations can be effectively detected using the proposed logic circuit based approach. Moreover, we discuss how Boolean Satisfiability (SAT) solvers can be utilized for detecting equivalent mutants. Finally, we propose a scalable solution for the switch monitoring on the basis of logic circuits and related operations.

The paper is organized as follows. Section 2 contains the necessary background and notations. Section 3 summarizes the related work in the area of SDN switch testing and verification. The logic circuit based approach for switch testing is presented in Sect. 4. Preliminary experimental results for a set of switch rules are shown in Sect. 5. Section 6 concludes the paper.

---

[1] Version 2.0.2 used with the ONOS controller version 1.10.4.

2   Background and Notations

2.1   Software Defined Networking

In Software Defined Networking architectures, the control plane is decoupled from the forwarding (data) plane [20], i.e., a logically centralized control function maintains the state of the network and provides instructions to the data plane (packet forwarding devices). Switches located in the data plane then forward data packets according to these control instructions, more specifically, forwarding and filtering rules [23]. Each switch should process the received packets according to the installed forwarding rules. A *forwarding rule* consists of three parts: a packet matching part, an action part, and a location/priority part. The *matching part* describes the values a received network packet should have in order for the rule to be applied (to the packet). The *action part* indicates how to process the matched network packets; the *location/priority part* controls the rule hierarchy using tables and priorities. In SDN, to steer network packets in the data plane, forwarding rules are 'pushed' to the switches by the controller that has a global view of the network; switches are configured remotely and dynamically through interfaces using protocols such as the OpenFlow (OF) protocol [16]. The forwarding rules are grouped in different flow tables and are considered to be the *configurations* of switches with respect to packets and application flow management.

As an example of rules installed in a switch, consider the set of rules defined in Table 1. The table includes the following matching parameters: *Flow Table*, a virtual partition for the installed rules; *Priority*, the order attributed to the rule to be applied with respect to other rules in the flow table; *Input Port* (In_port), the ingress port of the incoming packets; *Ethernet Type* (Eth_type), the type of traffic carried by the Ethernet datagram; *Source and Destination IP Addresses* respectively (IP_source, IP_dest), that define the IP protocol source and destination addresses. The *output ports* (Output) defines the set of ports where a matching packet should be forwarded.

Table 1. Switch example

Flow table	Priority	In_port	Eth_type	IP_source	IP_dest	Output
0	500	*	ARP (0x806)	*	*	Port 1
0	500	1	ARP (0x806)	*	*	"All"
1	501	1	IP (0x800)	10.0.0.1/32	10.0.0.2/32	Port 2
1	501	2	IP (0x800)	10.0.0.2/32	10.0.0.1/32	Port 1

For example, according to Table 1, the third rule is specified in the flow table 1 with the priority 501. When the packets having the source IP address 10.0.0.1 and destination IP address 10.0.0.2 arrive to Port 1 of the switch, these packets have to be forwarded via the (output) Port 2 of the switch.

2.2   Logic Circuits and Related Fault Models

A *combinational circuit* is composed of logic gates; each logic gate implements a Boolean function. Sequential circuits include on one hand, a combinational logic, and on the other, memory elements, namely latches. In this paper, we consider circuits 'without memory', i.e., combinational circuits where the circuit output significantly depends only on its current input.

Following [12], we consider three types of faults that can occur in the circuit implementation, namely Single Stuck-At Faults, Single Bridge Faults, and Hardly Detectable Faults. A circuit that contains a fault is referred to as a *mutant*, as usual.

- Single Stuck-At Fault (SSF) Mutants occur when one circuit gate gets 'stuck' at a given logical value ("1" or "0");
- Single Bridge Fault (SBF) Mutants occur when a given input of a given logical gate is wrongly wired (bridged), i.e., taking the input from the wrong gate;
- Hardly Detectable Fault (HDF) Mutants occur when a single gate changes its output for a single input.

A number of test generation strategies against the faults listed above have been proposed in the last decades. The interested reader can, for example refer to [15,21]. Moreover, test suites derived against the SSFs are claimed to have high fault coverage with respect to other types of circuit mutants. In this paper, we investigate the fault coverage of these techniques when testing SDN-enabled switches effectively described by corresponding logic circuits.

2.3   Notations

A *rule* R defined in the switch configuration is represented by the following implication: $(p_1 \in V_1 \ \& \ p_2 \in V_2 \ \& \ \ldots \ \& \ p_i \in V_i \ \& \ \ldots \ \& \ p_n \in V_n) \implies output\_ports = \{o_1, o_2, \ldots, o_m\}$. In this case, p_i refers to an input parameter, o_i refers to an output port and the sets $V_1, V_2, \ldots, V_n$ define a range or an interval for each switch parameter $p_1, p_2, \ldots, p_n$, correspondingly[2]. For convenience, we denote as Π the projection operator, characterized with a parameter p_i such that for a given rule $R = (p_1 \in V_1 \ \& \ p_2 \in V_2 \ \& \ \ldots \ \& \ p_i \in V_i \ \& \ \ldots \ \& \ p_n \in V_n) \implies output\_ports = \{o_1, o_2, \ldots, o_m\}$, $\Pi_{p_i} = V_i$. Similarly, we denote the output projection of R as $\Pi_{out} = \{o_1, o_2, \ldots, o_m\}$.

An *output mutant* for the rule R is defined as follows: $(p_1 \in V_1 \ \& \ p_2 \in V_2 \ \& \ \ldots \ \& \ p_i \in V_i \ \& \ \ldots \ \& \ p_n \in V_n) \implies output\_ports = \{o'_1, \ldots, o'_{m'}\}$, and $\{o'_1, \ldots, o'_{m'}\} \neq \{o_1, \ldots, o_m\}$.

A *parameter value mutant* for the rule R is defined as follows: $(p_1 \in V_1 \ \& \ p_2 \in V_2 \ \& \ \ldots \ \& \ p_i \in V'_i \ \& \ \ldots \ \& \ p_n \in V_n) \implies output\_ports = \{o_1, o_2, \ldots, o_m\}$, and $V'_i \neq V_i$.

---

[2] The defined intervals are assumed to contain integers, without loss of generality.

In the example illustrated in Table 1, the number of parameters is $n = 6$, and $|V_i| = 1, i \in \{1, \ldots, 6\}$. Note that $m = 3$ (the number of output ports) for the rules in Table 1.

3   Related Work

A number of publications and online presentations have been previously devoted to the verification and testing of SDN switches. In particular, a number of works are dedicated to the validation of the consistency of the switch rules [1,9].

There exist a large number of publications that concern the overall verification of the data plane. Different techniques can be applied in this case, for instance, Header Space Analysis of network packets [10] or Model Checking and Symbolic Execution [6]. Several properties for the whole data plane can be checked in this case, such as reachability issues, absence of loops/holes, etc.

Data plane analysis has also been performed in an *active* mode. In this case, the packets to be sent through the switches have been specifically generated to capture various network failures. The approaches of this set mostly cover automatic network traffic or flow generation (see, for example [5,7,25]). We however note that the analysis is usually performed for checking the paths/networks implemented in the data plane rather than checking the functionality of a given critical forwarding device.

Existing works on testing a given switch can be mostly divided into two groups. The approaches of the first group have a number of pre-defined test purposes that either cover some stress situations for the switch (such as, for example, a flow table capacity) or verify given scenarios formally described in the OpenFlow specification [19]. The approaches of the second group rely on formal models. In particular, in [24] so called Pipelined Extended Finite State Machines are introduced for describing a switch behavior. Note that in this case, a switch is considered as a stateful system which immediately complicates the process of test generation and execution.

We also note that the idea of expressing a switch or a composition of those with the use of Boolean algebra or a system of (partially specified) Boolean functions has been employed before. For example, in [1] a set of switch rules is described by a corresponding Binary Decision Diagram that later is used for verifying their consistency. Moreover, a set of Boolean expressions have been constructed in [14] for the data plane verification based on the SAT problem.

However, to the best of our knowledge, there does not exist an approach which proposes the use of Boolean satisfiability or related logic circuits/networks for deriving *active* test suites with guaranteed fault coverage. Moreover, 'classical' logic circuit based testing strategies such as for example, SSF detection, have not been previously used for checking the functionality of SDN-enabled switches. Likewise, the authors are not aware of any works where logic circuits and their software and/or hardware implementations are used for a *passive* testing/monitoring of an SDN-enabled switch behavior.

4   Logic Circuit Based Approach for Test Suite Generation

4.1   Introducing a Fault Model

We assume that the switch implementation has no faults if each packet is processed exactly in the way that the switch configuration requires. Moreover, if for a given packet pkt there is no rule R in the switch configuration such that the matching part $(p_1 \in V_1 \ \& \ p_2 \in V_2 \ \& \ \dots \ \& \ p_n \in V_n)$ contains the necessary preamble, the packet pkt is simply dropped by the switch, i.e., should not be forwarded anywhere. We note however that a switch can output the packet to 'consult' with the SDN controller about the action applied to an 'unknown' packet [16]; the controller might alter the rules in the switch configuration as a result. We assume this is a different *specification*; further, in this work, we do not focus on such case. The proposed fault model has three items, as usual, namely $FM = \langle S, =, FD \rangle$ where S, the specification, is the set of switch rules, i.e., the rule forwarding configuration of the switch (referred in this paper simply as switch configuration); $=$ is the conformance relation represented by the equality, and FD is the fault domain where the potential switch implementations are explicitly enumerated. As usual, we are interested in deriving *exhaustive* test suites, such that $\forall I \in FD, I \neq S$, is detected by the test suite.

We also note that the system specification in this case can be complete (completely specified) or partial. The set S of switch rules is said to be *complete* if for each preamble $(p_1 \in V_1 \ \& \ p_2 \in V_2 \ \& \ \dots \ \& \ p_n \in V_n)$ there exists a rule $R \in S$ such that $R = ((p_1 \in V_1 \ \& \ p_2 \in V_2 \ \& \ \dots \ \& \ p_n \in V_n) \implies output\_ports = \{o_1, o_2, \dots, o_m\})$. Otherwise, the specification S in the fault model FM is *partial*. We further discuss how completeness and partiality of S affect the exhaustiveness of the test suites derived using well-known logic circuit based fault models.

4.2   Deriving a Logic Circuit for a Switch Specification

The specification S represented by a set of switch rules is not scalable for solving different problems, such as for example, searching for two rules in possibly different tables that coincide or that on the contrary, contradict each other. We therefore, propose to build a logic circuit that preserves the behavior of S on one hand, but allows taking advantage of several scalable manipulations over the Boolean vectors (logic circuits) on the other hand. Such logic circuit LC can be derived in different ways and in this work, we focus on a somehow straightforward approach for this purpose, i.e., we propose to use logic synthesis solutions from a Look-up-Table (LUT) for a system of (partially specified) Boolean functions[3]. The corresponding procedure is described in Algorithm 1.

---

[3] It is intuitively right to consider Boolean representations for values transmitted in network packets as they represent data in binary strings.

Algorithm 1. Logic circuit derivation from a set of switch rules

---

Input : A specification S represented by a set of switch rules
Output: A logic circuit LC simulating S
Define the set of parameters $P = \{p_1, p_2, \ldots, p_n\}$ such that each parameter
$p_i \in P$ is used in at least one preamble of at least one rule $R \in S$.
Determine the number of the primary inputs for the logic circuit as
$\sum_{i=1}^{n} \lceil log_2(1 + max(\bigcup_{R \in S} \Pi_{p_i})) \rceil$, $max(\bigcup_{R \in S} \Pi_{p_i})$ is the maximal element in
all sets for the parameter p_i where all values of p_i are non-negative, and $\lceil x \rceil$
denotes the ceiling function applied to x.
The number of the primary outputs for the logic circuit equals to
$max(\bigcup_{R \in S} \Pi_{out})$, where $max(\bigcup_{R \in S} \Pi_{out})$ denotes the maximum output port
number used in S.
Derive an empty LUT L for a system of $max(\bigcup_{R \in S} \Pi_{out})$ partially specified
Boolean functions of $\sum_{i=1}^{n} \lceil log_2(1 + max(\bigcup_{R \in S} \Pi_{p_i})) \rceil$ variables
foreach *rule* $R \in S$ **do**
  foreach $r = (v_1, v_2, \ldots, v_n) \in V_1 \times V_2 \times \ldots \times V_n$, *where*
  $V_i = \Pi_{p_i}, \forall i \in \{1, 2, \ldots, n\}$ **do**
    Encode each v_i, $i \in \{1, 2, \ldots, n\}$ by a Boolean vector B_i of length
    $\lceil log_2(1 + max(\bigcup_{R \in S} \Pi_{p_i})) \rceil$
    Set the Boolean vector B_port to $(00 \ldots 0)$, $|B\_port| = max(\bigcup_{R \in S} \Pi_{out})$
    foreach *output port* $o_j \in \{o_1, \ldots, o_m\}$ **do**
      Set o_j-th bit of B_port to 1 (the first bit starts at the rightmost
      position with index 1)
    Add a new line to the LUT, i.e., set L to $L \cup \{B_1 B_2 \ldots B_n | B\_port\}$

Run a logic synthesis solution for deriving a logic circuit LC from the LUT L
return LC

For the running example of the set of switch rules listed in Table 1, the LUT
derived by Algorithm 1 has four lines illustrated in Table 2. Note that dashes $(-)$
denote 'don't care' terms[4].

Table 2. LUT for the switch running example

$x_1 x_2 \cdots x_{89}$	$f_1 f_2 f_3$
0111110100--100000000110---	001
011111010001100000000110---	110
111111010101100000000000000101000000000000000000000000001000010100000000000000000000000010	010
111111010110110000000000000101000000000000000000000000001000010100000000000000000000000001	001

4.3   Test Suite Generation

Once a logic circuit LC that simulates the behavior of the switch with the rules S
is derived, one can apply different techniques for test generation. On one hand,
'classical' logic circuit testing strategies such as for example, test derivation

---

[4] The netmasks of the IP addresses are taken into consideration by the dashes in the
corresponding field.

techniques for SSF detection can be exploited. In this case, the circuit LC is mutated in order to obtain a set of mutants of different kinds, such as for example SSF or HDF. The test suite derived to kill each mutant of a particular type can later be applied to the implementation of an SDN switch. The goal of deriving such test suite is to distinguish the output of a correct implementation from an assumed incorrect implementation (mutant)[5]. The advantage of this approach is that logic circuit testing techniques are well studied and elaborated and there exist a number of tools for such test derivation. In this work, we used the tool developed in [12] together with the logic synthesis and verification tool called ABC [4]. Preliminary experimental results for such test generation strategy are presented in Sect. 5.

On the other hand, in some cases, certain properties for a test suite fault coverage can be guaranteed. For example, for SSF mutants the following statements hold.

Proposition 1. *If S is complete and $\exists\, i \in \{1, \dots m\}$ such that $\exists!\, R \in S$, $R = ((p_1 \in V_1 \ \& \ p_2 \in V_2 \ \& \ \dots \ \& \ p_n \in V_n) \implies output\_ports = \{o_1, o_2, \dots, o_m\})$ and $o_i \notin \{o_1, o_2, \dots, o_m\}$, then each output fault in the rule R is detected by an exhaustive test suite w.r.t. SSFs.*

Proof. The completeness of the specification S automatically implies the completeness of the system of Boolean functions implemented by the circuit LC (Algorithm 1). Each output fault $(p_1 \in V_1 \ \& \ p_2 \in V_2 \ \& \ \dots \ \& \ p_n \in V_n) \implies output\_ports = \{o'_1, o'_2, \dots, o'_{m'}\}$, and $\{o'_1, o'_2, \dots, o'_{m'}\} \neq \{o_1, o_2, \dots, o_m\}$ is only detected by a test suite if this test suite includes the input pattern $B_1 B_2 \dots B_n$ that corresponds to the rule R. As the test suite TS contains a pattern that distinguishes each SSF mutant of the logic circuit LC, for the output i of LC this pattern can only be $B_1 B_2 \dots B_n$, otherwise the stuck-at-one fault in the i-th output cannot be detected (due to the uniqueness of the rule R). □

Note that whenever the set S of switch rules is not complete, the logic circuit LC is derived for a system of partially specified Boolean functions. Therefore, the behavior of the circuit over the undefined patterns can be specified in different ways. In our approach and in our experiments, we use ABC, which sets the corresponding outputs to 0. This fact allows to guarantee the fault coverage for output mutants of the rules when initially the specification S is not complete.

Proposition 2. *If for a set of rules $S\ \exists\, i \in \{1, \dots m\}$ such that $\exists!\, R \in S$, $R = ((p_1 \in V_1 \ \& \ p_2 \in V_2 \ \& \ \dots \ \& \ p_n \in V_n) \implies output\_ports = \{o_1, o_2, \dots, o_m\})$ and $o_i \in \{o_1, o_2, \dots, o_m\}$, then each output fault in the rule R is detected by an exhaustive test suite w.r.t. SSFs.*

Proof. Similar to Proposition 1, a test suite TS which detects each stuck-at-zero fault on the i-th output of LC must contain a pattern $B_1 B_2 \dots B_n$ that

---

[5] Note that we do not focus in this work on testing unsupported ports: the port number(-s) of an IUT should belong to the set of supported port numbers.

corresponds to the preamble ($p_1 \in V_1$ & $p_2 \in V_2$ & ... & $p_n \in V_n$) of rule R. This exact pattern detects each output fault in the rule R.

Corollary 1. *If in the set S of switch rules, each output port is used in at most one rule, then an exhaustive test suite w.r.t. SSFs is also exhaustive w.r.t. rule output mutants.*

We note however, that the above statements do not necessarily hold for the parameter value mutations. Such faults can in some cases be detected by other mutants of logic circuits such as bridges or hardly detectable faults. Nevertheless, thorough investigation of the correlation between the mutations of rules and those of logic circuit still needs to be performed. Such investigation is left for future work.

4.4 SAT Solving for Equivalent Mutant Detection

Whenever possible rule mutations are enumerated explicitly and therefore, a test suite TS is derived under the White Box testing assumption aiming at killing all the mutants of certain type, the question of *equivalent mutants* automatically rises [8]. Indeed, mutations of different orders (especially second and higher) have a high probability of deriving an equivalent mutant. However, as the number of patterns can be rather high ($2^{\sum_{i=1}^{n} \lceil log_2(1+max(\bigcup_{R\in S} \Pi_{p_i}))\rceil}$), applying/checking all such patterns can be a time consuming task, and thus, detecting equivalent mutants by direct (brute force) search becomes unfeasible.

Correspondingly, such equivalent mutants can be effectively detected whenever two logic circuits LC and LC_M for both the specification S and the mutant M under investigation, are derived. Indeed, the equivalence decision problem can be reduced to the well-known SAT problem. For this reason, a *miter* of two circuits can be derived. For two logic circuits LC and LC_M with the set $X = \{x_1, \ldots, x_k\}$ of inputs and the sets $O = \{o_1, \ldots, o_p\}$ and $O' = \{o'_1, \ldots, o'_p\}$ of outputs, a *miter Mit* with the set $X = \{x_1, \ldots, x_k\}$ of inputs and a single output is derived as follows. The output function of Mit is the result of a logic OR operation of the functions $f_1, \ldots, f_p$ that are implemented as the XORs of output functions $g_1, \ldots, g_p$ and $h_1, \ldots, h_p$ of the circuits LC and LC_M correspondingly, i.e., $f_j = g_j \oplus h_j$, $j \in \{1, 2, \ldots, p\}$. Circuits LC and LC_M are equivalent, and so are the sets of rules S and M, if each output of the miter Mit always equals 0, i.e., when the corresponding Boolean function is UNSAT. Algorithm 2 implements this strategy to detect equivalent mutants.

The correctness of the proposed equivalence check is established by the following proposition.

Proposition 3. *For a given set S of switch rules and a given mutant M of this specification, Algorithm 2 returns a test case killing M if and only if the mutant M is not equivalent to S.*

Algorithm 2. Equivalence check for a switch mutant

Input : A specification S represented by a set of switch rules and its mutant M

Output: The verdict about the mutant equivalence or a test case killing M

Run Algorithm 1 for both, specification S and its mutant M, obtain the logic circuits LC and LC_M, correspondingly.

Construct the miter Mit on the circuits LC and LC_M.

Run a SAT solver for the Boolean function f implemented by Mit.

if *UNSAT* **then**

⌊ **return** *the verdict 'The mutant M is equivalent to S'.*

return *A satisfying pattern B for the Boolean function f*

Proof. Indeed, the circuit Mit implements a constant 0 if and only if the outputs B_port coincide for all input patterns $B_1 B_2 \ldots B_n$ (Algorithm 1). Thus, a satisfying pattern B for the function f returns an input $B_1 B_2 \ldots B_n$ for the preamble $(p_1 \in V_1 \ \& \ p_2 \in V_2 \ \& \ \ldots \ \& \ p_n \in V_n)$ where the output ports differ.

We note that such equivalence check can be performed over the logic circuit representations in a scalable way. The reason is that both circuits LC and LC_M are combinational, i.e., without latches or internal memory. For sequential circuits, the derivation of the miter as well as the SAT problem formulation is in fact much more complex. The latter means, that if modelling a switch as a stateful system, for example when taking into account its potential communication with an SDN controller, the solution of the equivalence check might not be scalable. More research and experiments are needed in this area, and these tasks are left for the future work.

4.5   Logic Circuits for Switch Monitoring

We previously discussed the use of logic circuits for *active* test generation for an SDN switch. In fact, whenever the access to the switch is limited and its behavior can only be observed, a logic circuit LC modelling the specification S can still be effectively utilized. The reason is that the simulation of LC can in some cases be much faster than the search of the particular switch rule and its further application to conclude about the expected output port(-s). In other words, the task of the switch monitoring that verifies that the packets are forwarded to the exact ports specified by S, can be reduced to the problem of the circuit simulation[6], i.e., obtaining an output pattern for a given input (pattern). This approach is described in Algorithm 3.

As discussed in Sect. 5, in many cases, the verdict about the correct or incorrect application of a given switch rule can be made much faster when the logic circuit representation is exploited.

---

[6] Under the assumption that the circuit simulation is correct.

Algorithm 3. SDN switch monitoring

Input   : The switch implementation under test $\mathcal{I}$ and the corresponding
                specification S that $\mathcal{I}$ must implement
Output: Alerts for the packets processed wrongly by the given IUT
Run Algorithm 1 on S, obtain a logic circuit LC
while *working* **do**
> // *working* **is a Boolean flag to control the execution of the**
> **monitoring process**
> *packet_observed* $\leftarrow$ *input*($\mathcal{I}$).// *input* **returns the processed input of**
> **the IUT**
> Extract the Boolean vector B_packet from the *packet_observed* header
> parameters, including the encoded value for the input port of the IUT.
> *port_observed* $\leftarrow$ *output*($\mathcal{I}$).// *output* **returns the port number for the**
> *input*
> Encode *port_observed* as the Boolean vector B_port.
> **if** *port_observed* $\neq$ *sim*(LC,B_packet) // *sim* **is a function that**
> **simulates the circuit behavior over a given input**
> **then**
> > *alert*(*packet_observed*).// **Alert an incorrect processing of**
> > *packet_observed*

---

5   Preliminary Experimental Results for Open vSwitch

The experiments have been performed on the widely-known SDN-enabled switch,
Open vSwitch (OVS) [22] version 2.0.2. To simulate a 'close-to-real' switch
behavior, the popular Mininet [17] tool was utilized; Mininet provides an easy
way to simulate and prototype SDN networks (using OVS). The topology of
the simulated network is similar to the one presented in our previous work [3]
and shown in Fig. 1. This topology models the data plane as a graph where
all switches are connected to an SDN controller. In Fig. 1, hosts and switches
are labeled with strings starting with the letters h and s respectively. For each
edge in the graph, the corresponding port number used by the two nodes is
depicted; for example, in the edge (s_2, s_3), the label '33' indicates that the port
3 at switch s_2 is connected to the port 3 at switch s_3. In addition, the Ethernet
MAC addresses for each of the hosts are shown above or below each host. For our
experiments, without loss of generality, we chose the switch s_3 (depicted with a
dotted pattern) as the system under test. The ONOS [2] controller version 1.10.4
was used for all the experiments. The experiments were executed under different
virtual machines running under a VirtualBox Version 5.2.8 r121009 for Mac OS
X 10.13.4. The virtual machines have the characteristics shown in Table 3.

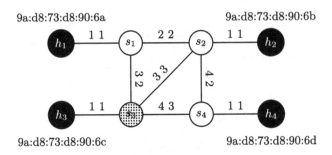

Fig. 1. Experimental setup topology

Table 3. Experimental platform

ID	Operating system	CPUs	RAM
$VM1$	CentOS 6.9 2	Intel(R) Core(TM) i5-2415M CPU @ 2.30 GHz processors	3 GB
$VM2$	Ubuntu 14.04.4 LTS (mininet dist.)	Intel(R) Core(TM) i5-2415M CPU @ 2.30 GHz processors	2 GB

5.1 Logic Circuit Fault Models for SDN-Enabled Switch Fault Model

There exist a large number of possibilities how an SDN network can be (re-) configured, and therefore how to obtain the switch rule set specification S. The SDN controller by itself is not 'responsible' for this configuration. In an SDN architecture, applications query the controller for information of the data plane and request the implementation of different rule sets for the forwarding devices (e.g., SDN-enabled switches). The applications can have different goals; for example, one application can monitor the data plane in order to balance the load between the network links (edges). One of the most common applications for an SDN network is the Layer 2 switching application; this application forwards Layer 2 packets (e.g., Ethernet) between hosts using the shortest paths.

To provide meaningful results, we programmed the data plane with a Layer 2 switching application. The rules were pushed through the controller using the REST interface. As an example, one rule $R \in S$ installed on s_1 is the following: $R = ((\text{INPUT\_PORT} \in \{1\}\&\text{ETH\_SRC} \in \{9a:d8:73:d8:90:6a\}\&\ \text{ETH\_DST} \in \{ff:ff:ff:ff:ff:ff\} \implies output\_ports = \{2,3\})$. After the rules were pushed, communication from / to any host was successfully achieved via the Ethernet protocol.

A logic circuit LC was derived from the specification S using Algorithm 1. The logic synthesis tool used for deriving LC was ABC [4]. After the synthesis, LC has 99 inputs and 4 gates. The logic circuit was then saved into the Berkeley Logic Interchange Format (BLIF), and a BLIF Mutant Generator (BMG) [12] tool was executed to generate mutants for the SSF, SBF, and HDF types. The total number of mutants is 214, where 206 mutants are all SSF mutants, 4 are randomly chosen SBF, and likewise 4 are randomly chosen HDF mutants. A distinguishing pattern was found for each non-equivalent mutant. For each of the fault models, a test suite was obtained, i.e., TS_{SSF}, TS_{SBF}, and TS_{HDF}; furthermore, the union of all 3 test suites was used to obtain TS_{ACF}, a test suite for all circuit faults[7]. The original BLIF circuit contains a sum of products, hence, only 4 gates (the output gates). In order to check if the fault coverage increases with different circuit representations, the original BLIF file was re-synthesized as an AND-INVERTER graph (AIG), we hereafter refer to this circuit as S' (functionally equivalent to S). S' has 99 inputs and 395 gates, and therefore, the total number of mutants is 1778, where 998 mutants are all SSF mutants, 395 are randomly chosen SBF, and likewise 395 are randomly chosen HBF mutants. The same procedure was performed on S' to obtain the corresponding test suites.

To check the fault coverage of traditional digital circuit fault models, a set $\mathcal{M}$ of 45 mutants of S was generated. The set of mutants contains different order mutants. After running Algorithm 2 to remove from $\mathcal{M}$ the equivalent mutants (1 was removed), each pattern p in each of the test suites TS_{SSF}, TS_{SBF}, TS_{HDF}, TS_{ACF} was used to simulate the behavior of S and compare it to the behavior of each mutant M in the non-equivalent mutant set $\forall M \in \mathcal{M}$. The fault coverage[8] obtained for each of the test suites is shown in Table 4.

Table 4. Fault coverage for traditional digital circuit fault models

Circuit	SSF	SBF	HDF	ACF (total)
S	79%	45%	18%	86%
S'	95%	97%	95%	100%

As seen in Table 4, the fault coverage of traditional logic circuit fault models reaches 100% for a Layer 2 switching specification. Therefore, we conclude that test suites derived based on traditional logic circuit fault models have a high fault coverage for SDN-enabled switch faults. An interesting aspect is that the fault coverage highly increases when the original circuit specification is transformed into an AIG. It is reasonable to assume that AIGs have more gates, and therefore more mutants and distinguishing patterns are obtained with such representations. Thus, different functional errors in the switch rules can be covered by a larger test suite when derived based on such AIGs.

5.2   Using Logic Circuits for Monitoring

When monitoring functional properties of a given IUT $\mathcal{I}$, there are two modes of operation (off-line and on-line/run-time). As discussed before, run-time monitoring requires that the monitor (in this case LC) is not slower than $\mathcal{I}$. A large body

---

[7] ACF stands for 'all circuit faults'.

[8] Calculated as the ratio of killed mutants to total number of (non-equivalent) mutants.

of studies has been dedicated to the proposal of fast monitoring algorithms (see, for example [13]) and heuristics (see, for example [11]) to enhance the performance of monitoring solutions. It is presumable that a combinational circuit has a constant (or near to constant) computational time for any input pattern. On the other hand, switch implementations such as Open vSwitch effectively work by caching the corresponding actions to be applied to a matching packet, and thus, these cached actions are applied to subsequent packets matching the rule [22]. The match lookup (and corresponding action to be applied) is done using a set of hash tables which are increased with each unique match [22]. Therefore, a priori the simulation of a logic circuit for the implementation of the switch behavior should be faster than the described caching mechanism.

To verify that logic circuits are indeed suitable for run-time monitoring of SDN-enabled switches, we performed the following experiment. On one hand, 10000 rules were pushed into the switch s_3 (IUT) using the ONOS controller. On the other hand, a logic circuit was obtained using Algorithm 1 for the specification containing the same 10000 rules installed in the IUT. The time Open vSwitch takes to process one packet and the time taken to simulate a single pattern of the logic circuit are measured as follows. To determine the time to process one packet, monitors were installed on each switch port (interface). The time difference between the packet ingress and the packet egress was measured to be ∼0.29 ms, executing Open vSwitch under $VM2$. As the time to simulate a single pattern in ABC (given a synthesized circuit) is considerably low, precision issues may occur while measuring the time to simulate a single pattern. Furthermore, reading the file and writing the response to the standard output take most of the simulation time. For that reason, the relevant values were extracted from the packet used, and the Open vSwitch was simulated one thousand times. The time taken to simulate a single pattern was measured to be ∼0.003408 ms.

Discussion. As a conclusion of the presented experiments, it can be seen that the logic circuit simulation is more than 85 times faster (compared to the switch packet processing). Arguably, the difference in the input/output interfaces for the different environments (packet input in a switch vs. file read in a circuit simulation) can also affect the time estimations. However, capturing packets at a network interface is done when the packet has been processed by the interface and processed by the operating system, therefore, reading a packet is done from the internal (RAM) memory of the devices. On the other hand, the file used to simulate a pattern in the circuit simulation is performed from a hard drive (HD). For that reason, it is reasonable to assume the time measurements performed over the switch have an inherent advantage (RAM access is much faster than HD access). Therefore, theoretically, the speed-up may be even larger when considering the same input/output interfaces.

It is of special interest to accurately estimate the obtained speed-up due to its potential applications not only for testing reasons but, for optimizing the switch implementations. Performing such investigation of the speed-up obtained via the logic circuit representation of a set of rules is left for the future work.

6   Conclusion

In this paper, we proposed a logic circuit based approach for testing SDN-enabled devices. It allows to take advantage of well established test generation strategies for logic circuits as well as of scalable manipulation over Boolean vectors and functions. We also introduced some mutation operators over the switch rules and discussed how logic circuit and related SAT solving can be utilized for detecting equivalent mutants. Finally, we considered run-time verification of switches and investigated the use of logic circuits in this case. Preliminary experiments with Open vSwitch confirm the effectiveness of the proposed approaches.

As future work, we foresee a number of directions. First, as the main focus of the paper is on test case derivation, important aspects of test execution are left for future work. Additionally, we plan to thoroughly investigate the correlation between the mutants of the switch rules and those of logic circuits. At the same time, it is interesting to analyze which kind of bugs and inconsistencies in an SDN controller or a controller-to-switch communication can be detected via proposed 'stateless' approach. Equivalent mutants for switches and the corresponding SAT solving solution also need further investigation. Likewise, it is interesting to study related complexity issues in this case to see if the SAT solving can scale in a general case or specific classes over switch rules should be defined. Finally, we would like to perform more experiments on other real SDN infrastructures and environments with software and/or hardware implementations for checking the effectiveness of logic circuit solutions.

Acknowledgments. This research was partially funded by the Celtic-Plus European project SENDATE, ID C2015/3-1.

References

1. Al-Shaer, E., Al-Haj, S.: FlowChecker: configuration analysis and verification of federated OpenFlow infrastructures. In: Proceedings of the 3rd ACM Workshop on Assurable and Usable Security Configuration, pp. 37–44. ACM (2010)
2. Berde, P., et al.: ONOS: towards an open, distributed SDN OS. In: Proceedings of the Third Workshop on Hot Topics in Software Defined Networking, pp. 1–6. ACM (2014)
3. Berriri, A., López, J., Kushik, N., Yevtushenko, N., Zeghlache, D.: Towards model based testing for software defined networks. In: Proceedings of the 13th International Conference on Evaluation of Novel Approaches to Software Engineering, ENASE 2018, Funchal, Madeira, Portugal, 23–24 March 2018, pp. 440–446 (2018)
4. Brayton, R., Mishchenko, A.: ABC: an academic industrial-strength verification tool. In: Touili, T., Cook, B., Jackson, P. (eds.) CAV 2010. LNCS, vol. 6174, pp. 24–40. Springer, Heidelberg (2010). https://doi.org/10.1007/978-3-642-14295-6_5
5. David, L., Stefano, V., Olivier, B.: Towards test-driven software defined networking. In: 2014 IEEE Network Operations and Management Symposium, pp. 1–9 (2014)
6. Dobrescu, M., Argyraki, K.: Toward a verifiable software dataplane. In: Proceedings of the Twelfth ACM Workshop on Hot Topics in Networks, p. 18. ACM (2013)

7. Fayaz, S.K., Yu, T., Tobioka, Y., Chaki, S., Sekar, V.: BUZZ: testing context-dependent policies in stateful networks. In: 13th USENIX Symposium on Networked Systems Design and Implementation, pp. 275–289 (2016)
8. Grün, B.J.M., Schuler, D., Zeller, A.: The impact of equivalent mutants. In: Proceedings of Second International Conference on Software Testing Verification and Validation Workshops, ICST 2009, pp. 192–199 (2009)
9. Han, J.H., et al.: BlueSwitch: enabling provably consistent configuration of network switches. In: Proceedings of the Eleventh ACM/IEEE Symposium on Architectures for Networking And Communications Systems, pp. 17–27 (2015)
10. Kazemian, P., Varghese, G., McKeown, N.: Header space analysis: static checking for networks. NSDI **12**, 113–126 (2012)
11. Kushik, N., López, J., Cavalli, A., Yevtushenko, N.: Improving protocol passive testing through "gedanken" experiments with finite state machines. In: IEEE International Conference on Software Quality, Reliability and Security, pp. 315–322 (2016)
12. Kushik, N.G., López, J.E., Yevtushenko, N.V.: Investigation of correlation of test sequences for reliability testing of digital physical system components. Russ. Phys. J. **59**(8), 1274–1280 (2016)
13. Lopez, J., Maag, S., Morales, G.: Behavior evaluation for trust management based on formal distributed network monitoring. World Wide Web **19**(1), 21–39 (2016)
14. Mai, H., Khurshid, A., Agarwal, R., Caesar, M., Godfrey, P.B., King, S.T.: Debugging the data plane with anteater. In: Proceedings of the ACM SIGCOMM 2011 Conference, SIGCOMM 2011, New York, NY, USA, pp. 290–301 (2011)
15. Matrosova, A., Mitrofanov, E., Shah, T.: Multiple stuck-at fault testability of a combinational circuit derived by covering ROBDD nodes by invert-and-or subcircuits. In: IEEE East-West Design & Test Symposium, pp. 1–4 (2015)
16. McKeown, N., et al.: OpenFlow: enabling innovation in campus networks. ACM SIGCOMM Comput. Commun. Rev. **38**(2), 69–74 (2008)
17. de Oliveira, R.L.S., Schweitzer, C.M., Shinoda, A.A., Prete, L.R.: Using mininet for emulation and prototyping software-defined networks. In: 2014 IEEE Colombian Conference on Communications and Computing (COLCOM), pp. 1–6 (2014)
18. Open-Networking-Foundation: Openflow switch specification v1. 4.0 (2013). https://www.opennetworking.org/images/stories/downloads/sdn-resources/onf-specifications/openflow/openflow-spec-v1.4.0.pdf
19. Open-Networking-Foundation: SDN testing & validation ONF SDN solutions showcase theme demonstrations (2014). https://www.opennetworking.org/wp-content/uploads/2014/07/IXIA-demo.pdf
20. OpenNetworking: Software-defined networking: the new norm for networks. ONF White Paper (2012). https://www.opennetworking.org
21. Patel, J.H.: Stuck-at Fault: a fault model for the next millennium? (2005). http://web.stanford.edu/class/ee386/public/stuck_at_fault_6per_page
22. Pfaff, B., et al.: The design and implementation of Open vSwitch. In: 12th USENIX Symposium on Networked Systems Design and Implementation (NSDI 15), pp. 117–130. USENIX Association (2015)
23. Sezer, S., et al.: Are we ready for SDN? Implementation challenges for software-defined networks. IEEE Commun. Mag. **51**(7), 36–43 (2013)
24. Yao, J., Wang, Z., Yin, X., Shiyz, X., Wu, J.: Formal modeling and systematic black-box testing of SDN data plane. In: The IEEE 22nd International Conference on Network Protocols (ICNP), pp. 179–190 (2014)
25. Zeng, H., Kazemian, P., Varghese, G., McKeown, N.: Automatic test packet generation. In: Proceedings of the 8th International Conference on Emerging Networking Experiments and Technologies, pp. 241–252 (2012)

An Energy Aware Testing Framework for Smart-Spaces

Teruhiro Mizumoto[1], Khaled El-Fakih[2(✉)], Keiichi Yasumoto[1],
and Teruo Higashino[3]

[1] Graduate School of Science and Technology,
Nara Institute of Science and Technology Ikoma, Nara 630-0192, Japan
[2] Department of Computer Science and Engineering,
American University of Sharjah, PO Box 26666, Sharjah, UAE
kelfakih@aus.edu
[3] Graduate School of Information Science and Technology,
Osaka University, Osaka, Japan

Abstract. We propose a novel energy based framework for the validation of smart-spaces. The framework includes, in addition to the given smart-space SS, an exterior environment (Env) that mimics a typical real environment where the SS can be deployed, and a $Tester$ for determining which pre-post condition requirements are satisfied by the SS in the considered Env contexts. The $Tester$ appropriately uses an energy aware simulator to derive device operation sequences (or tests), with minimal power consumptions cost, that can be used to move Env to the intended exterior context and the SS to a context satisfying the given pre-condition. In addition, the $Tester$ monitors the relevant SS context attributes to release verdicts about which pre-post conditions are met under each considered Env context. The framework is deployed in a real SS environment to assess the actual energy consumption of derived tests in practice. Experiments show that the actual power consumption of the derived tests is close to the estimated values. Furthermore, a detailed case study is provided to assess the gains in using energy aware tests in comparison to tests derived using non-energy aware alternatives.

Keywords: Ubiquitous computing systems · Smart-spaces
Minimal energy context move
Energy based simulation and testing framework

1 Introduction

Ubiquitous computing systems [19] or context-aware pervasive systems [6] are systems that can sense their surrounding physical environment and accordingly adapt their behavior. The space or home where the ubiquitous computing system is deployed is called *smart-space* (or *smart-home*) [4]. A smart-space (SS) consists

I. Medina-Bulo et al. (Eds.): ICTSS 2018, LNCS 11146, pp. 85–101, 2018.
https://doi.org/10.1007/978-3-319-99927-2_8

of a *physical-space* or a location with physical attributes such as temperature, humidity, etc., representing the *environment* of the SS. A SS also includes a set of *physical devices* such as sensors, actuators, home appliances, etc., that are distributed all over the physical space. Devices are controlled by an embedded software and they communicate with each other through the network to provide services to the SS users. A user has a behavior such as position in the room, activity, etc. A *context* of a smart-space is defined by a set of values of variables representing current status of devices, values of environment variables, position and activity of users, and others.

Users of a SS usually define, according to their preferences, a set of *testing requirements* that should be provided as services by the SS to its users. These requirements, are usually defined over attributes of the smart-space context variables. For example, the requirements specification are given as a set of pre-post condition properties that should hold in (or provided by) the system such as "If a user A is in a room R, room R's temperature and humidity should be set to 25 °C and 50%, respectively."

In practice, a SS is deployed in a realistic exterior environment which has an impact on the SS environment attributes such as temperature and humidity. However, the SS attributes such as humidity and temperature have no effect on *Env*. The values of *Env* temperature and humidity significantly vary within the same day, from day to day, from one season to another, and from one physical location to another. So, it is necessary to determine which of the SS testing requirements are satisfied over the different *Env* conditions (contexts).

Today, energy consumption is regarded an important aspect of research and development in ubiquitous computing. Accordingly, in this paper, we present a novel energy-aware approach for the validation of smart-spaces taking into account the minimization of energy consumption encountered during testing. More precisely, given a set of pre-post conditions as testing requirements that should be satisfied by the SS over various exterior environment contexts, a method is proposed that appropriately derives and executes operations sequences (or tests) and monitors the appropriate attributes of the SS contexts to determine which of the pre-post conditions are satisfied by the SS under specific exterior environment conditions. The method is implemented as a *Tester* in the framework that includes the considered SS devices and context-aware control system, and an *exterior environment Env* that is built and can be controlled by *Tester* to represent and mimic the exterior environment conditions where the SS can be deployed. Thus, *Env* includes appropriate devices and sensors to measure the required exterior environment attributes. The *Tester* interacts with both the SS and the *Env* devices and has the capability of observing their context attributes, mostly humidity and temperature, as needed. The *Tester*, for checking the given set of pre-post conditions under a certain exterior environment context, it first derives and uses a test (sequence of operations with minimal power consumption cost) that move *Env* to the intended exterior environment context. After reaching the intended context, the *Tester* derives and executes another minimal cost test that moves the SS from its current context into a context satisfying the pre-condition of a selected pre-post condition. After the SS reaches the intended context, the *Tester* gives control back to the SS and its software and hardware components, and thus the SS is left to run by itself according to its (black-box) possibly distributed implementation software and hardware components. Afterwards, at an appropriate time instance, determined in advance by the test case, the *Tester* checks if the current reached context attributes of the SS satisfy the post-condition of the considered pre-post requirement. If so, the SS is declared to satisfy the pre-post requirement under the current exterior environment context. Otherwise, no conclusion is made about the considered pre-post condition, and testing proceeds to examine another pre-post condition.

We note that in general multiple devices are deployed in a SS and there are many different sequences of device operations (tests) that can be used to move the SS from a context to another, and these sequences greatly differ in their consumption of energy. In addition, the behavior of the SS, in terms of contexts and events connecting contexts with their associated power consumption and duration (time), is not known in advance. Accordingly, we rely on a simulator to explore (part) of this behavior and derive minimal cost tests. We assess the energy consumption of tests derived by the simulator when executed in a real environment. According to these experiments, the difference, between the estimated and actual costs obtained when executing the derived tests in the real environment is reasonable (the difference is 20–30%). Our testing method can be used to determine and compare the actual energy cost obtained by the SS while covering a certain pre-post requirement to a possible energy-aware SS implementation. We provide a case study that considers many possible non-energy aware implementations (or alternatives) that cover the given SS testing requirements. We also compare these alternatives with respect the energy aware implementation used in the framework.

Related Work: There are some studies for context modeling and reasoning [2] and simulating context movement [13]. In [2], three context models are introduced as basic models: object-role based models, spatial models, and ontology-based models. These models can formally represent arbitrary context, but moves between contexts are not formally defined. UbiREAL [13] is a simulator for smart-spaces; However, unlike *PathSim* used in this paper, UbiREAL does not have a function to derive an optimal cost event sequence to reach an intended context. Recently, some studies try to optimize energy consumption in controlling devices in a smart home [7,8]. However this work does not support validation of requirements considering energy costs. Many approaches are used for testing smart-spaces based on altering and adapting previous related work on other related domains taking into account different aspects of SSs. Satoh [16] used a simulation centered validation technique of context-aware application. Further, a considerate number of specification-based validation techniques are proposed based on different formalisms. Axelsen et al. [1] model components as algebraic specifications Chan et al. [3] used metamorphic relations in testing context-aware applications. Lu et al. [10], and Lai et al. [9] used the traditional data-flow-graph model to represent context aware entities and proposed coverage criteria to dynamically verify the definition and use of variables. Wang et al. [18] also worked on the development of test suites based on some proposed coverage criteria. Further, many validation approaches are proposed based on formal specifications; for example, Heimdahl and George [5] obtain tests based on formal software specifications and von Ronne [14] derives requirements such that each testing item needs to be covered multiple times before it is considered sufficiently exercised. Sama et al. [15] uses a finite state model approach Our testing method can be regarded as a combination of a simulation and a requirements based validation technique specifically designed for checking if certain pre-post conditions are satisfied in a given SS taking into account energy consumption costs of test execution. In some sense, the novelty of our proposed work stems from the fact that we consider energy consumption is an important aspect that should be considered in test derivation and assessing SS implementations.

This paper is organized as follows. Section 2 includes preliminaries related to smart-spaces, and Sect. 3 addresses the testing framework. Section 4 gives the experimental evaluation and and Sect. 5 concludes the paper.

2   Smart-Space: Definitions and Requirements

In this section, we first introduce a behavioral representation of a smart-space and requirements specification that should hold in the smart-space.

2.1   Behavioral Representation of Smart-Spaces

Contexts: In general, a SS includes one or more physical locations (or rooms) R. Further, a SS has a set of devices such as TVs, Air Conditioners (ACs), Humidifiers (Hms), Dehumidifiers (Dhs), etc., deployed in R. Let $D = \{d_1, \ldots, d_m\}$ denote the set of m devices deployed in R. A device $d_i \in D$, has n attributes $A^{d_i}(j)$, $j = 1, \ldots, n$. For example, let Status, Current-Channel and Volume-Level be two attributes of a TV, then $A^{TV}(1)$ = Status and $A^{TV}(2)$ = Current-Channel. In addition, each attribute of a device $A^{d_i}(j)$ has a domain of values $Dom(A^{d_i}(j))$. For example, possible domains of the TV attributes are $Dom(A^{TV}(1)) = \{ON, OFF\}$ and $Dom(A^{TV}(2)) = \{1, \ldots, 300\}$.

A current state c of a device d_i is a valuation vector of attributes of the device. That is, a current state c of a device d_i is represented by a valuation vector $\mathbf{v}_c^{d_i} = \langle \mathbf{v}_c^{d_i}(1), \ldots, \mathbf{v}_c^{d_i}(n) \rangle$, $\mathbf{v}_c^{d_i}(j) \in Dom(A^{d_i}(j))$, for $j = 1, \ldots, n$. For example, the valuation vector $\mathbf{v}_c^{TV} = \langle \mathbf{v}^{TV}(1) = \text{"ON"}, \mathbf{v}^{TV}(2) = 10, \mathbf{v}^{TV}(3) = 30 \rangle$, represents a current state c of the TV where Status is "ON", Current-Channel is 10, and Volume-Level is 30. A current state c of the m devices in R is a vector of valuations $\langle \mathbf{v}_c^{d_1}, \ldots, \mathbf{v}_c^{d_m} \rangle$.

In addition, a SS usually has a set of l users $u_1, \ldots, u_l$. We properly partition the SS into a (finite) set of positions (or locations) representing disjoint sublocations of R. For every such user u_i, $i = 1, \ldots, l$, we let $u_i.pos$ denote the location of the user in R. Let $u_i.attr$ denote the other attributes of the user such as user ID and activity. Special devices, such as sensors, can be deployed in the SS to recognize users and determine activity status of users. A current state c of user u_i is represented as the vector $\mathbf{v}_c^{u_i} = \langle u_i.pos, u_i.attr \rangle$ and current state c of the l users can be represented by the vector $\langle \mathbf{v}_c^{u_1}, \ldots, \mathbf{v}_c^{u_l} \rangle$.

Further, we assume that a SS has environment attributes associated with each sublocation of R. Let $r_1, \ldots, r_k$ be sublocations of R. As environment variables, we consider temperature and humidity[1] and we denote the values of these variables at sublocation r_i by $r_i.temp$ and $r_i.humidity$, respectively. Values of these attributes can be set implicitly through other devices as will be described later. Current state c of sublocation r_i is represented as $\mathbf{v}_c^{r_i} = \langle r_i.temp, r_i.humidity \rangle$ and current state of R (k sublocations) can be represented by the vector $\langle \mathbf{v}_c^{r_1}, \ldots, \mathbf{v}_c^{r_k} \rangle$. A *context* (or a *current state*) c of the whole SS represents current states of its m devices, l users, and environment variables of k sublocations of R. That is $c = \langle \mathbf{v}_c^{d_1}, \ldots, \mathbf{v}_c^{d_m}, \mathbf{v}_c^{u_1}, \ldots, \mathbf{v}_c^{u_l}, \mathbf{v}_c^{r_1}, \ldots, \mathbf{v}_c^{r_k} \rangle$.

Events and Transitions: The behavior of the SS can be represented in terms of contexts and edges representing transitions connecting contexts. An edge connecting two contexts is labeled by an event which can move the system between these contexts and each such an event has a cost and time duration representing the energy cost and time of such a move as will be described later.

We consider three types of events of a SS: non-environment devise events, environment device events, and the environment spontaneous event.

An event is a *non-environment device event*, denoted by DE, if the event can be generated by setting the value of an attribute of a non-environment device within the domain of the attribute. A device, such as TV, is a *smart-space non-environment device* as it has negligible effect on the SS environment temperature and humidity attributes. As an example of non-environment device events, a TV Status can be set "ON" based on an event "SetON" which can be issued using the TV remote control. We note that we regard the event of setting the user location in R, by letting the user move into that location, as a non-environment event. An event is an *environment device event*, denoted by E, if the event can be generated by setting a value of an attribute of an environment device. A device, such as AC, Hm, and Dh, is considered a *smart-space environment device* if it can be used to change the SS environment temperature and humidity attributes. For example, the status of an AC can be turned "OFF" based on an appropriate environment device event that turns the AC "OFF".

Non-environment and environment events can instantly be executed, and thus have no related cost nor duration.

An event is called an *environment spontaneous event*, denoted by τ, if it represents a move of the system from a context to another due to change from one range to the following range of an environment (temperature or humidity) variable. This changes takes time and has an associated power consumption cost according to the current context humidity and temperature attributes and the effect of Env on the SS. Thus, it is clear that an appropriate selection

---

[1] We can easily add other environment variables such as illuminance, dust level, noise level, and so on, but as we focus on energy consumption, we focus on temperature and humidity in this paper.

of environment events and their execution order has an affect on the power consumption of the system.

It is worth mentioning that the behavior of a SS is in general infinite if the devices attributes, the user positions/attributes, or the environment variables have real value domains. Thus, an appropriate discretization of a SS behavior considering a finite number of ranges of continuous variables is necessary. Hereafter, we assume that the domain of each continuous variable of the SS is appropriately divided into finite number of ranges. We note that the range size must be carefully decided so that the perceptual quality of the context-aware service is not deteriorated.

Another important issue related to the representation of a SS behavior is that such a behavior is not known in advance. Thus there is the practice of deriving part of this behavior through simulation. Usually part of such a behavior is derived, based on certain intended goals, as the number of contexts and transitions can be so huge and the computation of the power consumption costs of spontaneous events is rather complex.

2.2   Energy-Aware Test Cases

A test case is a (finite) sequence of events. The *cost* of a test case is the total sum of the power consumption costs of the test case events. The (estimated) *time duration* or simply the *time* or *duration* of the test case is the total sum of the estimated durations of the events of the test case events. In this paper, we seek energy aware test cases that cover certain test purposes with least energy consumption costs.

Test Purposes: We consider user defined testing requirements that need to be checked over many realistic exterior environment conditions.

Smart-Space Testing Requirements: We specify a set of properties called *requirements specification* which should be satisfied in a given SS. Let $Properties = \{Proper_1, \ldots, Property_h\}$ denote the requirements specification, where $Property_i$ denotes a property. Each property is specified as a tuple of a *pre-condition* and a *post-condition* as follows: $Property_i = (Pre_i, Post_i)$

Here, Pre_i and $Post_i$ are specified as linear inequalities with variables and constants in configurations, comparison operators such as $>, \geq, \leq, <, =$, logic operator $\wedge$, and set operator $\in$.

For example, in a property "When Alice is in the living room, the room temperature and humidity should be around $27\,^{\circ}\mathrm{C}$ and 60%, respectively," *Pre* and *Post* can be described as follows. Here, we assume that temperature and humidity ranges are divided by 1 centigrade and 1% steps, respectively. Pre: $u_{Alice}.pos = r_{Living}, Post : r_{Living}.temp \in \{[26, 27), [27, 28)\} \wedge r_{Living}.humidity \in \{[59, 60), [60, 61)\}$

Smart-Space Exterior Environment Conditions: As a SS is deployed in a realistic *Env* which has an impact on the SS environment temperature and humidity attributes. As these attributes may significantly vary from one season

to another and with the same day. Thus, we consider checking the SS requirements over various realistic *Env* conditions. Accordingly, we consider a set of
exterior *Env* contexts $ExtContexts = \{C_1, \ldots C_n\}$ that are properly selected to
represent the different actual *Env* conditions where the SS can be deployed.

3 Testing Framework

3.1 Testing Architecture

In order to determine if a given SS satisfies a given set of user defined pre-post
conditions over some considered *Env* conditions, we use the *testing environment*,
depicted in Fig. 1, that includes the given SS environment with its corresponding
devices and control program. In addition, the environment includes an *exterior
environment Env* and a *Tester* that derives and executes (minimal energy) tests
to move *Env* to the intended contexts and then determine which of the pre-post
conditions are satisfied by the SS over each considered *Env* context.

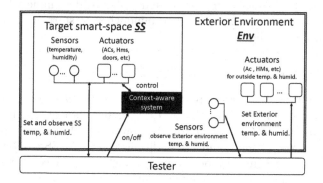

Fig. 1. Architecture of the testing environment

A SS deploys many sensors to sense the physical quantities and detect the
inhabitant locations. In addition, it implements a context-aware system, including, devices and appliances such as ACs, Hms, controllable doors and windows,
etc., and SS control program(s). Each device and sensor sends information to
the control program(s) through the network. The control-program(s) can observe
contexts and events of the system based on obtained information and also can
control the devices; thus, indirectly controls humidity and temperature, by issuing related environment device events as programmed in the controller(s).

In practice, a SS is deployed in an *Env* which has an impact on the SS
environment temperature and humidity attributes, then it is necessary to test a
SS in various *Env* conditions (or contexts). Accordingly, in order to test a SS,
we necessarily build in addition to the SS an *Env* that depicts the real exterior
environment of the SS. Thus, in *Env* temperature and humidity sensors and
several actuators including ACs and Hms are deployed as shown in the outer box

of Fig. 1. In addition, the testing environment includes a *Tester* that is connected
to the sensors and actuators of both the SS and *Env*. The *Tester* derives and
executes tests needed to move *Env* to a selected exterior context and also move
the SS to a context satisfying the pre-condition of a certain pre-post requirement.
In addition, the *Tester* makes conclusions about the status of the executed
tests. That is, the *Tester* can observe, as needed and determined by the relevant
tests, both the SS and the *Env* context temperature and humidity attributes.
In addition, the *Tester* can actuate and control both these environments by
issuing appropriate messages (or events) to related devices and control programs.
For example, *Tester* can stop or enable the SS or *Env* controllers as needed
and as specified by the derived test cases. Further, in order to test the system
in various *Env* contexts, *Tester* derives test cases that can move *Env* from
a given context and to another; and as *Env* can be controlled in our case,
such moves are always possible. However, while testing a given SS, it is not
guaranteed that we can always move the SS from a given context to an intended
context. Accordingly, our testing method takes into consideration these facts
while deriving and executing tests. Further the tester employs a timer that can
be used appropriately (according to related tests) to determine when to send
commands or observe contexts or to determine when to start or reset the timer
to start executing another test.

3.2   Testing Method

Given a set of user defined pre-post conditions $Properties = \{Proper_1, \ldots,$
$Property_h\}$, $Property_i = (Pre_i, Post_i)$, $i = 1..h$, and a set of exterior Env contexts $ExtContexts = \{C_1, \ldots C_n\}$ that are properly selected to represent the
different actual exterior environment conditions where the SS can be deployed.

Testing a given SS involves determining which pre-post conditions are satisfied by the SS under each considered Env context. In addition, our method
is an energy-aware method in the sense that it works on reducing the power
consumption needed for testing.

For each $(Pre_i, Post_i)$ and each exterior environment context C_j, we determine if $(Pre_i, Post_i)$ is satisfied in C_j. A pre-post condition $(Pre_i, Post_i)$ *is
satisfied* in a particular C_j if the SS can move, by itself, as implemented by its
designers, from a context that satisfies Pre_i to a context that satisfies $Post_i$
while Env is at C_j. Thus, there is a need to move Env from one to another
context, and also move the SS from a current context to another; for instance to
move the SS from the context that satisfies the pre-condition of a given pre-post
requirement. This requires the derivation and execution of test cases derived by
the simulator *PathSim* which is explained in the next sub section. In addition,
a test case includes commands to stop or enable the SS control system and commands that allow observing the context attributes as needed. If an event of a
test is explicit, the *Tester* executes the event by taking an appropriate action
command, such as issuing command to the appropriate device to actuate the
event, such as turn on or off AC, Hm, etc. However, if the event is the implicit
τ event, then the *Tester* waits an appropriate period of time (associated with

the event) in order to handle the next event of the test case. Thus, based on the durations associated with the implicit τ events of a test case, the *Tester* can determine when to observe the system current context temperature and humidity attributes.

3.3   PathSim: A Simulator for Deriving Tests with Minimal Costs

The proposed testing method uses the simulator *PathSim* [12] to derive minimal cost test cases that are used, for different purposes, in the testing method provided. More precisely, for each considered *Env* context in the set *ExtContexts*, the simulator is used to derive a minimal energy test that (a) can move *Env* from a current context to the intended context, or (b) move the SS from its current context to a context satisfying the pre-condition of a selected pre-post requirement from the set *Properties*. In addition, the simulator is used to estimate when the *Tester* can observe the SS context to determine if in fact it has moved from the context satisfying the pre-condition to a context satisfying the corresponding post-condition.

In fact *PathSim* uses a strategy that employs many functions to determine a minimal cost path (with related operation events). As the behavior, contexts and transitions between these contexts with associated power consumption costs, are not known, *PathSim* explores part of this behavior in such a way that a minimal cost path is derived. A known heuristic to solve such a problem is the A* algorithm; hence, *PathSim* employs a modified version of the A* utilizing functions to derive possible events that can be executed at a current context, a context move function that simulates context movement to a neighboring context upon the execution of an event. In addition, it includes functions that estimate for a τ event related power consumption and duration taking into account the volume (size) and heat conductivity of walls (including windows and roofs) of the SS outside air temperature and heat and moisture emitted by devices, and so on.

3.4   Testing Method in Detail

A detailed description of the testing method is provided as Algorithm 1.

3.5   Implementation of the Testing Environment

We have implemented the proposed test environment in a SS which is built in Nara Institute of Science and Technology [17]. This smart home is built in an experiment room (76 square meters) in the university building. The experimental room is equipped with temperature and humidity sensors and an air conditioner to imitate the temperature outside the smart home. A server is also deployed in the room and used to run both the context-aware system under test and our tester. The SS is equipped with home appliances, and temperature and humidity sensors. All sensors continuously upload the measured sensor values to the server every few seconds. Appliances can be operated via the home network.

Algorithm 1. *TestingMethod*

Input: A set of pre-post conditions $Properties = \{Property_1, \ldots, Property_h\}$, $Property_i = (Pre_i, Post_i)$, $i = 1..h$, a set $ExtContexts$ of exterior environment contexts C_j, $j = 1..n$, a current initial external environment context C_{cur}, and a current initial context c of the target SS.
Output: Verdicts about which $(Pre_i, Post_i)$ conditions are satisfied by the SS under each considered exterior environment context C_j

1: **for all** $C_j \in ExtContexts$ **do**
2:     Derive, using $PathSim$, a minimal cost path with corresponding test case that can move Env from the current exterior environment context C_{cur} to C_j
3:     Execute the derived test case; Wait appropriate time as specified in the test case for Env to reach the intended context C_j
4:     **for all** $Property_i \in Properties$ **do**
5:         Determine, using $PathSim$, if there is a minimal cost path, with the corresponding test case, that can move the SS from its current context c to a context c_i that satisfies the pre-condition Pre_i of $Property_i$
6:         **if** there is such path (test case) **then**
7:             Disable the target SS controller
8:             Execute the derived test case that moves SS to c_i which satisfies Pre_i of $Property_i$
9:             Wait appropriate time as specified by the test case (to let the SS move by itself to the context that satisfies $Post_i$)
            Observe the (reached) SS context
10:            **if** the SS reaches a context that satisfies $Post_i$ **then**
11:                Declare (or issue a verdict) that SS satisfied $Property_i$ in the current considered exterior environment context C_j
12:            **end if**
13:        **end if**
14:     **end for**
15: **end for**
16: End Algorithm 1

We also implemented the above proposed testing approach where a *Tester* is implemented that derives and executes tests as in the proposed approach. At the implementation level the events of the tests are appropriately coded using a device control language that we defined for this purpose.

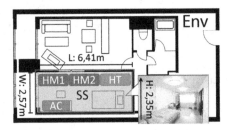

Fig. 2. *Env* and *SS* in the real environment (Color figure online)

4   Experimental Evaluation

In this section, we provide two case studies relevant to the proposed work.

4.1   Case Study 1: Real vs Simulated Environment Tests

In this case study, we consider the estimated energy consumption and execution times of tests derived by *PathSim* and compare these with respect to the

Table 1. Configuration of devices of the real target smart-space

	Power consumption	Heat capacity
AC	HOT: 1420 W	HOT: 4.1 kW
Heater	1500 W	1500 W
Humidifier-1	47 W	550 mL/h
Humidifier-2	35 W	450 mL/h

Table 2. Energy consumption and transition time

	Energy consumption (kW)	Transition time (s)
Simulation based	323.229	1262
Real environment	416.775	1868

actual values obtained by running these tests on a real SS environment that was explained in Sect. 3.5.

Real Environment of Case Study 1. We consider the SS shown within a red box shown in Fig. 2. The target SS (in gray area surrounded by red line) has 2.57 m width, 6.41 m length, and 2.35 m height. The all rooms outside the SS are supposed as an Env in this case study. Windows and doors are closed during the experiment.

The SS includes four devices (appliances): An AC with heating and cool modes, a heater and two humidifiers. In addition, for each device, we constructed a model of power consumption versus rated capacity (output) based on its device specification catalog as shown in Table 1.

In *PathSim*, we empirically defined the thermal conductivity by 0.2 $W/(m \cdot K)$ for a glass window and 0.15 $W/(m \cdot K)$ for the wood walls and the roof connecting to the exterior environment *Env*.

In order to calculate inflow and outflow moisture amounts in the SS, we conducted a preliminary experiment to measure the actual humidity variations in the SS and got an air quantity of ventilation $Vol_{ven} = 0.0762$.

Smart-Space Source and Target Contexts. The experiments were conducted under keeping *Env* with approximately 14–16 °C of temperature and 40–45% of humidity. The temperature and humidity in the SS were stable in the ranges of 16–18 °C and 20–25% after one-hour ventilation with turning off all appliances. This experiment was conducted in a daytime of winter (January) in Nara Japan.

Therefore, we divided the temperature domain into ranges of 2 °C, and the humidity domain into ranges of 5%, and we define the SS source context with [16 °C, 18 °C) in temperature range and [20%, 25%) in humidity range. The ministry of the Environment of Japan recommends 20 °C as the standard room temperature and 40–60% as the suitable room humidity, in winter. Accordingly, we defined the target context temperature to be in the range [20 °C, 22 °C) and humidity range in [50%, 55%).

Experimental Method and Results. Here we assess and compare the difference in energy consumption and execution time of running sequences obtained by the simulated *PathSim* environment and our real smart-home environment described in Sect. 4.1.

The experiments were conducted based on the following simple procedure.

1. Set the temperature and humidity ranges in the real home smart-space as those of the considered source context temperature and humidity ranges by ventilation with turning off all appliances.
2. Derive a sequence of events using *PathSim* for moving from the considered source context to the target context.
3. Use the derived sequence to move the real smart-home space to the intended target context.
4. Compare the energy consumption and transition time of the sequence obtained by *PathSim* in (2) with the corresponding real smart-home energy consumption and time obtained in (3).

In order to minimize errors in measurement results and the influence of the change of the temperature and humidity of the outside air, we repeated the above steps three times and compute the average of all obtained results. According to the conducted experiments, the real smart-home always reached the intended target context using the sequences derived by *PathSim*.

Table 2 shows the average results of the conducted experiments. According to these results, the difference between the energy consumption and the transitions duration (time) of the simulation and real smart-home environment are 20–30%. In this experiment, we defined the power consumptions and capacities for each appliance in PathSim based on the catalog specification, and this caused the difference. We believe that building a more realistic model of power consumption and capacity will reduce the difference.

Table 3. Source and target contexts

Pair #	Category		Source context	Target context	Description
1	Daytime	DT	17.8 °C, 27.35% (160 mL)	22.8 °C, 20.35% (160 mL)	+5 °C
2			17.8 °C, 27.35% (160 mL)	27.8 °C, 15.37% (160 mL)	+10 °C
3		DH	17.8 °C, 27.35% (160 mL)	17.8 °C, 37.35% (219 mL)	+10%
4			17.8 °C, 27.35% (160 mL)	17.8 °C, 47.35% (277 mL)	+20%
5		DP	17.8 °C, 27.35% (160 mL)	20.0 °C, 40% (300 mL)	Low T & H
6			17.8 °C, 27.35% (160 mL)	24.0 °C, 50% (470 mL)	High T & H
7			17.8 °C, 27.35% (160 mL)	22.0 °C, 45% (378 mL)	Middle T & H
8	Night	DT	13.6 °C, 27.38% (124 mL)	22.8 °C, 27.38% (124 mL)	+5 °C
9			13.6 °C, 27.38% (124 mL)	27.8 °C, 27.38% (124 mL)	+10 °C
10		DH	13.6 °C, 27.38% (124 mL)	13.6 °C, 37.38% (170 mL)	+10%
11			13.6 °C, 27.38% (124 mL)	13.6 °C, 47.38% (215 mL)	+20%
12		DP	13.6 °C, 27.38% (124 mL)	20.0 °C, 40% (267 mL)	Low T & H
13			13.6 °C, 27.38% (124 mL)	24.0 °C, 50% (420 mL)	High T & H
14			13.6 °C, 27.38% (124 mL)	22.0 °C, 45% (337 mL)	Middle T & H

DT: Different temperature, DH: Different humidity, DP: Different preference
T: Temperature, H: Humidity

Table 4. Simulation parameters

Parameter		Value
Env environment	Daytime	$temp = 8.7\,°C,\ humid = 48\%$
	Night	$temp = 1.5\,°C,\ humid = 60\%$
Temperature range boundary k	$k1$	$1\,°C$
	$k2$	$1\,°C(temp < 18\,°C), 0.5\,°C(temp \geq 18\,°C)$

4.2 Case Study 2: Assessing Energy Gains in Using Energy Aware Tests

In this section, we assess the gains (in terms of energy cost) of using minimal cost test cases, derived with the simulator *PathSim* used in our testing method, in comparison to test cases derived using some non energy-aware adhoc methods. To this end, we consider deriving tests for moving the SS from a given source to a target context using the following hypotheses:

(1) *Minmal Energy Cost Tests:* Here *PathSim* is used to derive minimal energy cost tests as described above.

(2) *Minimal Time Cost Tests:* Here *PathSim* is also used; however, to derive minimal time test to reach the intended context range by changing the cost function of *PathSim* to consider durations of the τ events.

(3) *Temprature-First Focus Tests:* Tests are derived by turning All ACs and heaters on with the Heat (Cool) mode to reach the intended target context temperature if the source context temperature range is higher (lower) than that of the target context. In addition, all humidifiers then are used afterwards to reach the intended context humidity.

(4) *Humidty-First Focus Tests:* Opposite to (3); i.e., all humidifiers are used to reach the intended humidity given in the target context and then all ACs and heaters are used to reach the intended temperature.

We consider many source and target context pairs, as given below, and for each pair tests are derived using each of the above options and their corresponding energy and time costs are captured.

In this case study, we set the temperature and humidity by supposing the typical winter in Tokyo, Japan based on [11]. We used the same *SS* and *Env* with the same devices as in Case Study 1 (see Fig. 2 and Table 1).

Tables 3 and 4 show the source and target contexts and simulation variables used in this case study. We consider two time periods of a day (daytime and night time), three types of the target contexts (supposing different persons with different preferences), and two types of range widths.

Daytime and Night in a day have different outside temperature and humidity. Accordingly, the natural room temperature also differs between daytime and night. Moreover, the room temperature and the outside temperature will greatly differ as long as the window(s) of the room is closed. Here, we assume that the relative humidity of a room has the same absolute humidity as that outside unless (de)humidification is not done. Consequently, we consider two types of source contexts (in *SS* and *Env* environment, respectively, with different temperature and humidity to assess the difference between daytime and night.

The target contexts are set by considering different temperature, different humidity, and different user's preference, respectively. To consider temperature difference, 5 or 10 °C more than the source context is set to the temperature in the target contexts where the (absolute) humidity is left unchanged. To consider the humidity difference in the target contexts, 10 or 20% humidity more than the source context is set to the target humidity while the temperature is left unchanged. To assess the realistic case supposing user's preferences/demands, we consider three target contexts with comfortable temperature and humidity: the case with a user of type 1 who dislikes hot and high humidity, the case with another user of type 2 who dislikes cold and low humidity, and the case of the two users with type 1 and 2 being in the same room, respectively.

The finer the ranges are divided, the more finely the tester can monitor context changes and control devices. However, if the source context is far from the target context, processing resources of the tester will be wasted and the path derivation time by PathSim will be increased. Therefore, we consider two types of the temperature range widths. k_1 divides all ranges every 1 °C temperature. k_2 divides ranges every 1 °C if less than 18 °C, and every 0.5 °C if more than or equals to 18 °C that corresponds to the comfortable winter temperature range.

In summary, we consider 14 different source and target context pairs for the considered two types of range widths, thus, we evaluate the total of 28 pairs with respect to energy consumption, transition time, and the path length for each test derivation hypothesis.

Table 5 shows the results for these 28 pairs (numbered from 1 to 14 to compare between $k1$ and $k2$ cases in each pair). In the table, gray cells show the best cases among all methods.

According to the results depicted in Table 5, for all considered pairs, tests derived using the Minimal Energy Cost Tests (EC) hypothesis have less energy costs than those derived using the other methods. In addition, Minimal Time Cost Tests (TC) have less time durations, except for the pair #14 with k_1, than the tests derived by the other methods. For the pair #14 the target context range is far apart from the source context, thus TC did not derive the test with minimal time. This is due to the fact that *PathSim* is a heuristic.

For the pairs where source and target differ only in temperature (DT: # 1 & 2), all except the *EC* test derivation method derived minimal time tests. The reason why only *EC* derived tests with longer time costs is that it derives the tests without using low energy efficiency devices to achieve the minimal **energy** cost. In these cases and in the cases where the humidity of the target context is closer to that in the source target, Temperature-First Focus Tests (TF) and Humidity-First Focus Tests (HF) derived the same tests.

For the pairs where source and target contexts differ only in humidity (DH: # 3 & 4), the same tests were obtained by all test derivation methods. This is due

Table 5. Results of simulation (gray cells show the best cases)

Pair#	Category		k	Energy(kW)				Time(s)				Path Length			
				EC	TC	TF	HF	EC	TC	TF	HF	EC	TC	TF	HF
1	DT	+5 °C	k_1	154	188	188	188	109	68	68	68	8	10	10	10
			k_2	162	198	198	198	115	71	71	71	13	15	15	15
2		+10 °C	k_1	319	388	388	388	224	136	136	136	13	15	15	15
			k_2	327	398	398	398	230	139	139	139	23	25	25	25
3	DH	+10%	k_1	21	21	21	21	230	230	230	230	7	7	7	7
			k_2	21	21	21	21	230	230	230	230	7	7	7	7
4		+20%	k_1	49	49	49	49	513	513	513	513	9	9	9	9
			k_2	49	49	49	49	513	513	513	513	9	9	9	9
5	DP	Low	k_1	129	142	143	143	431	367	407	407	13	14	15	15
			k_2	120	132	133	133	425	366	404	404	15	16	17	17
6		High	k_1	439	1473	487	549	2420	2255	2359	3000	21	41	23	28
			k_2	431	638	477	538	2416	2224	2356	2987	29	46	29	34
7		Middle	k_1	255	679	288	288	1061	993	1102	1103	17	29	19	19
			k_2	246	474	278	278	1124	931	1099	1099	23	38	23	23
8	DT	+5 °C	k_1	161	196	196	196	114	70	70	70	8	10	10	10
			k_2	169	206	206	206	120	74	74	74	9	11	11	11
9		+10 °C	k_1	325	396	396	396	229	138	138	138	13	15	15	15
			k_2	334	406	406	406	234	142	142	142	19	21	21	21
10	DH	+10%	k_1	16	16	16	16	176	176	176	176	7	7	7	7
			k_2	16	16	16	16	176	176	176	176	7	7	7	7
11		+20%	k_1	36	36	36	36	380	380	380	380	9	9	9	9
			k_2	36	36	36	36	380	380	380	380	9	9	9	9
12	DP	Low	k_1	280	320	329	329	713	624	651	651	18	21	20	20
			k_2	277	310	319	319	710	620	648	648	22	23	22	22
13		High	k_1	761	1842	839	1645	4397	3542	4319	12610	25	66	28	37
			k_2	753	2163	829	1967	4395	3740	4315	16022	31	104	34	43
14		Middle	k_1	427	582	492	517	1240	1259	1537	1794	23	32	24	33
			k_2	422	988	482	506	1567	1284	1534	1784	30	56	28	37

EC: Minimal Energy Cost Tests, TC: Minimal Time Cost Tests,
TF: Temperature-First Focus Tests, HF: Humidity-First Focus Tests
DT: Different temperature, DH: Different humidity, DP: Different preference

to the fact that there is no significant difference in efficiency of humidification between humidifiers and the temperature ranges of source contexts are as those of the corresponding target contexts.

For the pairs supposing the user's preference (DP: # 5–7 & 12–14), TF derived tests with less energy and time costs than HF. Moreover, EC derived tests with less energy costs than other methods, and TC derived tests with less time costs than other methods. In all these cases, the fine range width (k_2) significantly reduced the energy cost for EC; but, for most pairs, this significant improvement was not obtained by the other methods.

5   Conclusion

An energy-based framework for the validation of smart-spaces is proposed. The framework includes in addition to the considered SS environment an exterior environment *Env* representing a typical environment where the SS can be deployed and a *Tester* for test derivation, execution and monitoring. Given a set of *Env* contexts, the *Tester* appropriately derives minimal cost tests for moving *Env* to the considered exterior contexts and also it derived tests for moving the SS to contexts satisfying the pre-conditions of a given set of user defined pre-post condition requirements. The *Tester* controls and appropriately observes both the SS and *Env* to release verdicts about which pre-post conditions are satisfied by the SS. A case study that considers real SS and *Env* environments is provided. In addition, another study is given to show the gains (in terms of energy reduction) in using energy aware tests in comparison to adhoc non-energy aware tests.

Acknowledgment. This work was partially supported by JSPS KAKENHI Grant Numbers 26220001, 16H01721.

References

1. Axelsen, E.W., Johnsen, E.B., Owe, O.: Toward reflective application testing in open environments. In: Proceedings of the Norwegian Informatics Conference (NIK 2004), pp. 192–203 (2004)
2. Bettini, C., et al.: A survey of context modelling and reasoning techniques. Pervasive Mob. Comput. **6**(2), 161–180 (2010)
3. Chan, W., Chen, T.Y., Lu, H., Tse, T., Yau, S.S.: Integration testing of context-sensitive middleware-based applications: a metamorphic approach. Int. J. Softw. Eng. Knowl. Eng. **16**(05), 677–703 (2006)
4. Edwards, W.K., Grinter, R.E.: At home with ubiquitous computing: seven challenges. In: Abowd, G.D., Brumitt, B., Shafer, S. (eds.) UbiComp 2001. LNCS, vol. 2201, pp. 256–272. Springer, Heidelberg (2001). https://doi.org/10.1007/3-540-45427-6_22
5. Heimdahl, M.P., George, D.: Test-suite reduction for model based tests: effects on test quality and implications for testing. In: Proceedings of the 19th IEEE International Conference on Automated Software Engineering, pp. 176–185. IEEE Computer Society (2004)
6. Henricksen, K., Indulska, J.: Developing context-aware pervasive computing applications: models and approach. Pervasive Mob. Comput. **2**(1), 37–64 (2006)
7. Jahn, M., Jentsch, M., Prause, C.R., Pramudianto, F., Al-Akkad, A., Reiners, R.: The energy aware smart home. In: 2010 5th International Conference on Future Information Technology, pp. 1–8. IEEE (2010)
8. Kashimoto, Y., Ogura, K., Yamamoto, S., Yasumoto, K., Ito, M.: Saving energy in smart homes with minimal comfort level reduction. In: 2013 IEEE International Conference on Pervasive Computing and Communications Workshops, pp. 372–376. IEEE (2013)
9. Lai, Z., Cheung, S.C., Chan, W.K.: Inter-context control-flow and data-flow test adequacy criteria for nesC applications. In: Proceedings of the 16th ACM SIGSOFT International Symposium on Foundations of Software Engineering, pp. 94–104. ACM (2008)
10. Lu, H., Chan, W., Tse, T.: Testing context-aware middleware-centric programs: a data flow approach and an RFID-based experimentation. In: Proceedings of the 14th ACM SIGSOFT International Symposium on Foundations of Software Engineering, pp. 242–252. ACM (2006)

11. M., U.: Simplified method for calculating annual space heating load in residential houses. In: Transactions of the Society of Heating, Air-Conditioning and Sanitary Engineers of Japan, pp. 117–130 (1982), http://www.jma.go.jp/jma/indexe.html

12. Mizumoto, T., El-Fakih, K., Yasumoto, K.: PathSim: a tool for finding minimal energy device operation sequence for reaching a target context in a smart-home. In: 2013 IEEE 10th International Conference on Ubiquitous Intelligence and Computing and 2013 IEEE 10th International Conference on Autonomic and Trusted Computing, pp. 64–71, December 2013

13. Nishikawa, H., et al.: UbiREAL: realistic smartspace simulator for systematic testing. In: Dourish, P., Friday, A. (eds.) UbiComp 2006. LNCS, vol. 4206, pp. 459–476. Springer, Heidelberg (2006). https://doi.org/10.1007/11853565_27

14. von Ronne, J.: Test suite minimization: an empirical investigation (1999). http://www.ics.uci.edu/jronne/pubs/jvronneuhc-thesis.pdf

15. Sama, M., Elbaum, S., Raimondi, F., Rosenblum, D.S., Wang, Z.: Context-aware adaptive applications: fault patterns and their automated identification. IEEE Trans. Softw. Eng. **36**(5), 644–661 (2010)

16. Satoh, I.: A testing framework for mobile computing software. IEEE Trans. Softw. Eng. **29**(12), 1112–1121 (2003)

17. Ueda, K., Tamai, M., Yasumoto, K.: A method for recognizing living activities in homes using positioning sensor and power meters. In: 2015 IEEE International Conference on Pervasive Computing and Communication Workshops, pp. 354–359. IEEE (2015)

18. Wang, H., Chan, W., Tse, T.: Improving the effectiveness of testing pervasive software via context diversity. ACM Trans. Auton. Adapt. Syst. (TAAS) **9**(2), 9 (2014)

19. Weiser, M.: Some computer science issues in ubiquitous computing. Commun. ACM **36**(7), 75–84 (1993)

C++11/14 Mutation Operators Based on Common Fault Patterns

Ali Parsai$^{(\boxtimes)}$ ⃝, Serge Demeyer ⃝, and Seph De Busser

University of Antwerp, Middelheimlaan 1, 2020 Antwerp, Belgium
{ali.parsai,serge.demeyer}@uantwerpen.be, seph.debusser@gmail.com

Abstract. The C++11/14 standard offers a wealth of features aimed at helping programmers write better code. Unfortunately, some of these features may cause subtle programming faults, likely to go unnoticed during code reviews. In this paper we propose four new mutation operators for C++11/14 based on common fault patterns, which allow to verify whether a unit test suite is capable of testing against such faults. We validate the relevance of the proposed mutation operators by performing a case study on seven real-life software systems.

Keywords: Software testing · Mutation testing · C++11/14
Mutation operators

1 Introduction

Nowadays, the process of software development relies more and more on automated software tests due to the developers interest in testing their software components early and often. The level of confidence in this process depends on the quality of the test suite. Therefore, measuring and improving the quality of the test suite has been an important subject in literature. Among many of the studied techniques, mutation testing is known to perform well for improving the quality of the test suite [10].

The idea of mutation testing is to help identify software faults indirectly by improving the quality of the test suite through injecting an artificial fault (i.e. generating a *mutant*) and executing the unit test suite to see whether the fault is detected [19]. If any of the tests fail, the mutant is said to detected, thus *killed*. On the other hand, if all the tests pass, the test suite failed to detect the mutant, thus the mutant *survived*. However, some mutants result in code which does not pass the compiler and these are called *invalid mutants*. And in other situations, a mutant fails to change the output of a program for any given input hence can never be detected—these are called *equivalent mutants*.

A mutant is created by applying a transformation rule (i.e. *mutation operator*) to the code that results in a syntactic change of the program [9]. Given an effective set of mutation operators, mutation testing can help developers identify the weaknesses in the test suite [1]. Nevertheless, designing effective mutation

I. Medina-Bulo et al. (Eds.): ICTSS 2018, LNCS 11146, pp. 102–118, 2018.
https://doi.org/10.1007/978-3-319-99927-2_9

operators requires considerable knowledge about the coding idioms and the common programming faults often made in the language [9]. More importantly, good mutation operators should maximize the likelihood of *valid* and *non-equivalent* mutants [4].

The first set of mutation operators were reported in King et al. [12]. They were later implemented in the tool Mothra which was designed to mutate the programming language FORTRAN77. With the advent of the object-oriented programming paradigm, new mutation operators were proposed to cope with specific programming faults therein [11]. This is a common trend in mutation testing: languages evolve to get new language constructs; some of these constructs cause subtle programming faults; after which new mutation operators get designed to shield against these common faults. For example, with the evolution of Java related languages, mutation operators have been designed to account for concurrent code [2], aspect-oriented programming [7], graphical user interfaces [18], and Android applications [6].

The C++11/14 standard (created in 2011 and 2014 respectively) offers a wealth of features aimed at helping programmers write better code [20]. Most notably there is more type-safety and compile-time checking (e.g. static_assert, override). Unfortunately, the standard also provides a few features that may cause subtle faults (e.g. lambda expressions, list initialization, ...). Our goal is to identify these sources of common faults and introduce new mutation operators that address them. While it is possible that some subset of these faults are addressed by C++99 mutation operators, previous experience shows targeted mutation operators prove useful in improving the test suite quality further [3,5]. In this study, we seek to answer the following research questions:

- **RQ1.** Which categories of C++11/14 faults are most likely to be made by programmers, and what are the corresponding mutation operators?
- **RQ2.** To what extent do these mutation operators create valid, non-equivalent mutants?

The rest of this paper is structured as follows: In Sect. 2 we provide the necessary background information about this study, and briefly discuss the related work. In Sect. 3 we discuss our approach to answering our research questions, and show our results in Sect. 4. Finally, we present our conclusions in Sect. 5 and highlight the future research directions rooted in this work.

2 Background and Related Work

In this section we provide the necessary background information needed to comprehend the rest of the article and discuss the related work. First, we describe mutation testing and its related concepts. Then, we describe the new C++11/14 features, focusing on subtle faults that may be revealed via mutation testing.

2.1   Mutation Testing

Mutation testing is the process of inserting bugs into software(*Mutants*) using a set of rules(*Mutation Operators*) and then running the accompanying test suite for each inserted mutant. If all tests pass, the mutant survived. If at least one test fails, the mutant is killed. If the mutant causes an error during compilation of the production code, it is invalid. A valid mutant that does not change the semantics of the program, thus making it impossible to detect, is called equivalent.

An equivalent mutant is a mutant that does not change the semantics of the program, i.e. its output is the same as the original program for any possible input. Therefore, no test case can differentiate between an equivalent mutant and the original program, which makes it undesirable. The detection of equivalent mutants is undecidable due to the halting problem [16]. The only way to make sure there are no equivalent mutants in the mutant set is to manually inspect and remove all the equivalent mutants. However, this is impractical in practice. Therefore, the aim is to generate as few equivalent mutants as possible.

Mutation operators are the rules mutation testing tools use to inject syntactic changes into software. Most operators are defined as a transformation on a certain pattern found in the source code. The first set of mutation operators ever designed were reported in King et al. [12]. These mutation operators work on basic syntactic entities of the programming language such as arithmetic, logical, and relational operators. Offutt et al. came up with a selection of few mutation operators that are enough to produce high quality test suites with a four-fold reduction of the number of mutants [17]. Kim et al. extended the set of mutation operators for object-oriented programming constructs [11].

Because of the complexity of parsing C++, building a mutation testing tool for C++ is almost equivalent to building a complete compiler [8]. It is only with modern tooling, e.g. the Clang/LLVM compiler platform, that it became possible to write such tools without an internal parser.

Kusano et al. developed CCmutator, a mutation tool for multi-threaded C/C++ programs that mutates usages of POSIX threads and the C++11 concurrency constructs, but works on LLVM's intermediate representation instead of directly on C++ source code [13]. Delgado-Perez et al. have expanded on the work done for the C language by adding class mutation operators, and created a set of C++ mutation operators [5]. In addition, they show that the class mutation operators compliment the traditional ones and help testers in developing better test suites.

2.2   C++11/14

C++11 was introduced in 2011 with the goal of adapting C++ and its core libraries to modern use cases of the language (e.g. multi-threading, genetic algorithms, ...). This release was followed by C++14 in 2014 with similar goals. The introduction of C++11/14 has changed the language to the point that earlier iterations of the language are dubbed the classical C++, and modern C++[1]

---

[1] http://www.modernescpp.com/index.php/what-is-modern-c.

starts with C++11/14. The release of the standard was followed by real-time adoption in compilers such as Clang and G++.

Unfortunately, the C++11/14 standard also provides a few features that may cause subtle faults, thus where support in the form of new mutation operators would be desirable. In this subsection we briefly explain these features of C++11/14.

Range-Based for Loop. [http://en.cppreference.com/] is syntactic sugar made to simplify looping over a range of elements. For example, the following two loops are similar:

```
for(int i : v) {
std::cout << i << '\n'; }
```

```
for(int i=0; i<v.size(); i++) {
std::cout << v.at(i) << '\n'; }
```

Lambda Expressions. [http://en.cppreference.com/] allow for the definition of unnamed in-line functions. For example, in the following piece of code, lambda contains a function which *captures* a and b (they are available in the body of lambda as const expressions), takes an input parameter x, and returns a bool.

```
int a, b;
auto lambda = [a, b](int x) {return x > a + b;}
```

It is possible to have a default capture at the start of the capture list, e.g. '=' for by-value, or '&' for by-reference capture. This causes all variables referenced in the lambda body to be captured the specified way.

Move Semantics. [http://en.cppreference.com/] are introduced in C++11/14 to address the inefficiencies of copy construction when the copied value is deleted after the execution of the constructor. For example, the following code would be inefficient in C++03:

```
std::vector<int> v(ComputeLargeVector(1000));
```

In C++03, this code would create the vector in ComputeLargeVector, call the copy constructor for v, which copies all elements into a newly allocated buffer, and then destroys the original. With move semantics, v would simply copy the internal size, capacity, and pointer to the elements in the temporary vector and set the members of the temporary vector to 0.

To enable this, value categories[2] got redefined in C++11. Every expression is either an lvalue, an xvalue, or a prvalue. The difference between these value categories lies in two properties: whether or not they have identity (i.e. it is possible to determine whether two expressions are the same using an address), and whether they can be moved from (move semantics can bind to the expression).

---

[2] http://en.cppreference.com/w/cpp/language/value_category.

lvalues and xvalues have identity, while xvalues and prvalues can be moved from. All rvalues can bind to rvalue references, which are denoted by &&. For example, the signature of the move constructor of vector is:

```
vector<T> (vector<T>&&);
```

It is possible to convert an lvalue to an xvalue through std::move, which casts the object to an rvalue reference type.

Perfect Forwarding. [http://en.cppreference.com/] allow for forwarding of input arguments to other functions as-is. For example, the emplace family of functions in the standard containers accept any number of arguments and forward them to the constructor of the element type. The following template function constructs an object of type T with a given argument:

```
template<typename T, typename Arg>
T construct(Arg&& argument) {
    return T{std::forward<Arg>(argument)};
}
```

Because Arg is a template parameter, Arg&& is a forwarding reference [22]. This means that it will resolve to either an lvalue or an rvalue reference depending on argument. If argument is an lvalue, std::forward is a no-op, and if argument is an rvalue reference, it behaves the same way std::move does.

List Initialization. [http://en.cppreference.com/] is a new syntax introduced in C++11 that allows the initialization of an object from braced initial values. It expands the ability to construct structs and arrays using braced initializer to all types in C++. For example, the following is a valid syntax for creating and initializing an array of *int*:

```
int b {1,2,3,4,5};
```

Also, a type with a constructor that takes std::initializer_list as an argument can be initialized using this new syntax. For example, the following declaration of a std::vector creates a vector of integers with 5 elements:

```
std::vector<int> v{1,2,3,4,5};
```

3   Study Design

In this section, we discuss the design of our study. First, we explain our evaluation criteria, and then we describe the process by which we determine the fault categories and create mutation operators. Finally, we present the details of our data set.

3.1   Evaluation Criteria

RQ1. Which categories of C++11/14 faults are most likely to be made by programmers, and what are the corresponding mutation operators?
To evaluate the results of this question, the mutation operator needs to fulfill the following criteria:

- Can the mutation operator simulate a fault from the fault category we identified?
- Is it reasonable to assume that the software developer can create faulty code similar to the generated fault?

We look at guidelines provided by experts concerning the new standards and the common pitfalls mentioned therein. We search for such patterns and select those that can be reconstructed into a mutation operator.

RQ2. To what extent do these mutation operators create valid, non-equivalent mutants?

$$Mutation\ Operator\ Score = 1 - \frac{E - D}{T - I - D} \qquad (1)$$

T = Total Number of Mutants, E = Number of Equivalent Mutants, D = Number of Easily-Detectable Equivalent Mutants, I = Number of Invalid Mutants

An effective mutation operator generates valid semantic faults. This means that mutation operators need to generate as few equivalent mutants as possible. We borrow this criterion from Delgado-Perez et al. who used it in their study [4]. It is also important for each mutant to be valid, i.e. the mutated program compiles without errors. To quantify the effectiveness of each mutation operator, we calculate the percentage of equivalent mutants among the valid mutants after filtering the easily-detectable equivalent mutants. The mutation operator score is then calculated by deducting the mentioned percentage from 100% (see Eq. 1). For each mutation operator, we provide methods to filter easily-detectable equivalent mutants.

To see how our operators work in real-life scenarios, we looked at seven open source projects that are using C++11/14 (see Table 1). Our analysis consists of applying our mutation operators to create all possible mutants. We do this by manually searching for the code patterns that match (using grep). Then, we manually categorize the resulting mutants into invalid, equivalent, and valid non-equivalent mutants. If a mutant did not change the semantics of the program, we classified it as an equivalent mutant. If the operator created a non-compilable program, we classified the mutant as invalid. Otherwise, we considered the mutant as valid non-equivalent.

3.2   Data Set

In this subsection, we present the details of our data set. Our data set is publicly available in the replication package available at https://www.parsai.net/files/research/ICTSSRepPak.zip.

In order to find the common fault patterns related to C++11/14, we looked at the authoritative sources of fault patterns such as those suggested by Scott Meyers in his book titled Effective Modern C++ [15], and C++ Core Guidelines by Bjarne Stroustrup [21]. We also took into account the standard proposal N3853 by Lavavej [14] which points out problems with range-based for loop syntax.

Table 1. Project statistics

Project	Commit	Size (Lines of Code)		Number of commits	Team size
		Production	Test		
i-score	c86cd3d	108K	3.5K	5358	14
C++React	1f6ddb7	11K	2K	417	1
EntityX	6389b1f	9K	1K	296	28
Antonie	59deb0d	9K	0.1K	306	2
Json	a09193e	8K	18K	1973	59
Corrade	ff3b351	6.5K	9.1K	1898	10
termdb	bd0fb4a	783	153	26	2

For the evaluation of the mutation operators, we looked at seven open source projects that use C++11/14 (Table 1). These projects range from a small, several hundred lines of code header-only library, to a full application with over 100,000 lines of code with years of active development:

– i-score is an interactive intermedia sequencer, built in Qt.
– *C++React* is a C++11 reactive programming library, based on signals and event streams.
– *EntityX* is an Entity Component System that uses C++11 features.
– *Antonie* is a processor of DNA reads, developed at the Bertus Beaumontlab of the Bionanoscience Department of Delft University of Technology.
– *Json* is a single-header library for working with Json with modern C++.
– *Corrade* is a C++11/14 utility library, including several container classes, a signal-slot connection library, a unit test framework, a plugin management library and a collection of other small utilities.
– *termdb* is a small C++11 library for parsing command-line arguments.

4   Results

In this section, we present the results of our research. For each mutation operator, first we give its definition, then we discuss the motivation behind it to answer RQ1, and finally we provide our analysis of the data set to answer RQ2.

4.1 For

The range-based "for" reference removal (FOR) operator finds instances of range-based for loops of the form `for (T& elem : range)` or `for (T&& elem : range)`, where T is either `auto` or a concrete type, and removes the reference qualifier from the range declaration. Table 2 shows the results for this mutation operator.

Code Excerpt 1.1. Original For	**Code Excerpt 1.2.** Mutated For
`for(auto& elem : range) { ... }`	`for(auto elem : range) { ... }`

Motivation (RQ1). FOR operator is based on the possibility of confusion over the default value semantics of the new range-based for loop, whereas previous methods of looping over containers resulted in reference semantics. This was noted previously by Stephan Lavavej [14]. In his standard proposal, he lists three problems with the most idiomatic-looking range-based for loop, `for (auto elem : range)`, namely:

- It might not compile - for example, `unique_ptr`[3] elements are not copyable. This is problematic both for users who won't understand the resulting compiler errors, and for users writing generic code that'll happily compile until someone instantiates it for movable-only elements.
- It might misbehave at runtime - for example, `elem = val;` will modify the copy, but not the original element in the range. Additionally, `&elem` will be invalidated after each iteration.
- It might be inefficient - for example, unnecessarily copying `std::string`.

From a mutation testing perspective, the second reason is the main motivation to create a mutation operator. In the case of a range-based for loop that modifies the elements of a container in-place, the correct and generic way to write it is `for (auto&& elem : range)`. For all cases except for proxy objects and move-only ranges, `for (auto& elem : range)` works as well.

This operator is only a minor syntactic change that is easily overlooked even in code review if such fault pattern is not actively looked for. Surviving mutants of this type can pinpoint the loops whose side effects on container elements are not tested.

Analysis (RQ2). *Invalid Mutants:* The invalid mutants are comprised of two groups. The majority of the invalid loops were over containers of move-only types. Of the invalid mutants in *i-score*, 33 were containers of pointers to virtual interface classes with custom dereferencing iterators, making the mutant try to

---

[3] http://en.cppreference.com/w/cpp/memory/unique_ptr.

Table 2. Results of FOR operator

Project	Total	Invalid	Equivalent	Easily detectable	Score
i-score	251	101	115	110	87.5%
Corrade	24	1	13	13	100%
Json	1	0	0	0	100%
EntityX	2	0	2	2	N/A
termdb	0	0	0	0	N/A
C++React	8	0	6	6	100%
Antonie	39	10	18	18	100%

instantiate a non-instantiable type. Both of these cases can be easily checked when generating the mutants.

Equivalent Mutants: In the majority of equivalent cases, the body of the loop did not mutate the referenced element in the container, thus making it equivalent to a loop with an added `const` qualifier. This is relatively easy to verify automatically, hence such mutants are listed as detectable. Only a handful of equivalent cases were loops that did mutate the elements of the container, but the container never gets used after the loop finishes. This would require more complicated static analysis.

4.2 LMB

The lambda reference capture (LMB) operator changes a default *value* capture to a default *reference* capture. Table 3 shows the results for this mutation operator.

Code Excerpt 1.3. Original Lambda

```
[=](int x) { return x + a; };
```

Code Excerpt 1.4. Mutated Lambda

```
[&](int x) { return x + a; };
```

Motivation (RQ1). This operator is based on the warnings on default capture modes in Core Guideline F53 and Meyers' 31st item [15,21]. This mutation operator results in code that leads to undefined behavior if the lambda is executed in a non-local context, because the references to local variables are not valid. This can happen when the lambda is pushed up the call stack or sent to a different thread for asynchronous execution.

Just like the FOR operator, this operator is only a minor syntactical change that can easily be overlooked, and results in faults that are not necessarily easy to detect; thus it is worth testing for its absence. Mutants created by this operator are not easy to detect either, because they invoke undefined behavior which is highly dependent on compiler optimization levels and runtime circumstances.

Table 3. Results of LMB operator

Project	Total	Invalid	Equivalent	Easily detectable	Score
i-score	189	0	113	101	86.3%
Corrade	0	0	0	0	N/A
Json	0	0	0	0	N/A
EntityX	0	0	0	0	N/A
termdb	0	0	0	0	N/A
C++React	1	0	0	0	100%
Antonie	0	0	0	0	N/A

Analysis (RQ2). *Invalid Mutants:* We did not witness any invalid mutants generated by this operator in our data set.

Equivalent Mutants: All undetectable equivalent mutations were ones where the lambda gets passed into a function that executes it within its own scope. While it is theoretically possible to detect them, we classify them as undetectable because it would require complicated non-local reasoning. The other equivalent mutants are detectable by taking into account what the capture list actually captures. For example, in Code Excerpt 1.5, the minimal capture list is empty, whereas in Code Excerpt 1.6 the minimal capture list is [a] and in Code Excerpt 1.7 the minimal capture list is [this]. In the first and third examples, replacing the default value-capture with reference-capture changes nothing about the capture list. In i-score, these made up the majority of equivalent cases, hence the high percentage of detectable equivalent mutants.

Code Excerpt 1.5. Empty Capture

```
[=](int x) {return x < 1;};
```

Code Excerpt 1.6. Local Capture

```
int a; [=](int x) {return x < a;};
```

Code Excerpt 1.7. 'this' Capture

```
struct Foo {
  int a;
  auto getFilter() {
    return [=](int x) {return x < a;};
  }
};
```

4.3 FWD

The forced **rvalue** forwarding (FWD) operator replaces `std::forward` instances with `std::move` to force moving from forwarded arguments. Table 4 shows the results for this mutation operator.

Code Excerpt 1.8. Original Forwarding **Code Excerpt 1.9.** Mutated Forwarding

```
template<class T>
void wrapper(T&& arg)
{
    foo(std::forward<T>(arg));
}
```

```
template<class T>
void wrapper(T&& arg)
{
    foo(std::move(arg));
}
```

Motivation (RQ1). There are often two possible errors in relation to forwarding semantics (which Meyers warns about in his items 24 and 25 [15]): forgetting to use `std::forward` (and thus passing both lvalues and rvalues on as lvalues) or moving instead of forwarding (and thus passing lvalues on as rvalues to be moved from).

As an example, the following function constructs an object of type T using uniform initialization by forwarding the variadic list of arguments using perfect forwarding:

```
template<typename T, typename... Args>
T construct(Args&&... args) {
    return T{std::forward<Args>(args)...};
}
```

We then use the following type, chosen because `std::string` has a destructive move constructor and `std::unique_ptr` is a move-only type:

```
struct Widget
{
    std::string text;
    std::unique_ptr<int> value;
};
```

Then the following code constructs two Widgets with the same text and different values:

```
std::string text{64,'a'}; //Long enough to disable SSO
auto w1 = construct<Widget>(text, std::make_unique<int>(0));
auto w2 = construct<Widget>(text, std::make_unique<int>(1));
```

Both calls result in `Args` being `[std::string&,std::unique_ptr<int>&&]`, which makes `std::forward` correctly forward the first argument as lvalue and the second as rvalue. Forgetting to use `std::forward` results in both arguments being forwarded as lvalues, which fails to compile since `std::unique_ptr` is a move-only type. When forgetting to forward, code will always either compile and default to copying the types, or fail to compile because a move-only type is used. Since for all types, the only visible effect of doing a copy instead of a move is a performance degradation, this would not be a useful operator for testing purposes.

Table 4. Results of FWD operator

Project	Total	Invalid	Equivalent	Easily detectable	Score
i-score	71	13	18	9	81.6%
Corrade	5	0	0	0	100%
Json	14	0	14	6	0%
EntityX	7	0	1	1	100%
termdb	0	0	0	0	N/A
C++React	160	0	17	15	98.6%
Antonie	0	0	0	0	N/A

Replacing the `std::forward` with `std::move`, however, does has the potential to change program behavior. With `construct` mutated as in the code sample above, the string `text` will be moved from in the first call, and the second call results in unspecified behavior. In most standard library implementations, `w2` will end up with an empty text. Meyers argues that it is easy to confuse `rvalue` and forwarding references because of their identical syntax, making this a likely fault for developers to make.

A large part of these mutants can be targeted by using forwarding on a non-const `lvalue` argument, since it cannot bind to an `rvalue` reference. Another way of testing these is to use a type with a destructive move, and test the state of the original object after passing it into the function as an `lvalue`.

Analysis (RQ2). *Invalid Mutants:* The invalid mutants were comprised of two groups: fixed template argument and non-const `lvalue` reference callee arguments. The first group forwards to another template function while explicitly stating the template argument as seen in Code Excerpt 1.10. This causes the code to not compile when called with a non-const `lvalue`. If it is called with const `lvalues` or `rvalue` references it will have the same runtime behavior as the original.

Code Excerpt 1.10. Fixed Template Argument Forwarding

```cpp
template<typename T>
void foo(T&&);

template<typename T>
void bar(T&& t) {
   foo<T>(std::forward<T>(t));
}
```

The second group forwards into a function with fixed arguments, at least one of which is a non-const `lvalue` reference, as seen in Code Excerpt 1.11 which defines a function that calls another with a prepended integer argument. Because the second argument is a non-const `lvalue` reference, applying the operator here results in an invalid mutant because it cannot bind to an `rvalue` reference.

Code Excerpt 1.11. Forwarding into Non-Const Lvalue Reference

```
void  foo(int ,int &,int );

template<typename ...  Args>
void  bar(Args&&... args)  {
   foo (1 ,std :: forward<Args>(args )...);
}
```

Equivalent Mutants: There are three categories of equivalence for this operator. The first is where std::forward gets used within a `decltype` or `noexcept` context, where the operator either changes nothing, or makes the code fail to compile. This is why we classify these as detectable equivalent mutants. The second case is where the forwarded argument never gets stored, which makes irrelevant the difference between `std::forward`, `std::move`, and passing by reference. The third and final category is where the callees are guaranteed to not take `rvalue` references or value parameters of movable types. Of these three categories, the first is easily detectable by filtering out mutants within a `decltype` or `noexcept` expression. The second would require sophisticated flow analysis which is why we listed them as not easily-detectable. The last category can be detected if it is feasible to find all possible callees and see whether they take any `rvalue` references or value parameters of movable types. This is only feasible for mutants calling functions that cannot be overloaded by external code, since it is otherwise theoretically possible to introduce a new overload of the called function that takes a parameter of a type with a destructive move, making the mutant non-equivalent. The mutants for which this analysis is possible are listed as detectable in our analysis.

4.4   INI

The initializer list constructor (INI) operator checks constructor calls of types with an initializer list constructor and changes to/from uniform initialization in order to provoke calling a different constructor. Table 5 shows the results for this mutation operator.

Code Excerpt 1.12. Original Initializer   **Code Excerpt 1.13.** Mutated Initializer

`std :: vector<int> v(3 ,2);`	`std :: vector<int> v{3 ,2};`

Motivation (RQ1). While initializer list constructors are helpful in defining container contents, they are possible sources of faults as well. For example, when using uniform initialization one needs to pay attention to the correct syntax,

Table 5. Results of INI operator

Project	Total	Invalid	Equivalent	Easily detectable	Score
i-score	1	0	0	0	100%
Corrade	0	0	0	0	N/A
Json	0	0	0	0	N/A
EntityX	0	0	0	0	N/A
termdb	1	0	0	0	100%
C++React	0	0	0	0	N/A
Antonie	18	0	0	0	100%

since using {} instead of () by mistake changes the semantics of the expression drastically. A prominent example of this problem is `std::vector` of integer types, which Meyers points out in his 7th item [15]. The non-mutated version in Code Excerpt 1.12 defines a vector of three elements with value 2, whereas the mutated vector in Code Excerpt 1.13 has only two elements: 3 and 2.

Analysis (RQ2). *Invalid Mutants:* This operator has no way of creating invalid mutants by design, because it checks whether or not a different constructor is called when it is applied. This includes checking for narrowing conversions; e.g. when trying to mutate `std::vector<char>(10,'a');`.

Code Excerpt 1.14. Equivalence Cases for INI

```
struct Default1 {
int foo = 1;
Default() = default;
Default(int f) : foo(f) {};
};

std::vector<Default1> v1(1); //v1{1}
std::vector<int> v2(2,2); //v2{2,2}
```

Equivalent Mutants: There are only a few corner cases for `std::vector` where this operator results in equivalence (e.g. Code Excerpt 1.14).

In both of these cases, the mutated initializer results in the same vector as the original. Given the number of times this pattern was observed in our data set (20 instances in all projects), it is unlikely that such equivalent mutants are found in any significant number.

4.5 Discussion

We have aggregated the number of all generated mutants per kind for each mutation operator in Fig. 1. The FOR operator generates the highest number of mutants, most of which are either invalid or easily detectable equivalent. Hence, it is possible to filter most of these mutants easily. This is why this mutation operator is promising. The most promising mutation operator is INI, which generated no invalid or equivalent mutants in our data set. However, the low number of mutants generated by this mutation operator means that it might not be applicable in every case. FWD is the operator that generates the most valid, non-equivalent mutants along with a low number of equivalent and invalid mutants, while LMB generates no invalid mutants at all but has a slightly higher ratio of equivalent mutants that are hard to detect.

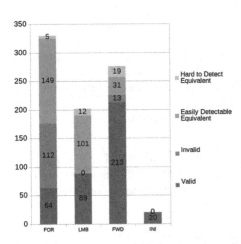

Fig. 1. Generated mutants

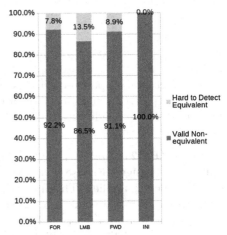

Fig. 2. Mutation operator scores

Figure 2 shows the mutation operator score for each mutation operator. It is clear that all mutation operators are within reasonable boundaries regarding the percentage of generated hard to detect equivalent mutants when compared to other C++ mutation operators (e.g. Delgado-Perez et al. [4]). Overall, we found that these mutation operators have a high mutation operator score, with all of them generating very few equivalent mutants (13.5% or less of the total number of mutants).

One of the noticeable trends among these mutation operators is their tendency to generate lots of mutants in a single project, and few in others. For example, INI generated 18 mutants in Antonie, and 2 in all other projects, while LMB generated 189 mutants in i-score and only 1 in others. Other than the size of the projects, we found that the adoption of the new syntax has not been uniform in all of the projects, i.e. some projects make use of mostly a single new syntactic feature and not all of them.

5   Conclusions and Future Work

In this study, we created a set of mutation operators that target the common faults introduced by C++11/14 syntactic features. We collected advice about the new C++11/14 syntax from authoritative sources, and created four new statement-level mutation operators (FOR, LMB, FWD, and INI). For each mutation operator, we discussed the motivation behind its creation and the type of faults they generate. We used Mutation Operator Score as a way to measure the effectiveness of each mutation operator. For this, we selected 7 real-life C++11/14 projects, and counted the number of valid, invalid, easily detectable and hard to detect equivalent mutants generated by each mutation operator for each project. Our results show that all of the introduced mutation operators generate at most 13.5% hard to detect equivalent mutants. The high operator scores indicate that these mutation operators are a useful addition to the mutation operators suggested previously in literature.

Several aspects of this study can be researched further. In particular, the use of our proposed mutation operators alongside traditional and class mutation operators may result in finding multiple redundancies among these mutation operators. In addition, a comparative study similar to Delgado-Perez et al. [5] between these mutation operator sets would provide more insight into the usefulness of each set of operators depending on the context.

Acknowledgments. This work is sponsored by (a) the ITEA3 ReVaMP² Project (number 15010), sponsored by VLAIO—Flanders Innovation Sponsoring Agency; (b) Flanders Make vzw, the strategic research centre for the manufacturing industry.

References

1. Baker, R., Habli, I.: An empirical evaluation of mutation testing for improving the test quality of safety-critical software. IEEE Trans. Softw. Eng. **39**(6), 787–805 (2013). https://doi.org/10.1109/TSE.2012.56
2. Bradbury, J.S., Cordy, J.R., Dingel, J.: Mutation operators for concurrent java (J2SE 5.0). In: Second Workshop on Mutation Analysis (Mutation 2006 - ISSRE Workshops 2006), p. 11, November 2006. https://doi.org/10.1109/MUTATION.2006.10
3. Chekam, T.T., Papadakis, M., Traon, Y.L., Harman, M.: An empirical study on mutation, statement and branch coverage fault revelation that avoids the unreliable clean program assumption. In: 2017 IEEE/ACM 39th International Conference on Software Engineering (ICSE), pp. 597–608, May 2017. https://doi.org/10.1109/ICSE.2017.61
4. Delgado-Pérez, P., Medina-Bulo, I., Domínguez-Jiménez, J.J., García-Domínguez, A., Palomo-Lozano, F.: Class mutation operators for C++ object-oriented systems. Ann. Telecommun. - annales des télécommunications **70**(3), 137–148 (2015). https://doi.org/10.1007/s12243-014-0445-4
5. Delgado-Pérez, P., Medina-Bulo, I., Palomo-Lozano, F., García-Domínguez, A., Domínguez-Jiménez, J.J.: Assessment of class mutation operators for C++ with the MuCPP mutation system. Inf. Softw. Technol. **81**, 169–184 (2017). https://doi.org/10.1016/j.infsof.2016.07.002

6. Deng, L., Offutt, J., Ammann, P., Mirzaei, N.: Mutation operators for testing android apps. Inf. Softw. Technol. **81**, 154–168 (2017). https://doi.org/10.1016/j. infsof.2016.04.012

7. Ferrari, F.C., Maldonado, J.C., Rashid, A.: Mutation testing for Aspect-Oriented programs. In: 2008 1st International Conference on Software Testing, Verification, and Validation, pp. 52–61, April 2008. https://doi.org/10.1109/ICST.2008.37

8. Irwin, W., Churcher, N.: A generated parser of C++. NZ J. Comput. **8**(3), 26–37 (2001)

9. Jia, Y., Harman, M.: An analysis and survey of the development of mutation testing. IEEE Trans. Softw. Eng. **37**(5), 649–678 (2011). https://doi.org/10.1109/ TSE.2010.62

10. Just, R., Jalali, D., Inozemtseva, L., Ernst, M.D., Holmes, R., Fraser, G.: Are mutants a valid substitute for real faults in software testing? In: Proceedings of the 22nd ACM SIGSOFT International Symposium on Foundations of Software Engineering, FSE 2014, pp. 654–665. ACM, New York (2014). https://doi.org/10. 1145/2635868.2635929

11. Kim, S., Clark, J.A., McDermid, J.A.: Class mutation: mutation testing for object-oriented programs. In: Proceedings of Net Object Days 2000, pp. 9–12 (2000). http://citeseerx.ist.psu.edu/viewdoc/summary?doi=10.1.1.16.6116&rank=1

12. King, K.N., Offutt, A.J.: A Fortran language system for mutation-based software testing. Softw.: Practice Exp. **21**(7), 685–718 (1991). https://doi.org/10.1002/spe. 4380210704

13. Kusano, M., Wang, C.: CCmutator: a mutation generator for concurrency constructs in multithreaded C/C++ applications. In: Proceedings of 2013 28th IEEE/ACM International Conference on Automated Software Engineering, ASE 2013, pp. 722–725 (2013). https://doi.org/10.1109/ASE.2013.6693142

14. Lavavej, S.T.: ISO/IEC JTC1/SC22/WG21 N3853: Range-Based For-Loops: The Next Generation (2014). http://open-std.org/jtc1/sc22/wg21/docs/papers/2014/ n3853.htm

15. Meyers, S.: Effective Modern C++: 42 Specific Ways to Improve Your Use of C++11 and C++14, 1st edn. O'Reilly Media Inc., Sebastopol (2014)

16. Offutt, A.J., Pan, J.: Automatically detecting equivalent mutants and infeasible paths. Softw. Test. Verif. Reliab. **7**(3), 165–192 (1997). https://doi.org/10.1002/ (sici)1099-1689(199709)7:3⟨165::aid-stvr143⟩3.0.co;2-u

17. Offutt, A.J., Voas, J.M.: Subsumption of condition coverage techniques by mutation testing. Technical report, George Mason University (1996)

18. Oliveira, R.A.P., Alégroth, E., Gao, Z., Memon, A.: Definition and evaluation of mutation operators for GUI-level mutation analysis. In: 2015 IEEE Eighth International Conference on Software Testing, Verification and Validation Workshops (ICSTW), pp. 1–10, April 2015. https://doi.org/10.1109/ICSTW.2015.7107457

19. Papadakis, M., Kintis, M., Zhang, J., Jia, Y., Traon, Y.L., Harman, M.: Mutation testing advances: an analysis and survey. In: Advances in Computers (2018). https://doi.org/10.1016/bs.adcom.2018.03.015

20. Stroustrup, B.: Programming: Principles and Practice Using C++, 2nd edn. Addison-Wesley Professional, Boston (2014)

21. Stroustrup, B.: C++ Core Guidelines (2017). http://isocpp.github.io/ CppCoreGuidelines/CppCoreGuidelines

22. Sutter, H., Stroustrup, B., Reis, G.D.: ISO/IEC JTC1/SC22/WG21 N4262: Wording for Forwarding References (2014). http://open-std.org/jtc1/sc22/wg21/docs/ papers/2014/n4262.pdf

Conformance Testing and Inference
of Embedded Components

Alexandre Petrenko[(✉)] and Florent Avellaneda

CRIM, Montreal, Canada
{Alexandre.Petrenko,Florent.Avellaneda}@crim.ca

Abstract. The problems of active inference (learning) and conformance testing of a system modelled by an automaton have actively been studied for decades, however, much less attention has been paid to modular systems, modelled by communicating automata. In this paper, we consider a system of two communicating FSMs, one machine represents an embedded component and another the remaining part of the system, the context. Assuming that the context FSM is known, we want to learn the embedded FSM without directly interacting with it. This problem can be viewed as a generalization of the classical automata inference in isolation, i.e., it is the grey box learning problem. The proposed approach to solve this problem relies on a SAT-solving method for FSM inference from traces. It does not depend on the composition topology and allows at the same time to solve a related problem of conformance testing in context. The latter is to test whether an embedded implementation FSM composed with the given context is equivalent to the embedded specification FSM also composed with the context. The novelty of the conformance testing method is that it directly generates a complete test suite for the embedded machine and avoids using nondeterministic approximations with their tests, eliminating thus several sources of test redundancy inherent in the existing methods.

Keywords: Active inference · FSM learning · Conformance testing
Component-based systems · Embedded testing · Testing in context
SAT solving

1 Introduction

Componentization is an important engineering principle. Top-down design approaches brake down large systems into smaller parts, components, and bottom-up approaches compose existing components into larger systems. While practitioners are mostly using ad hoc techniques, model-based software engineering is investigating formal approaches which can offer automation to various phases of modular system development, including testing and using legacy components and components of the shelf, COTS.

The existing model-based testing approaches focus mostly on a holistic view of a modular system, based on a single state-oriented model, see, e.g., [7]. Conformance tests are then generated from a state machine, which models either a component in isolation or a whole system as observed on external interfaces [4, 5, 7]. On the other hand, when a system is built using existing components, testing efforts should be

© IFIP International Federation for Information Processing 2018
Published by Springer Nature Switzerland AG 2018. All Rights Reserved
I. Medina-Bulo et al. (Eds.): ICTSS 2018, LNCS 11146, pp. 119–134, 2018.
https://doi.org/10.1007/978-3-319-99927-2_10

focused only on new components [17]. This motivates research in conformance testing in context aka embedded testing, which aims to check whether an embedded implementation FSM composed with the given context is equivalent to the embedded specification FSM also composed with the context.

All the known methods for complete tests generation for testing in context first construct from the context and embedded machine an embedded equivalent or the largest solution to the appropriate FSM equation, which represents the behavior of the embedded machine as can be controlled and observed via context [2, 11, 12, 14]. The resulting partial machine is a nondeterministic approximation of the embedded deterministic machine, it is then used to derive complete internal tests, which are finally translated into external ones executed on external interfaces of a modular system.

Conformance testing is closely related to active inference, aka query learning, as already been understood, see, e.g., [10], for the case when a system is considered "as a whole", i.e., modelled as an FSM.

Model inference helps in dealing with legacy components and COTS. Once a model is reengineered it can be used to perform verification with model checkers, regression and integration testing or redesign. Automata inference is an important topic addressed in many works, see, e.g., [1, 3, 8, 9, 13, 15], which treat a system as a single black box, even if it contains components with known models and only some need to be learned.

We propose to generalize the FSM inference problem to the case when an FSM to learn is a part of a modular system. Indeed, the traditional automaton/FSM inference problem statement is a particular case of this general situation, namely, when the rest of the system is a single state machine performing just a bijection of external and internal inputs. We know the only work [18] addressing the grey box learning problem, where the goal is to learn a tail FSM in the serial composition with the context FSM. We propose an approach for solving the grey box learning problem that does not depend on the composition topology, as opposed to the previous work [18].

To simplify the discussions, we model a system with two communicating FSMs, one machine represents an embedded component and another the remaining part of the system, the context. Assuming that the context FSM is known, we elaborate an approach to learn the embedded FSM without directly interacting with it. The proposed approach relies on a SAT-solving method for FSM inference from sample traces. The approach also allows to solve the problem of conformance testing in context, which is to check whether an embedded implementation FSM composed with the given context is equivalent to the embedded specification FSM also composed with the context. The novelty of the conformance testing method is that it directly generates a complete test suite for the embedded machine and avoids using nondeterministic approximations with their tests, eliminating thus several sources of test redundancy inherent in the existing methods.

The paper is organized as follows. Section 2 provides definitions related to state machines and automata needed to formalize the approach. Communicating FSMs are formally defined and illustrated on a working example in Sect. 3. A SAT-solving method for FSM inference from traces, which allows to obtain different conjectures [10] as required by the proposed methods, is recalled in Sect. 4. Section 5 presents our method for complete test generation for embedded components. In Sect. 6 we present some experimental results concerning test generation. Section 7 describes the method for embedded FSM inference and Sect. 8 concludes.

2 Definitions

A *Finite State Machine* or simple machine M is a 5-tuple (S, s_0, I, O, T), where S is a finite set of states with an initial state s_0; I and O are finite non-empty disjoint sets of inputs and outputs, respectively; T is a transition relation $T \subseteq S \times I \times O \times S$, $(s, a, o, s') \in T$ is a transition. When we need to refer to the machine being in state $s \in S$, we write M/s.

M is *complete* (completely specified) if for each tuple $(s, a) \in S \times I$ there exists transition $(s, a, o, s') \in T$, otherwise it is *partial*. It is *deterministic* if for each $(s, a) \in S \times I$ there exists at most one transition $(s, a, o, s') \in T$, otherwise it is *nondeterministic*. FSM M is a *submachine* of $M' = (S', s_0, I, O, T')$ if $S \subseteq S'$ and $T \subseteq T'$.

An *execution* of M/s is a finite sequence of transitions forming a path from s in the state transition diagram of M. The machine M is *initially* connected, if for any state $s \in S$ there exists an execution from s_0 to s. Henceforth, we consider only deterministic initially connected machines.

A *trace* of M/s is a string in $(IO)^*$ which labels an execution from s. Let $Tr(s)$ denote the set of all traces of M/s and Tr_M denote the set of traces of M/s_0. For trace $\omega \in Tr(s)$, we use s-after-ω to denote the state M reached after the execution of ω, for an empty trace ε, s-after-$\varepsilon = s$. When s is the initial state we write M-after-ω instead of s_0-after-ω.

Given a string $\omega \in (IO)^*$, the *I-restriction* of ω is a string obtained by deleting from ω all symbols that are not in I, denoted $\omega_{\downarrow I}$.

The I-restriction of a trace $\omega \in Tr(s)$ is said to be a *transfer* sequence from state s to state s-after-ω. The length of a trace is defined as the length of its I-restriction. A *prefix* of trace $\omega \in Tr(s)$ is a trace $\omega' \in Tr(s)$ such that the I-restriction of the latter is a prefix of the former.

Given an input sequence α, we let $out(s, \alpha)$ denote the O-restriction of the trace that has α as its I-restriction. States $s, s' \in S$ are *equivalent w.r.t.* α, if $out(s, \alpha) = out(s', \alpha)$, denoted $s \cong_\alpha s'$; they are *distinguishable* by α, if $out(s, \alpha) \neq out(s', \alpha)$, denoted $s \not\cong_\alpha s'$ or simply $s \not\cong s'$. States s and s' are *equivalent* if they are equivalent w.r.t. all input sequences, i.e., $Tr(s) = Tr(s')$, denoted $s \cong s'$. The equivalence and distinguishability relations between FSMs is similarly defined. Two FSMs are equivalent if their initial states are equivalent.

Given two FSMs $M = (S, s_0, I, O, T)$ and $M' = (S', s_0', I, O, T')$, their *product* $M \times M'$ is the FSM (P, p_0, I, O, H), where $p_0 = (s_0, s_0')$ such that P and H are the smallest sets satisfying the following rule: If $(s, s') \in P$, $(s, x, o, t) \in T$, $(s', x, o', t') \in T'$, and $o = o'$, then $(t, t') \in P$ and $((s, s'), x, o, (t, t')) \in H$. It is known that if M and M' are complete machines then they are equivalent if and only if the product $M \times M'$ is complete.

Two complete FSMs $M = (S, s_0, I, O, T)$ and $M' = (S', s_0', I, O, T')$ are called *isomorphic* if there exists a bijection $f: S \rightarrow S'$ such that $f(s_0) = s_{00}'$ and for all $a \in I$, $o \in O$, and $s \in S$, $f(s\text{-after-}ao) = f(s)\text{-after-}ao$. Isomorphic FSMs are equivalent, but the converse does not necessarily hold.

Given a string $\omega \in (IO)^*$ of length $|\omega|$, let $Pref(\omega)$ be the set of all prefixes of ω. We define a (linear) FSM $W(\omega) = (X, x_0, I, O, D_\omega)$, where D_ω is a transition relation, such that $|X| = |\omega| + 1$, and there exists a bijection $f: X \rightarrow Pref(\omega)$, such that $f(x_0) = \varepsilon$, $(x_i, a, o, x_{i+1}) \in D_\omega$ if $f(x_i)ao = f(x_{i+1})$ for all $i = 0, ..., |\omega|-1$, in other words, $W(\omega)$ has the set of traces $Pref(\omega)$. We call it the ω-*machine*. Similarly, given a finite prefix-closed set of traces $\Omega \subset (IO)^*$ of some deterministic FSM, let $W(\Omega) = (X, x_0, I, O, D_\Omega)$ be the acyclic deterministic FSM such that Ω is the set of its traces, called an Ω-*machine*. The bijection f relates states of this machine to traces in Ω.

While the set of traces of the Ω-machine is Ω, there are many FSMs which contain the set Ω among their traces. We restrict our attention to the set of all FSMs with at most n states and alphabets I and O, denoted $\mathfrak{J}(n, I, O)$. An FSM $C = (S, s_0, I, O, T)$, $C \in \mathfrak{J}(n, I, O)$ is called an Ω-*conjecture*, if $\Omega \subseteq Tr_C$.

The states of the Ω-machine $W(\Omega) = (X, x_0, I, O, D_\Omega)$ and an Ω-conjecture $C = (S, s_0, I, O, T)$ are closely related to each other. Formally, there exists a mapping $\mu: X \rightarrow S$, such that $\mu(x) = s_0\text{-after-}f(x)$, the state reached by C with the trace $f(x) \in \Omega$. The mapping μ is unique and induces a partition π_C on the set X such that x and x' belong to the same block of the partition π_C, denoted $x =_{\pi_C} x'$, if $\mu(x) = \mu(x')$.

Given an Ω-conjecture C with the partition π_C, let D be an Ω'-conjecture with the partition π_D, such that $\Omega' \subseteq \Omega$, we say that the partition π_C is an *expansion* of the partition π_D, if its projection onto states of Ω' coincides with the partition π_D.

A finite set of input sequences $L \subset I^*$ is a *checking experiment* for a complete FSM M with n states if for each FSM $N \in \mathfrak{J}(n, I, O)$, such that $N \cong_L M$, it holds that $N \cong M$. Checking experiments are also called *complete* (i.e., sound and exhaustive) tests.

We also use the classical automaton model. A *Finite Automaton* A is a 5-tuple (P, p_0, X, T, F), where P is a finite set of states with the initial state p_0; X is a finite alphabet; T is a transition relation $T \subseteq S \times X \cup \{\varepsilon\} \times S$, where ε represents an internal action, and F is a set of *final* or *accepting* states. We shall use several operations over automata, namely, expansion, restriction, and intersection, following [16].

Given an automaton A and a finite alphabet U, $U \cap X = \varnothing$, the U-*expansion* of automaton A is the automaton denoted $A_{\uparrow U}$ obtained by adding at each state a self-looping transition labeled with each action in U.

For an automaton A and an alphabet $U \subseteq X$, the U-*restriction* of automaton A is the automaton denoted $A_{\downarrow U}$ obtained by replacing each transition with the symbol in $X \backslash U$ by an ε-transition between the same states.

Given automata $A = (P, p_0, X, T, F_A)$ and $B = (R, r_0, Y, Z, F_B)$, such that $X \cap Y \neq \varnothing$, the *intersection* $A \cap B$ is the largest initially connected submachine of the automaton $(P \times R, (p_0, r_0), X \cap Y, Q, F_A \times F_B)$, where for each symbol $a \in X \cap Y$ and each state $(p, r) \in P \times R$, $((p, r), a, (p', r')) \in Q$, if $(p, a, p') \in T$ and $(r, a, r') \in Z$.

We also define an automaton corresponding to a given FSM M. The automaton, denoted by $A(M)$, is obtained by splitting each transition of M labeled by input/output into two transitions labeled by input and output, respectively, and connecting them with an auxiliary non-final state. The original states of M are only final states of $A(M)$, hence the language of $A(M)$ coincides with the set of traces of M.

3 Communicating FSMs

The behavior of a modular system composed of FSM components depends on its environment. The two together constitute a closed system. Communications in it can either be via messages or by method calls, using no queues. We restrict our attention to the case when queues are not used, which is possible with a so-called slow environment assuming that the closed system operates with a single message in transit [12]. This is a sufficient condition for the existence of a deterministic FSM modelling the external behavior of a modular system [12, 16]. Such an environment can be modelled by a (chaos) automaton Env with two states, out of which the initial state is the final state, shown in Fig. 1. After issuing an external input in X to the system it waits until an external output in O is produced before executing a next input. Its language is the set $(XO)^*$.

We further consider only two deterministic FSMs, one of them representing an embedded component E and another the remaining part of the modular system, aka context K, as shown in Fig. 1.

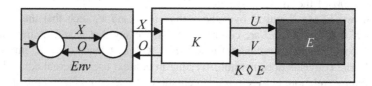

Fig. 1. Closed system of two FSMs K and E with the environment.

We assume that the sets X, O, U, and V are pairwise disjoint. The context FSM K assumed to be a complete machine interacts with the environment and can process an external input after it produces an internal output even before an external output is emitted. Since this violates the restriction of having a single message in transit, we constrain its behavior by composing it with the slow environment. Let $A(K)$ be the automaton of the context FSM K. Then the intersection of automata $A(K) \cap Env_{\uparrow U \cup V} = A(K)_{\text{slow}}$ represents the behavior of the context constrained by the slow environment. Then the intersection $A(K)_{\text{slow}} \cap A(E)_{\uparrow X \cup O}$ denoted by $A(K) \Diamond A$ (E) describes the behavior of the closed system, called the *composite automaton* of the modular system.

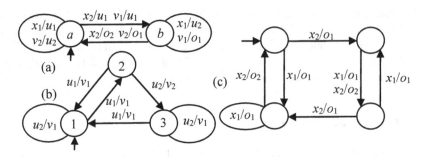

Fig. 2. The context FSM K (a), embedded FSM E (b) and composite FSM $K \Diamond E$ (c).

The language of $A(K) \Diamond A(E)$ is the set of all strings labelling all the executions of the system $L(A(K) \Diamond A(E))$. Restricting a string to the alphabets of a component FSM we obtain a trace of the context or embedded FSM. The external behavior of the system is expressed in terms of external inputs X and outputs O, so it is the set of $(X \cup O)$-restrictions of $A(K) \Diamond A(E)$, i.e., external traces of the system. They are traces of an FSM, provided that $A(K) \Diamond A(E)$ has no livelocks, i.e., cycles labelled by symbols in $U \cup V$ [16], the machine can be obtained by removing ε-transitions in $A(K) \Diamond A$ $(E)_{\downarrow X \cup O}$ and pairing each input with a subsequent output, if it exists, to an FSM transition's label. If some external input is not followed by an external output it is deleted from the corresponding state of $(A(K) \Diamond A(E))_{\downarrow X \cup O}$, as a result, the FSM becomes partial. If all inputs are deleted from the initial state then the machine has a single state and no transition. We let $K \Diamond E$ denote the resulting FSM, called the *composite FSM* of the modular system.

Given two FSMs E and E' over the alphabets U and V, such that the composite machines $K \Diamond E$ and $K \Diamond E'$ are complete FSMs, we say that E and E' are *externally equivalent* (or *equivalent in context*) if $K \Diamond E \cong K \Diamond E$. Clearly, $E \cong E'$ implies $K \Diamond E \cong K$, but the converse does not hold. Testing in context uses external equivalence as a conformance relation between implementations of a component embedded in a modular system and its specification.

A finite set of input sequences $L \subset X^*$ is an *external* checking experiment (complete test suite) for the embedded FSM E w.r.t. $\mathfrak{J}(n, U, V)$, if for each FSM $N \in \mathfrak{J}(n, U, V)$, where n is the number of states in E such that $K \Diamond N \cong_L K \Diamond E$, it holds that $K \Diamond N \cong K \Diamond E$.

Example. Consider the context FSM K and embedded FSM E shown in Fig. 2 together with the composite FSM $K \Diamond E$. The composite automaton $A(K) \Diamond A(E)$ is shown in Fig. 3.

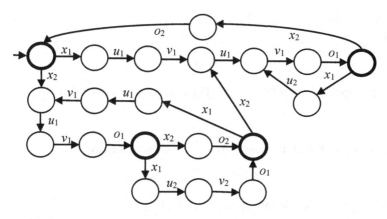

Fig. 3. The composite automaton $A(K) \lozenge A(E)$, final states are in bold.

4 Passive Inference with SAT-Solving

Henceforth, we first provide a brief overview of the SAT-solving based method for conjecture generation from a given set of traces avoiding regeneration of already considered conjectures which is the basic step of testing and learning an FSM in isolation [10] and an embedded FSM, as we show in Sect. 5. For a detailed presentation, the reader is referred to [10].

The basic step of conjecture inference from a given set of traces Ω is state merging of the Ω-machine. SAT-solving approaches [6, 9] encode the problem into Boolean constraints, a solution if it exists is a conjecture with a given number of states. We use an existing encoding of a set of traces Ω into a Boolean formula *formula* [6]. Let W $(\Omega) = (X, x_0, I, O, D_\Omega)$ be the Ω-machine. Each state of the Ω-machine is represented by a variable x, so $x_i \in \{0, ..., n - 1\}$. Since the Ω-machine is deterministic, the state variables satisfy the constraint [1]:

$$\forall x_i, x_j \in: \text{ if } x_i \ncong x_j \text{ then } x_i \neq x_j \text{ and}$$
$$\text{if } \exists a \in I \text{ s.t. } out(x_i, a) = out(x_j, a) = o \text{ then } x_i = x_j \Rightarrow x_i\text{-after-}ao = x_j\text{-after-}ao \quad (1)$$

An assignment of values to variables such that the formula (1) is satisfied defines a mapping $\mu: X \rightarrow S$, where S is the set of states of an Ω-conjecture, i.e., the mapping μ defines a partition of X into n blocks.

These CSP (constraint satisfaction problem) formulas are then translated to SAT using unary coding for integer variables, represented by n Boolean variables $v_{x,0}, ..., v_{x,n-1}$. For each $x \in X$, we have the clause:

$$v_{x,0} \vee ... \vee v_{x,n-1} \quad (2)$$

For each state $x \in X$ and all $i, j \in \{0, \ldots, n - 1\}$ such that $i \neq j$, we have the clauses:

$$\neg v_{x,i} \vee \neg v_{x,j} \tag{3}$$

We use auxiliary variables $e_{x, y}$ [6]. For every $x, y \in X$ such that $x \not\equiv y$ we have

$$\neg e_{x, y} \tag{4}$$

For all $x, y \in X$ such that $out(x, a) = out(y, a) = o$, we have

$$e_{x,y} \Rightarrow e_{x-after-ao, y-after-ao} \tag{5}$$

For every $x, y \in X$ and all $i \in \{0, \ldots, n - 1\}$

$$e_{x,y} \wedge v_{x,i} \Rightarrow v_{y,i} \tag{6}$$

$$\neg e_{x,y} \wedge v_{x,i} \Rightarrow \neg v_{y,i} \tag{7}$$

The resulting Boolean formula is the conjunction of clauses (2)–(7).

The traditional use of SAT solvers for state minimization aims at obtaining a single conjecture, while the problems of conformance testing and learning require that constraints should allow a solver to check, once a conjecture is found, whether another non-equivalent conjecture exists. Absence of a conjecture proves that a checking experiment is constructed and the machine is identified.

This is achieved by using the following procedure to infer a conjecture that differs from already considered conjectures. Isomorphic conjectures are identified by their common partition, encoded into an additional constraint. Recall that states of an Ω-machine form a partition defined by an Ω-conjecture. We let Π denote a set of partitions of states of Ω'-machines, where $\Omega' \subseteq \Omega$.

> **Algorithm 1.** *Infer_conjecture(Ω, n, Π)* [10]
> **Input:** A set of traces Ω, an integer n, and a set of partitions Π
> **Output:** An Ω-conjecture with at most n states such that its partition does not expand any partition in Π, or False.
> 1. *formula* = conjunction of the clauses (2) - (7)
> 2. **for all** $\pi \in \Pi$ **do**
> 3.   *clause* = False
> 4.   **for all** x, y such that $x =_\pi y$ **do**
> 5.   *clause* = *clause* $\vee \neg e_{x,y}$
> 6.   **end for**
> 7.   *formula* = *formula* $\wedge$ *clause*
> 8. **end for**
> 9. **return** *call-solver(formula)*

To check the satisfiability of a formula one can use any of the existing solvers, calling the function *call-solver(formula)*. If a solution exists then we have an Ω-conjecture with n or fewer states. The latter is obtained from the determined partition on X.

5   External Checking Experiment Construction

Solving the problem of external checking experiment generation, we use as in our previous work [10] Algorithm 1 for conjecture inference from a current set of traces. The difference, however, is that traces now no longer belong to a machine considered in isolation (this becomes even more crucial for active inference), they are produced by an embedded component. Accordingly, instead of checking the equivalence of a conjecture to the specification machine, we must check their external equivalence. To this end, we need to compose a conjecture C and the context K. As discussed above, if the resulting composite automaton $A(K) \lozenge A(C)$ has a livelock, its external behavior cannot be specified by an FSM, since an external input triggering livelock cannot be paired with any output. To deal with this issue we formulate a new constraint (in the form of a partition, as before) avoiding its regeneration by a solver. Once the current conjecture composed with the context yields a composite FSM $K \lozenge C$ an external input sequence distinguishing it from the given composite machine $K \lozenge E$ can be determined, if they are not equivalent. The found sequence is added to a current set of input sequences. The distinguishing external input sequence is the X-restriction of the word of the automaton $A(K) \lozenge A(C)$ from which a trace of the embedded component is obtained as the $(U \cup V)$-restriction and used to generate a next conjecture. If, however, no new trace of the embedded component is obtained and the state partition of the conjecture distinguishable from the specification machine is added as a constraint to avoid its regeneration. The process iterates until the constraints are no longer satisfiable. The procedure is implemented in Algorithm 2.

Algorithm 2. Generating external checking experiment
Input: Complete deterministic FSMs K and E such that the composite machine $K \lozenge E$ is a complete FSM

   Output: An external checking experiment Ψ for the embedded FSM E w.r.t. $\Im(n, U, V)$
1. $\Omega := \varnothing$
2. $\Psi := \varnothing$
3. $\Pi := \varnothing$
4. **while** an Ω-conjecture C is returned by *Infer_conjecture*(Ω, n, Π) **do**
5.   **if** $A(K) \lozenge A(C)$ has a livelock or $(K \lozenge C) \times (K \lozenge E)$ is complete **then**
6. $\Pi := \Pi \cup \{\pi_C\}$
7.   **else**
8.   Determine an input sequence βa such that β is the shortest transfer sequence to a state with the undefined input a in $(K \lozenge C) \times (K \lozenge E)$
9. $\Psi := \Psi \cup \{\beta a\}$
10.   Let $\sigma \in L(A(K) \lozenge A(E))$ such that $\sigma_{\downarrow X} = \beta a$
11.   **if** $\sigma_{\downarrow(U \cup V)} \in \Omega$ **then**
12. $\Pi := \Pi \cup \{\pi_C\}$
13.   **else**
14. $\Omega := \Omega \cup \{\sigma_{\downarrow(U \cup V)}\}$
15.   **end if**
16.   **end if**
17. **end while**
18. **return** Ψ

Algorithm 2 calls *Infer_conjecture*(Ω, n, Π), which in turn calls a SAT solver constraining it to avoid solutions of already considered conjectures.

Note that the Boolean formula used by the SAT solver is built incrementally; a current formula is saved and new clauses are added when a set Ω or Π is augmented.

Example. We illustrate Algorithm 2 using the context and embedded machines in Fig. 2. We assume $n = 2$. Initially, the set of external input sequences Ψ is empty, so is the set of internal input sequences Ω. The function *Infer_conjecture*(Ω, n, Π) for the empty set Π returns a Ω-conjecture C_0 as an FSM with a single state and no transitions. The composite machine $K \Diamond C$ has no transitions either. We choose the external input x_1, so $\Psi = \{x_1\}$. This input is the X-restriction of the word $\sigma = x_1 u_1 v_1 u_1 v_1 o_1$ in A $(K) \Diamond A(E)$. Its restriction onto the alphabets of the embedded component is $\sigma_{\downarrow(U \cup V)} = u_1 v_1 u_1 v_1$. $\Omega = \{u_1 v_1 u_1 v_1\}$. The function *Infer_conjecture*(Ω, n, Π) for the empty set Π returns a Ω-conjecture C_1 as an FSM with a single state and transition labelled u_1/v_1. The composite FSM $K \Diamond C_1$ is shown in Fig. 4(a).

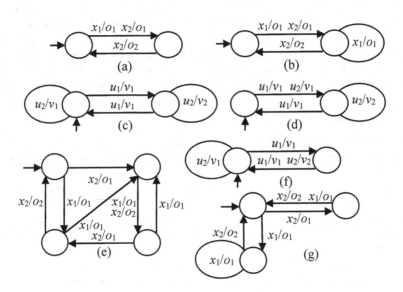

Fig. 4. Constructing the external checking experiment.

The FSM $K \Diamond C_1$ has an undefined input x_1 in the second state, we take the external input sequence $x_1 x_1$, so now $\Psi = \{x_1 x_1\}$. It is the X-restriction of the word $\sigma = x_1 u_1 v_1 u_1 v_1 o_1 x_1 u_2 v_1 o_1$ in $A(K) \Diamond A(E)$. Its restriction onto the alphabets of the embedded component is $\sigma_{\downarrow(U \cup V)} = u_1 v_1 u_1 v_1 u_2 v_1$. $\Omega = \{u_1 v_1 u_1 v_1 u_2 v_1\}$. The function *Infer_conjecture*(Ω, n, Π) for the empty set Π returns a Ω-conjecture C_2 as an FSM with a single state and two transitions labelled u_1/v_1 and u_2/v_1. The composite FSM $K \Diamond C_2$ is shown in Fig. 4(b). It is a complete machine, however, the product $(K \Diamond C) \times (K \Diamond E)$ is a partial machine, since its behavior is not specified for the input sequence $x_2 x_1 x_2$. In fact, this sequence demonstrates that $K \Diamond C_2 \not\cong K \Diamond E$, since $K \Diamond C_2$ reacts with the $o_1 o_1 o_2$, while $K \Diamond E$ with $o_1 o_1 o_1$.

The input sequence $x_2 x_1 x_2$ is added to Ψ, which becomes $\{x_1 x_1, x_2 x_1 x_2\}$. The sequence $x_2 x_1 x_2$ is the X-restriction of the word $\sigma = x_2 u_1 v_1 o_1\ x_1 u_2 v_2 o_1 x_2 u_1 v_1 o_1$ in A $(K) \lozenge A(E)$. Its restriction onto the alphabets of the embedded component is $\sigma_{\downarrow(U \cup V)} = u_1 v_1 u_2 v_2 u_1 v_1$. $\Omega = \{u_1 v_1 u_1 v_1 u_2 v_1, u_1 v_1 u_2 v_2 u_1 v_1\}$. Next Ω-conjecture C_3 is shown in Fig. 4(c). The composite FSM $K \lozenge C_3$ is isomorphic to $K \lozenge E$. Now the set of partitions Π should include the following partition of prefixes of Ω, as each of them is a state of the Ω-machine:

$$\pi_1 = \{\varepsilon,\ u_1 v_1 u_1 v_1,\ u_1 v_1 u_1 v_1 u_2 v_1,\ u_1 v_1 u_2 v_2 u_1 v_1;\ u_1 v_1,\ u_1 v_1 u_2 v_2\}.$$

In the next iteration, *Infer_conjecture*(Ω, n, Π) returns the Ω-conjecture C_4 shown in Fig. 4(d). The composite FSM $K \lozenge C_4$ is shown in Fig. 4(e). It is not equivalent to $K \lozenge E$, and the shortest input sequence distinguishing them is $x_1 x_1 x_1 x_2$, it extends the existing sequence $x_1 x_1$.

The input sequence $x_1 x_1 x_1 x_2$ is added to Ψ, which becomes $\{x_1 x_1 x_1 x_2, x_2 x_1 x_2\}$. It is the X-restriction of the word $\sigma = x_1 u_1 v_1 u_1 v_1 o_1 x_1 u_2 v_1 o_1 x_1 u_2 v_1 o_1 x_2 o_2$ in $A(K) \lozenge A(E)$. We have $\sigma_{\downarrow(U \cup V)} = u_1 v_1 u_1 v_1 u_2 v_1 u_2 v_1$. $\Omega = \{u_1 v_1 u_1 v_1 u_2 v_1 u_2 v_1, u_1 v_1 u_2 v_2 u_1 v_1\}$. Next Ω-conjecture C_5 is shown in Fig. 4(f). The composite FSM $K \lozenge C_5$ is shown in Fig. 4 (g). It is not equivalent to $K \lozenge E$, and the shortest input sequence distinguishing them is $x_2 x_1 x_2 x_1 x_2$, it extends the existing sequence $x_2 x_1 x_2$.

The input sequence $x_2 x_1 x_2 x_1 x_2$ is added to Ψ, which becomes $\{x_1 x_1 x_1 x_2,$ $x_2 x_1 x_2 x_1 x_2\}$. It is the X-restriction of the word $\sigma = x_2 u_1 v_1 o_1\ x_1 u_2 v_2 o_1 x_2 u_1 v_1 o_1 x_1\text{-}$ $u_2 v_1 o_1 x_2 o_2$. We have $\sigma_{\downarrow(U \cup V)} = u_1 v_1 u_2 v_2 u_1 v_1 u_2 v_1$. $\Omega = \{u_1 v_1 u_1 v_1 u_2 v_1 u_2 v_1, u_1 v_1 u_2 v_2$ $u_1 u_2 v_1\}$. The function *Infer_conjecture*(Ω, n, Π) returns False, since there is no solution which does not extend the partition π_1. Algorithm 2 terminates with the external checking experiment $\Psi = \{x_1 x_1 x_1 x_2, x_2 x_1 x_2 x_1 x_2\}$.

This example was used in the previous work [12] to illustrate a number of various approaches to construct complete tests for the embedded component, compared to them the SAT solving approach elaborated here generates a much smaller test suite. For comparison, we construct the same experiment assuming this time that $n = 3$. The prototype tool presented in Sect. 7 returns just seven tests.

Notice that the algorithm not only delivers an external checking experiment for the embedded component, but also infers an FSM that is externally equivalent to the given embedded FSM. In our example, the Ω-conjecture C_3 in Fig. 4(c) is externally equivalent to the FSM E in Fig. 2. This observation indicates that the approach should work for active inference of an embedded component. We elaborate a corresponding algorithm in Sect. 7.

Theorem 1. Given complete deterministic FSMs K and E such that the composite machine $K \lozenge E$ is a complete FSM, Algorithm 2 returns an external checking experiment for the embedded FSM E w.r.t. $\mathfrak{J}(n, U, V)$.

Sketch of Proof. When Algorithm 2 terminates the resulting set of external input sequence Ψ is indeed a checking experiment, since by the post-condition of *Infer_-conjecture* no conjecture exists that is not externally equivalent to the given embedded FSM E. Note that all complete conjectures externally equivalent to E are excluded because as soon as one if found (including E itself), its partition is added to Π. Algorithm 2 will not generate the same conjecture all over again and always terminates because the set of all possible conjectures with at most n states is finite.

6 Preliminary Experiments

The complexity of checking experiments for complete deterministic FSMs is well understood, however, no result exists yet on estimating complexity of external checking experiments for embedded FSMs. Considering a system of two communicating machines, context and embedded FSMs, the question arises which of them contribute more to the complexity of external checking experiments. We decided to perform experiments aiming at shedding some light on this.

Both machines are generated randomly for $|X| = |O| = |U| = |V| = 2$. In the first experiment, we fix the number of states of an embedded FSM to six and vary that of the context; in the second experiment, we fix the number of states of a context FSM to six and vary that of the embedded FSM. For each pair of values, the average of ten instances obtained with a prototype tool implementing Algorithm 2 is calculated and the results are illustrated in Fig. 5. They indicate that the length of experiments grows with the number of states in an embedded machine similar to an FSM considered in isolation, but the complexity of the context seems not to be a significant contributor. More experiments are needed to check this conclusion.

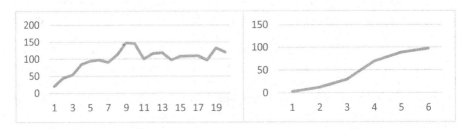

Fig. 5. The length of external checking experiments vs the number of states in the context (left hand side) and in the embedded machine (right hand side).

7 Active Inference of Embedded FSM

Given a composition of two complete deterministic FSMs K and E with the topology in Fig. 1, called a *grey box*, *GB*, where the context FSM K is known, while the embedded FSM E is not, we want to learn the machine E by applying external inputs I and observing external as well as internal outputs O, U, V, assuming that the embedded FSM E has at most n states.

External input sequences are applied to the grey box obeying the property of a slow environment *Env* (Fig. 1), i.e., inputs are interleaved with outputs. We assume that livelocks are removed from the grey box. The learning procedure is implemented in Algorithm 3. It is an enhancement of Algorithm 2 replacing the FSM E by a current conjecture.

Algorithm 3. Inferring the embedded FSM and determining an external checking experiment for it

Input A grey box GB and integer n

Output A minimal complete conjecture with at most n states and an external checking experiment w.r.t. $\Im(n, U, V)$

1: $\Omega := \varnothing$
2: $\Psi := \varnothing$
3: $\Pi := \varnothing$
4: $C := Infer\_conjecture(\Omega, n, \Pi)$
5: **while** an Ω-conjecture D is returned by *Infer_conjecture*(Ω, n, Π) **do**
6:    **if** $A(K) \lozenge A(D)$ has a livelock or $(K \lozenge D) \times (K \lozenge C)$ is complete **then**
7:        $\Pi := \Pi \cup \{\pi_D\}$
8:    **else**
9:        Determine an input sequence βa such that β is the shortest transfer sequence from a state of $K \lozenge C$ reached by an input sequence $\mu \in \Psi \cup \{\varepsilon\}$ to a state with the undefined input a in $(K \lozenge D) \times (K \lozenge C)$
10:       $\Psi := \Psi \cup \{\mu \beta a\}$
11:       Let σ be a trace observed in GB when the external input sequence $\mu \beta a$ is applied
12:       **if** $\sigma_{\downarrow(U \cup V)} \in \Omega$ **then**
13:           $\Pi := \Pi \cup \{\pi_D\}$
14:       **else**
15:           $\Omega := \Omega \cup \{\sigma_{\downarrow(U \cup V)}\}$
16:           **if** $\sigma_{\downarrow(U \cup V)} \notin Tr_C$ **then**
17:               $C := Infer\_conjecture(\Omega, n, \Pi)$
18:           **end if**
19:       **end if**
20: **end while**
21: **return** C and Ψ

Example. We illustrate Algorithm 3 using the context and embedded machines in Fig. 2. The embedded FSM is the one to be inferred and we use the composite automaton in Fig. 3 as the grey box. We assume that $n = 2$. Initially, the set of external input sequences Ψ is empty, so is the set of internal input sequences Ω. The function *Infer_conjecture*(Ω, n, Π) for the empty set Π returns a Ω-conjecture C_0 as an FSM with a single state and no transitions. Its second execution yields D_0 which has no transition. $(K \lozenge C_0) \times (K \lozenge D_0)$ has no transitions either. We choose the external input x_1, so $\Psi = \{x_1\}$. When this input is applied to the grey box, the trace $\sigma = x_1 u_1 v_1 u_1 v_1 o_1$ is observed. Its restriction onto the alphabets of the embedded component is $\sigma_{\downarrow(U \cup V)} = u_1 v_1 u_1 v_1$. $\Omega = \{u_1 v_1 u_1 v_1\}$. The function *Infer_conjecture*(Ω, n, Π) for the empty set Π returns a Ω-conjecture with a single state and transition labelled u_1/v_1. This machine becomes now the conjecture C_1. The composite FSM $K \lozenge C_1$ is shown in Fig. 4(a). Next execution of the loop yields the conjecture D_1 equivalent to C_1.

The product $(K \lozenge C_1) \times (K \lozenge D_1)$ has an undefined input x_1 in the second state, we take the external input sequence $x_1 x_1$, so now $\Psi = \{x_1 x_1\}$. When this input sequence is applied to the grey box, the trace $\sigma = x_1 u_1 v_1 u_1 v_1 o_1 x_1 u_2 v_1 o_1$ is observed. Its restriction onto the alphabets of the embedded component is $\sigma_{\downarrow(U \cup V)} = u_1 v_1 u_1 v_1 u_2 v_1 . \Omega = \{u_1 v_1 u_1 v_1 u_2 v_1\}$. The function $Infer\_conjecture(\Omega, n, \Pi)$ for the empty set Π returns a Ω-conjecture D_2 with a single state and two transitions labelled u_1/v_1 and u_2/v_1. This machine becomes now the conjecture C_2. The composite FSM $K \lozenge C_2$ is shown in Fig. 4 (b). The product $(K \lozenge C_2) \times (K \lozenge D_2)$ is a complete machine, $\Pi := \Pi \cup \{\pi_{D_2}\}$ is executed, where $\pi_{D_2} = \{\varepsilon, u_1 v_1, u_1 v_1 u_1 v_1, u_1 v_1 u_1 v_1 u_2 v_1\}$. The function $Infer\_conjecture$ (Ω, n, Π) for the set Π returns a Ω-conjecture D_3 shown in Fig. 6(a). The composite FSM $K \lozenge D_3$ is shown in Fig. 6(b). Its behavior is not specified for the input sequence $x_2 x_1$.

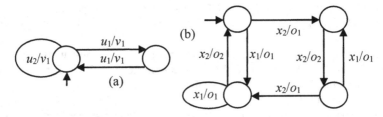

Fig. 6. Ω-conjecture D_3 (a) and the composite FSM $K \lozenge D_3$.

The input sequence $x_2 x_1$ is added to Ψ, which becomes $\{x_1 x_1, x_2 x_1\}$. The grey box produces the trace $\sigma = x_2 u_1 v_1 o_1 \ x_1 u_2 v_2 o_1$ when the sequence $x_2 x_1$ is applied. Its restriction onto the alphabets of the embedded component is $\sigma_{\downarrow(U \cup V)} = u_1 v_1 u_2 v_2 . \Omega = \{u_1 v_1 u_1 v_1 u_2 v_1, u_1 v_1 u_2 v_2\}$. Next Ω-conjecture D_4 is shown in Fig. 4(c). This machine becomes now the conjecture C_3. The composite FSM $K \lozenge C_3$ is isomorphic to the FSM in Fig. 2(c). Then the set of partitions Π should include the following partition: $\pi_{D_4} = \{\varepsilon, u_1 v_1 u_1 v_1, u_1 v_1 u_1 v_1 u_2 v_1; u_1 v_1, u_1 v_1 u_2 v_2\}$.

In the next iteration, $Infer\_conjecture(\Omega, n, \Pi)$ returns the Ω-conjecture D_5 shown in Fig. 4(d). The composite FSM $K \lozenge D_5$ is shown in Fig. 4(e). It is not equivalent to $K \lozenge C_3$, and the shortest input sequence distinguishing them is $x_1 x_1 x_1 x_2$, it extends the sequence $x_1 x_1$.

The input sequence $x_1 x_1 x_1 x_2$ is added to Ψ, which becomes $\{x_1 x_1 x_1 x_2, x_2 x_1\}$. The sequence applied to the grey box produces the trace $\sigma = x_1 u_1 v_1 u_1 v_1 o_1 x_1 u_2 v_1 o_1 x_1 u_2 v_1 o_1 x_2 o_2$. We have $\sigma_{\downarrow(U \cup V)} = u_1 v_1 u_1 v_1 u_2 v_1 u_2 v_1 . \Omega = \{u_1 v_1 u_1 v_1 u_2 v_1 u_2 v_1, u_1 v_1 u_2 v_2\}$. Next Ω-conjecture D_5 is shown in Fig. 4(f). The composite FSM $K \lozenge D_5$ is shown in Fig. 4(g). It is not equivalent to $K \lozenge E$, and the shortest sequence distinguishing them is $x_2 x_1 x_2 x_1 x_2$, it extends the sequence $x_2 x_1$.

The input sequence $x_2 x_1 x_2 x_1 x_2$ is added to Ψ, which becomes $\{x_1 x_1 x_1 x_2, x_2 x_1 x_2 x_1 x_2\}$. Applied to the grey box it produces the trace $\sigma = x_2 u_1 v_1 o_1 x_1 u_2 v_2 o_1 x_2 u_1 v_1 o_1 x_1 u_2 v_1 o_1 x_2 o_2$. We have $\sigma_{\downarrow(U \cup V)} = u_1 v_1 u_2 v_2 u_1 v_1 u_2 v_1 . \Omega = \{u_1 v_1 u_1 v_1 u_2 v_1 u_2 v_1, u_1 v_1 u_2 v_2 u_1 v_1 u_2 v_1\}$.

The function *Infer_conjecture*(Ω, n, Π) returns False, since no solution with a state partition which does not extend the partition π_{D_4} can be found. Algorithm 3 terminates with the conjecture C_3 (Fig. 4(c)) that is externally equivalent to the embedded FSM E in Fig. 3 and its external checking experiment $\Psi = \{x_1x_1x_1x_2, x_2x_1x_2x_1x_2\}$. In this example, both algorithms give the same experiment, though this should not be expected for other systems, since the function *call-solver(formula)* can make nondeterministic choices in solving constraints. Moreover, various input sequences can be chosen to deal with partial FSM products (see line 13 in Algorithm 3).

Theorem 2. If a grey box behaves as a complete FSM and the embedded FSM E has n states, Algorithm 3 infers a conjecture with at most n states that is externally equivalent to E and constructs an external checking experiment for it.

Sketch of Proof. Algorithm 3 follows the steps of Algorithm 2, just replacing the FSM E by a current conjecture. This does not influence its termination since it only occurs when no more externally distinguishable conjecture can be found. At some point, because the grey box behaves as a composite FSM of the known context FSM and the embedded machine with n states, an FSM that is externally equivalent to E will be returned by *Infer_conjecture*. The resulting set of external input sequences is an external checking experiment for the resulting FSM, as in Theorem 1.

8 Conclusions

We considered a system of communicating FSMs and investigated possibilities for active learning and testing of an embedded FSM without disassembling the system. The contribution of this paper is the generalization of the isolated FSM inference problem to that of an FSM embedded in a modular system (grey box learning) and an approach for solving this problem that does not depend on the composition topology. The approach also offers a novel solution to embedded testing by generating a complete test suite directly for the embedded machine that avoids intermediate testing of non-deterministic approximations, eliminating thus several sources of test redundancy inherent in the existing methods. We plan to perform more experiments to assess the proposed methods, especially for learning embedded components.

Acknowledgements. This work was partially supported by MESI (Ministère de l'Économie, Science et Innovation) of Gouvernement du Québec, NSERC of Canada and CAE.

References

1. Biermann, A.W., Feldman, J.A.: On the synthesis of finite-state machines from samples of their behavior. IEEE Trans. Comput. **100**(6), 592–597 (1972)
2. El-Fakih, K., Petrenko, A., Yevtushenko, N.: FSM test translation through context. In: Uyar, M.Ü., Duale, A.Y., Fecko, M.A. (eds.) TestCom 2006. LNCS, vol. 3964, pp. 245–258. Springer, Heidelberg (2006). https://doi.org/10.1007/11754008_16
3. Gold, E.M.: Complexity of automaton identification from given data. Inf. Control **37**(3), 302–320 (1978)

4. Groz, R., Li, K., Petrenko, A., Shahbaz, M.: Modular system verification by inference, testing and reachability analysis. In: Suzuki, K., Higashino, T., Ulrich, A., Hasegawa, T. (eds.) FATES/TestCom-2008. LNCS, vol. 5047, pp. 216–233. Springer, Heidelberg (2008). https://doi.org/10.1007/978-3-540-68524-1_16

5. Groz, R., Li, K., Petrenko, A.: Integration testing of communicating systems with unknown components. Ann. Telecommun. **70**(3), 107–125 (2015)

6. Heule, Marijn J.H., Verwer, S.: Exact DFA identification using SAT solvers. In: Sempere, J. M., García, P. (eds.) ICGI 2010. LNCS (LNAI), vol. 6339, pp. 66–79. Springer, Heidelberg (2010). https://doi.org/10.1007/978-3-642-15488-1_7

7. Luo, G., Bochmann, G.V., Petrenko, A.: Test selection based on communicating nondeterministic finite-state machines using a generalized Wp-method. IEEE Trans. Softw. Eng. **20**(2), 149–162 (1994)

8. Meinke, K.: CGE: a sequential learning algorithm for Mealy automata. In: Sempere, J.M., García, P. (eds.) ICGI 2010. LNCS (LNAI), vol. 6339, pp. 148–162. Springer, Heidelberg (2010). https://doi.org/10.1007/978-3-642-15488-1_13

9. Oliveira, A.L., Silva, J.P.M.: Efficient algorithms for the inference of minimum size DFAs. Mach. Learn. **4**(1), 93–119 (2001)

10. Petrenko, A., Avellaneda, F., Groz, R., Oriat, C.: From passive to active FSM inference via checking sequence construction. In: Yevtushenko, N., Cavalli, A.R., Yenigün, H. (eds.) ICTSS 2017. LNCS, vol. 10533, pp. 126–141. Springer, Cham (2017). https://doi.org/10.1007/978-3-319-67549-7_8

11. Petrenko, A., Yevtushenko, N., Bochmann, G.V., Dssouli, R.: Testing in context: framework and test derivation. Comput. Commun. **19**(14), 1236–1249 (1996)

12. Petrenko, A., Yevtushenko, N., Bochmann, G.V.: Fault models for testing in context. In: Gotzhein, R., Bredereke, J. (eds.) Formal Description Techniques IX. IFIP Advances in Information and Communication Technology. Springer, Heidelberg (1996). https://doi.org/10.1007/978-0-387-35079-0_10

13. Rivest, R.L., Schapire, R.E.: Inference of finite automata using homing sequences. In: Hanson, S.J., Remmele, W., Rivest, R.L. (eds.) Machine Learning: From Theory to Applications. LNCS, vol. 661, pp. 51–73. Springer, Heidelberg (1993). https://doi.org/10.1007/3-540-56483-7_22

14. Petrenko, A., Yevtushenko, N.: Testing faults in embedded components. In: 10th International Workshop on Testing of Communicating Systems, pp. 272–287 (1997)

15. Steffen, B., et al.: Active automata learning: from DFAs to interface programs and beyond. In: ICGI, pp. 195–209 (2012)

16. Villa, T., Petrenko, A., Yevtushenko, N., Mishchenko, A., Brayton, R.: Component based design by solving language equations. Proc. IEEE **103**(11), 2152–2167 (2015)

17. Jaffar-ur Rehman, M., Jabeen, F., Bertolino, A., Polini, A.: Testing software components for integration: a survey of issues and techniques. Softw. Test. Verif. Reliab. **17**, 95–133 (2007)

18. Abel, A., Reineke, J.: Gray-Box learning of serial compositions of mealy machines. In: Rayadurgam, S., Tkachuk, O. (eds.) NFM 2016. LNCS, vol. 9690, pp. 272–287. Springer, Cham (2016). https://doi.org/10.1007/978-3-319-40648-0_21

Neural Networks as Artificial Specifications

I. S. Wishnu B. Prasetya[(✉)] and Minh An Tran

Utrecht University, Utrecht, The Netherlands
s.w.b.prasetya@uu.nl

Abstract. In theory, a neural network can be trained to act as an artificial specification for a program by showing it samples of the programs executions. In practice, the training turns out to be very hard. Programs often operate on discrete domains for which patterns are difficult to discern. Earlier experiments reported too much false positives. This paper revisits an experiment by Vanmali et al. by investigating several aspects that were uninvestigated in the original work: the impact of using different learning modes, aggressiveness levels, and abstraction functions. The results are quite promising.

Keywords: Neural network for software testing · Automated oracles

1 Introduction

Nowadays, many systems make use of external services or components to do some of their tasks, allowing services to be shared, hence reducing cost. However, we also need to take into account that third parties services may be updated on the fly as our system is running in production. If such an update introduces an error, this may affect the correctness of our system as well. One way to guard against this is by doing run time verification [2]: at the runtime the outputs of these services are checked against their formal specifications. Unfortunately, in practice it is hard to persuade developers to write formal specifications.

A more pragmatic idea is to use 'artificial specifications' generated by a computer. Another use case is automated testing. Tools like QuickCheck, Evosuite, and T3 [3,6,13] are able to generate test inputs, but if no specification is given, only common correctness conditions such as absence of crashes can be checked. Using artificial specifications would extend their range.

Although we cannot expect a computer to be able to on its own specify the intent of a program, it can still try to guess this intent. One way to do this is by observing some training executions to predict general properties of the program, e.g. in the form of 'invariants' (state properties) [5], finite state machine [12], or algebraic properties [4]. These approaches cannot however capture the full functionality of a program, e.g. [5] can only infer predefined families of predicates,

I. Medina-Bulo et al. (Eds.): ICTSS 2018, LNCS 11146, pp. 135–141, 2018.
https://doi.org/10.1007/978-3-319-99927-2_11

many are simple predicates such as $o \neq$ null and $x + y \geq 0$. With respect to these approaches, neural networks offer an interesting alternative, since they can be trained to simulate a function [9].

The trade off of using artificial specifications is the additional overhead in debugging. When a production-time execution violates such a specification, the failure may be either caused by an error triggered by the execution, or by an error in the training executions that were reflected in the predictions, or due to inaccuracy of the predictions. The first two cases expose errors (though the second case would take more effort to debug). However, the failure in the last case is a false alarm (false positive). Since we do not know upfront if a violation is a real error or a false positive, we will need to investigate it (debugging), which is quite labour intensive. If it turns out to be a false positive, the effort is wasted. Despite the potential, studies on the use of neural networks as artificial specifications are few: [1,10,11,14]. They either reported unacceptably high rate of false positives, or do not address the issue.

In this paper we revisit an experiment by Vanmali et al. [14] that revealed $\approx 16\%$ rate of false positives—a rate of above 5% is likely to render any approach unusable in practice. The challenge lies in the discrete nature of the program used as the experiment subject, making it very hard to train a neural network. This paper explores several aspects that were left uninvestigated in the original work, namely the influence of different learning modes, aggressiveness levels, and abstraction. The results are quite promising.

2   Neural Network as an Artificial Specification

Consider a program P that behaves as a function $I \rightarrow O$. An artificial *specification* ϕ is a predicate $I \times O \rightarrow$ bool; $\phi(x, P(x)) = \mathsf{T}$ means that P's output is judged as correct, and else incorrect. With respect to the intended specification $\mathcal{G}$, ϕ's judgment is a *true positive* is when both ϕ and $\mathcal{G}$ judge a T, a *true negative* is when they agree on the judgement F, a *false positive* is when ϕ judges F and $\mathcal{G}$ judges T, and a *false negative* is when ϕ judges T and $\mathcal{G}$ judges F.

An *neural network* (NN) is a network of 'neurons' [9] that behaves as a function $\mathbb{R}^M \rightarrow \mathbb{R}^N$. We will restrict ourselves to *feed forward NNs* (FNNs) where the neurons are organized in linearly ordered layers [9]; an example is below:

The first layer is called the *input layer*, consisting of M neurons connected to the inputs. The last layer is the *output layer*, consisting of N neurons that produce the outputs. The layers in between are called *hidden layers*. An input neuron simply passes on its input, else it has k inputs and an additional input called 'bias' whose value is always 1 [9]. Each input connector has a weight w_i. The neuron's output is the weighted sum of its inputs, followed by applying a so-called *activation function*: $out = f\ (\Sigma_{0 \le i \le k}\ w_i.x_i)$. A commonly used f is the logistic function, which we also use in our experiments.

Any continuous numeric function $\mathbb{R}^M \to \mathbb{R}^N$, restricted within any closed subset of $\mathbb{R}^M$, can be simulated with arbitrary accuracy by an FNN [7], which implies that an FNN can indeed act as an artificial specification for P, if P is injectable into such a numeric function. That is, there exists a continuous numeric function $F{:}\mathbb{R}^M \to \mathbb{R}^N$ and injections $\pi_I{:}I \to \mathbb{R}^N$ and $\pi_O{:}O \to \mathbb{R}^N$ such that F encodes P: for all $x \in I$, $P(x) = \pi_O^{-1}(F(\pi_I(x)))$. However, finding a right FNN is hard. A common technique to find one is by training an FNN using a set of sample inputs and outputs, e.g. using the back propagation [9] algorithm. It might be easier to train the NN to simulate $\alpha \circ P$ instead, where α is some chosen abstraction on P's output values. The trade off is that we get a weaker specification.

Since an NN does not literally produce a bool, we couple its output vector $\bar{z}' = \mathrm{NN}(\pi_I(\bar{x}))$ to a so-called *comparator* $\mathcal{C} : \mathbb{R}^N \to \mathbb{R}^N \to$ bool to calculate the judgement by comparing $\bar{z}'$ with the observed output $\bar{z} = \pi_O(\alpha(P(\bar{x})))$. Basically, if their values are 'far' from each other, then the judgement is F, and else T. By adjusting what 'far' means we can tune the specification's aggressiveness without having to tamper with the NN's internals. In our experiments (below), the identity function $id = (\lambda x . x)$ will be used as the injector π_I and π_O. Because id simply passes on its input, it will be omitted from the formulas.

3   Experiments

Figure 1 shows a credit approval program from the financial domain that was used as the experiment subject by Vanmali et al. [14]. The program takes 8 input parameters describing a customer. The output is a pair (b, y) where b is a boolean indicating whether the credit request is approved, and if so y specifies the maximum allowed credit. We will ignore b since [14] already shows that an FNN can accurately predict its value. Despite its size, the subject is quite challenging for an NN to simulate because it operates on a discrete domain (the numeric values are all integers). The whole input domain has 224000 possible values. We will use an FNN with 8 inputs (representing approve's inputs) and a hidden layer with 24 neurons (adding more layers and neurons does not really improve the FNN's accuracy).

Five variations of the FNN will be used, as listed below, along with the used comparator $\mathcal{C}$. $\mathcal{C}$ is parameterized with aggressiveness level A (integer 0 (least aggressive) ... 5) that determines $\mathcal{C}$'s policy to deal with non clear-cut cases.

1. The FNN direct has one output, which is trained to simulate y. Its comparator $\mathcal{C}_A$ uses Euclidian distance, with sensitivity linearly scaled by A: $\mathcal{C}_A(y, y') = |y - y'| < \epsilon_{max} - 0.01A$, with $\epsilon_{max} = 0.09$.

```
1  approve(Citizenship ,State ,Region ,Sex ,Age,  Marital ,Dependents ,Income) {
2    if (Region==5 || Region==6) Amount=0 ;
3    else if (Age<18) Amount=0 ;
4    else {
5    if (Citizenship==0) {
6       Amount = 5000+1000*Income ;
7       if (State==0)
8          if (Region==3 || Region==4) Amount = Amount*2 ;
9          else  Amount = (int)(Amount*1.50) ;
10      else Amount = (int)(Amount*1.10) ;
11      if (Marital==0)
12         if (Dependents >0) Amount = Amount+200*Dependents ;
13         else Amount = Amount+500;
14      else Amount = Amount+1000 ;
15      if (Sex==0) Amount = Amount+500 ;
16      else Amount = Amount+1000;
17   }
18   else {
19      Amount = 1000 + 800 * Income;
20      if (Marital==0)
21         if (Dependents >2) Amount = Amount+100*Dependents ;
22         else Amount = Amount+100 ;
23      else Amount = Amount+300 ;
24      if (Sex==0) Amount = Amount+100 ;
25      else Amount = Amount+200 ;
26   }
27   if (Amount==0) Approved=F else Approved=T;
28   return (Approved ,Amount ); }
```

Fig. 1. The experiment subject: a credit approval program from [14].

2. The FNN uni_N has N outputs, trained to simulate $\alpha_N \circ$ approve. The abstraction α_N maps approve's y output to a vector $\bar{z} : [0.0..1.0]^N$ representing one of N uniform sized intervals in y's range $[0..18000]$, such that the k-th interval is represented by a vector of 0's except a single 1 at the k-th position. If $\bar{v} : [0.0..1.0]^N$, let winner($\bar{v}$) be the index of the greatest element in $\bar{v}$.

The comparator is more complicated. An obvious case is when $\bar{z}' = \mathrm{NN}(\bar{x})$ and $\bar{z} = \alpha_{10}(\text{approve}(\bar{x}))$ report the same winner. If the NN's winner is confident of itself, approve's output is judged as correct. When they produce different winners and the NN's winner is confident of itself, we judge approve to be incorrect. Other cases are non-clear-cut and judged depending on the aggressiveness level. The full definition of C_A is shown below. The original work Vanmali et al. [14] only uses $A = 3$ aggressiveness level.

function $C_A(\bar{z}, \bar{z}')$
  $k, j \leftarrow$ winner($\bar{z}$), winner($\bar{z}'$) ; $agree \leftarrow k = j$
  if $agree \wedge |agree - \bar{z}'_j| < th_{low}$ **then** (obvious match) T
  else if $\neg agree \wedge |agree - \bar{z}'_j| > th_{high}$ **then** (obvious mismatch) F
  else (non-clear-cut cases) **case** A **of**
    0 : (least aggressive: always accept) T
    1 : (reject when the NN contradicts agreement) $\neg(agree \wedge |\mathrm{T} - \bar{z}'_j| > th_{high})$
    2 : (always accept on agreement) $agree$
    3 : (Vanmali et al. [14]: accept on conflicting results) $\neg agree \vee |\mathrm{T} - \bar{z}'_j| > th_{high}$
    4 : (only accept if NN's winner supports $\bar{z}$) $|agree - \bar{z}'_j| < th_{low}$
    5 : (most aggressive: never accept) F
  end function

The thresholds th_{low} and th_{high} are set to 0.2/0.8.

3. The FNN $unimin_N$ is a less presumptuous variant of uni, with th_{low}/th_{high} set to 0.1/0.9. This will cause more cases to be regarded as non-clear-cut.
4. The FNN $lower_N$ is like uni_N, but trained to simulate $\alpha_N \circ low \circ$ approve. low is used to 'stretch' α_N to divide y into finer intervals in the lower region of y's range, e.g. if we believe the region to be more error prone, and growing coarser towards the other end. We use the log function to do this: $K * log(1 + y/a)$ with $K = 8000$ and $a = 100$ controlling the steepness.
5. The FNN $center_N$ is like uni_N, but trained to simulate $\alpha_N \circ ctr \circ$ approve. ctr is used to 'stretch' α_N to divide y into finer intervals in the center region of y's range. We use logistic function $ctr(y) = M/(1 + e^{-a(y-0.5M)})$ where $M = 18000$ (y's maximum) and $a = 0.0006$ control the function's steepness.

Training. We randomly generate 500 distinct inputs (from the space of 224000 values) and collect the corresponding approve's outputs. This set of 500 pairs (input,output) forms the training data. For every type of FNN above and every aggressiveness level an FNN is trained. N controls the granularity of the used abstraction, so we also try various N (10..60). For each FNN, the connections' weight is randomly initialized in $[-0.5..0.5]$. The training is done in a series of epochs using the back propagation algorithm [9]. We tried both the incremental learning mode [8,9], where the FNN's error is propagated back after each training input, and batch learning modes, where only the average error is propagated back, after the whole batch of training inputs (500 of them). Incremental learning is thus more sensitive to the influence of individual inputs.

Evaluation. To evaluate the FNNs' ability to detect errors, we run them on 21 erroneous variations (mutants) of the subject as in [14]—due to limited space they are not shown here. For each mutant, 500 distinct random inputs are generated, whose outputs are 'error exposing' (distinguishable from the corresponding outputs of the correct subject). As an artificial specification, an FNN should ideally reject all these error exposing outputs. Each rejection is a true positive. We also generate 500 distinct random inputs and feed it to the (unmutated) subject. The FNN should accepts the corresponding outputs—each rejection is a false positive.

Figure 2 shows some of the results. Except for direct, the training was done in 1500 epochs with learning rate 0.5. We can see that using abstraction improves the FNN's performance: compare direct with uni_{30}. The latter obtains a true positive rate 68% on aggressiveness 2, implying that out of two erroneous executions, uni_{30} is likely to detect at least one, while when the aggressiveness level is set low, its rate of false positives is only around 2%. Abstraction also makes training easier: after 1500 epochs uni_{30} produces a mean square error (MSE) of ≈ 0.0001, whereas the shown results for direct is obtained after 10000 epochs (incrementally) with 0.1 learning rate, yielding an MSE ≈ 0.0004.

The experiment in [14] uses $unimin_{10}$. We believe [14] used batch learning because the reported MSE after 1500 epochs matches, namely ≈ 0.05. However, as can be seen in Fig. 2, this leads to poor performance (batched $unimin_{10}$). Incremental learning yields a much more accurate FNN (≈ 0.0001 MSE), hence also better performance ($unimin_{10}$). The performance of the FNN in [14] under our setup is indicated by the vanmali-markers in Fig. 2.

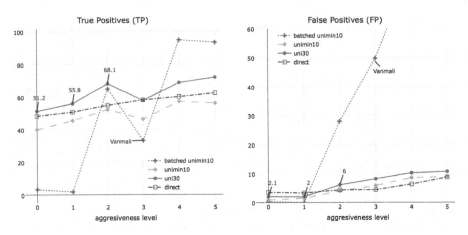

Fig. 2. The true positive and false positive rates (in %) of different FNNs.

The effect of using different abstractions and abstraction granularity (the N parameter) is shown in Fig. 3. Based on the results in Fig. 2, we now use the lowest aggressiveness level (0). The graph of uni shows that increasing N can greatly improve the FNN's ability to detect error, while keeping the false positive rate below 5%. We also see α_N and $\alpha_N \circ low$ perform significantly better than $\alpha_N \circ ctr$, implying that the choice of the abstraction function matters. Compared to α_N, $\alpha_N \circ low$ and $\alpha_N \circ ctr$ introduce non-linear granularity. The results suggest that introducing more granularity in the region (of P's output) which is more error prone pays off.

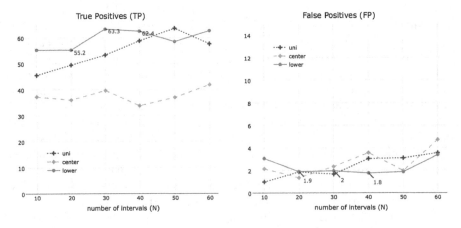

Fig. 3. The effect of different abstractions and the abstraction granularity (N).

4 Conclusion

The experiment showed that, contrary to earlier attempts, it is possible to train Neural Networks, given an appropriate abstraction, to become an artificial specification for a non-trivial discrete-domain program with acceptable precision. As future work, more case studies are needed to see how this generalizes.

References

1. Aggarwal, K., Singh, Y., Kaur, A., Sangwan, O.: A neural net based approach to test oracle. ACM SIGSOFT Softw. Eng. Notes **29**(3), 1–6 (2004)
2. Cao, T.D., Phan-Quang, T.T., Felix, P., Castanet, R.: Automated runtime verification for web services. In: International Conference on Web Services (ICWS). IEEE (2010)
3. Claessen, K., Hughes, J.: QuickCheck: a lightweight tool for random testing of Haskell programs. In: ACM SIGPLAN International Conference on Functional Programming (2000)
4. Elyasov, A., Prasetya, W., Hage, J., Rueda, U., Vos, T., Condori-Fernández, N.: AB=BA: execution equivalence as a new type of testing oracle. In: 30th ACM Symposium on Applied Computing. ACM (2015)
5. Ernst, M., et al.: The Daikon system for dynamic detection of likely invariants. Sci. Comput. Program. **69**(1), 35–45 (2007)
6. Fraser, G., Arcuri, A.: EvoSuite: automatic test suite generation for object-oriented software. In: SIGSOFT FSE, pp. 416–419 (2011)
7. Goodfellow, I., Bengio, Y., Courville, A.: Deep Learning. MIT Press, Cambridge (2016)
8. Joelself: FANN C# NeuralNet float. http://joelself.github.io/FannCSharp
9. Kriesel, D.: A brief Introduction on Neural Networks. dkriesel.com (2007)
10. Lu, Y., Ye, M.: Oracle model based on RBF neural networks for automated software testing. Inf. Technol. J. **6**(3), 469–474 (2007)
11. Mao, Y., Boqin, F., Li, Z., Yao, L.: Neural networks based automated test oracle for software testing. In: King, I., Wang, J., Chan, L.-W., Wang, D.L. (eds.) ICONIP 2006 Part III. LNCS, vol. 4234, pp. 498–507. Springer, Heidelberg (2006). https://doi.org/10.1007/11893295_55
12. Mariani, L., Pastore, F.: Automated identification of failure causes in system logs. In: 19th International Symposium on Software Reliability Engineering. IEEE (2008)
13. Prasetya, I.S.W.B.: T3i: a tool for generating and querying test suites for Java. In: 10th Joint Meeting on Foundations of Software Engineering (FSE). ACM (2015)
14. Vanmali, M., Last, M., Kandel, A.: Using a neural network in the software testing process. Int. J. Intell. Syst. **17**(1), 45–62 (2002)

Combining Model Learning and Data Analysis to Generate Models of Component-Based Systems

Sébastien Salva[✉], Elliott Blot, and Patrice Laurencot

LIMOS CNRS UMR 6158, Clermont Auvergne University, Clermont-Ferrand, France
sebastien.salva@uca.fr, {eblot,laurencot}@isima.fr

Abstract. Finding bugs in systems without model is well-known to be challenging and costly. But, most of today's developers think that writing models is also a hard and error-prone task. In this context, this paper addresses the problem of learning a model, from a component-based system, which captures and separates the behaviours of components and encodes their synchronisations. We present a passive model learning method called COnfECt to infer such models from execution traces in which no information is provided to identify components. We describe the two main steps of COnfECt in this paper and show some preliminary experimentations on real systems.

Keywords: Model learning · Passive learning · Reverse engineering Component-based systems

1 Introduction

Software testing aims at assessing the quality of the features offered by a system in terms of conformance, security, performance, etc., to discover and correct its defects. Nowadays, testing is essentially performed by means of test cases written by hand, which is often a long, difficult and error-prone task. To make this task easier, model learning approaches have proven to be valuable for recovering models that can be exploited by many software engineering stages, e.g. testing.

Although the generation of behavioural models has been greatly studied, little attention has been given to the learning of models from component-based systems. Yet, most of the systems being currently developed are made up of reusable features or communicating components that interact together. These observations motivate this work, which adresses the challenge of how to learn a model from its traces, in such a way that the model captures the behaviour of every component of the System Under Learning (SUL) and their synchronisations.

Research supported by the VASOC Project and the French Region Auvergne-Rhône-Alpes (https://vasoc.limos.fr/).

I. Medina-Bulo et al. (Eds.): ICTSS 2018, LNCS 11146, pp. 142–148, 2018.
https://doi.org/10.1007/978-3-319-99927-2_12

For this purpose, we designed the method COnfECt (COrrelate Extract Compose) for learning models of component-based systems. Its main originality is that it does not require any preliminary identification information about components. COnfECt learns a system of LTSs (Labelled Transition Systems) from traces (passive learning), which captures the behaviours of every component by a LTS and shows how they are synchronised together. COnfECt is composed of two main steps called *Trace Analysis & Extraction* and *LTS synchronisation* which are going to be developped in this paper.

Paper Organisation: Section 2 introduces the two steps of the COnfECt approach. The next section summarises the results of a preliminary evaluation on an IOT (Internet Of Things) device. Finally we conclude in Sect. 4.

2   The COnfECt Approach

Beforehand, we recall that the LTS model, we use in this paper, is defined in terms of states and transitions labelled by actions, taken from a general action set $\mathcal{L}$, which expresses what happens (a more complete definition can be found in [2]). We also define special actions of the form $call\_C_i$ and $return\_C_i$ to model component calls with C_i referring to a LTS. Actions of the form $call\_C_i$ and $return\_C_i$ synchronise pairs of LTSs as described in [1]. The execution of C_i starts with the label $call\_C_i$ and ends when the transition $return\_C_i$ is fired.

2.1   Overview of COnfECt

The COnfECt method aims to infer a system of LTSs SC from the traces of SUL, in such a way that SC captures the behaviours of the SUL components and their synchronisations. COnfECt initially requires the set of traces of SUL, denoted $Traces(SUL)$, to analyse the system behaviours and identify components. We suppose that each component can be identified by its behaviour, materialised by action sequences. And the more traces, the more correct the component detection will be. SUL can be indeterministic, uncontrollable or can have cycles among its internal states. However, we assume SUL and $Traces(SUL)$ obey certain restrictions. We consider that SUL has components whose observable behaviours are not carried out in parallel. One component is executed at a time from its initial state to one of its final states. Furthermore, we consider that traces are collected in a synchronous manner (by means of synchronous communications) to avoid the interleaving of actions. Traces can be collected by means of monitoring tools or extracted from log files. We assume that $Traces(SUL)$ does not include actions expressing the calls of components.

Furthermore, although this task is costly and important, we do not focus this work on the trace formatting, hence, we assume having a mapper, which is a tool often required in model learning to transform raw execution traces into higher level representations.

COnfECt has two main successive steps illustrated in Fig. 1. The first step, called *Trace Analysis & Extraction* tries to detect components in $Traces(SUL)$,

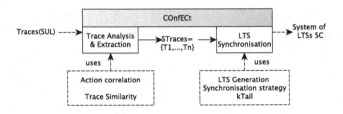

Fig. 1. The COnfECt approach overview

which is partitioned into a set of trace sets called *STraces*. Each trace set of *STraces* captures some behaviours of one component. The second step, called *LTS Synchronisation*, takes the set *STraces* and starts with the generation of one LTS for each trace set of *STraces*. This step also proposes different synchronisation strategies to generate a system of LTSs *SC*, before merging equivalent states with kTail.

2.2   Trace Analysis and Extraction

The aim of this step is to identify the different components in the traces of *Traces(SUL)*. The algorithm, which is given in [2] is divided into three procedures. The first one, *Inspect* analyses the traces and segments them in subsequences. We define a Correlation Coefficient to evaluate the correlation of successive actions in *Traces(SUL)*, i.e. the degree to which successive actions are associated with regard to *Traces(SUL)*. We define the Correlation coefficient between two actions by means of a utility function, which involves a weighting process for representing user priorities and preferences. We have chosen the technique *Simple Additive Weighting* (SAW) [3], which allows the interpretation of these preferences with weights. This factor must take a value between 0 and 1, and needs to be appraised, depending of the context.

From this Correlation coefficient, we define a relation to express the notion of strong correlation. We say that strong-corr(σ_1) holds when σ_1 has successive actions that strongly correlate. Besides, we compare two sequences with the relation σ_1 *mismatch* σ_2, which holds when the last event of σ_1 does not correlate strongly with the first one of σ_2.

The second procedure *Extract* whose algorithm is also given in [2] creates recursively different sequences to express component calls. It takes every trace σ, transforms it and stores the new trace into a set T_j, by the means of the coefficient correlation.

Example 1. Let us illustrate the procedure *Extract* with the example of Fig. 2a. The procedure takes as input a trace initially segmented into 4 sub-sequences by the correlation coefficient. (A) We start at σ_1 and suppose that no other subsequence is strongly correlated with σ_1. The sequence $\sigma_2\sigma_3\sigma_4$ is hence extracted and replaced by the actions *call_C2 return_C2*, which model the call of a component $C2$. The procedure is recursively called with Extract($\sigma' = \sigma_2\sigma_3\sigma_4, T_2$).

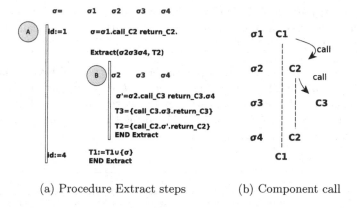

(a) Procedure Extract steps   (b) Component call

Fig. 2. Sequence extraction example.

(B) We now suppose $\sigma_2\sigma_4$ strongly correlate, thus σ_3 is extracted and the sequence σ' becomes $\sigma' = \sigma_2.call\_C3\ return\_C3.\sigma_4$. The extracted sequence σ_3 cannot be segmented. It is surrounded with the actions $call\_C3$ and $return\_C3$ to prepare the LTS synchronisation and to express that C3 is called by another component. The resulting sequence is added to the set T_3. As σ' is completely covered, σ' is surrounded with the actions $call\_C2$ and $return\_C2$ and added to the new trace set T_2. At the end of this process, we have recovered the hierarchical component call depicted in Fig. 2b and we get three trace sets.

The set T_1, which holds the modified traces of the initial trace set $Traces(SUL)$, may include traces resulting from several components. We call the third procedure *Separate* for trying to partition T1, to build the set $STraces$ such that a trace set T of $STraces$ is produced by one component. For that, we evaluate the trace similarity with regard to the actions shared between pairs of traces. Among the different available coefficients, we chose the Overlap coefficient because the action sets used by two traces may have different sizes. Then a clustering technique is used to get the equivalence classes. The procedure Separate is implemented with a Similarity threshold here.

2.3   LTS Synchronisation

The previous step of COnfECt has segmented, extracted and modified the traces of $Traces(SUL)$ in such a way that each trace set contains the behaviour of only one component. We generate a LTS from every trace set, where each trace represent a path of a tree-like LTS. These LTSs include actions of the form $call\_C_i$ and $return\_C_i$. These actions were added in the previous step to prepare the synchronisation of components with LTSs. We proposes different synchronisation strategies, which provide systems of LTSs with different levels of generalisation. The strict synchronisation limits over-generalisation, and used only kTail to merge equivalent states. The weak synchronisation aims at reducing the number of models and allows repetitive components calls, its uses a LTS similarly coefficient to merge models by means of a clustering technique. The strong synchronisation generate callable-complete LTSs, i.e., the LTS can call any other LTS of the system from any states.

Example 2. Let us illustrate this step with the set *STraces* of Fig. 3. The traces *T1* to *T4* are obtained from the step *Trace Analysis & Extraction* on a trace collected from a real smart thermostat device at the HTTP level. This trace, composed of 16 actions, was formatted to keep the Urls and some data, e.g., the temperature.

```
STraces = {
T1 {/devices call_C2 return_C2 Response(status:=200,data:=[1]) call_C3 return_C3 /devices
    Response(status:=200,data:=[1]) /hardware Response(status:=200,data:=[2]) /config call_C4
    return\_C4 Response(status:=200,data:=[2]) /tools Response(status:=200,data:=[3])}
T2 {call_C2 /json.htm(idx:=115,svalue:=15.00)=A Response(status:=200)=D return_C2}
T3 {call_C3 /json.htm(idx:=115,svalue:=16.00)=B Response(status:=200)=D return_C3}
T4 {call_C4 /json.htm(idx:=0,switchcmd:=On)=C Response(status:=200)=D return_C4} }
```

Fig. 3. Example of formatted trace segmented into 4 trace sets.

We choose to apply the Weak synchronization strategy. A similarity matrix is computed by means of the LTS Similarity coefficient. Figure 4a shows the matrix obtained with the four LTSs of our example. We can observe that two classes of similar LTSs emerge in this matrix: (C_1) and (C_2, C_3, C_4). A clustering technique is used to generate these classes. The LTSs of each cluster are then joined by means of a disjoint union.

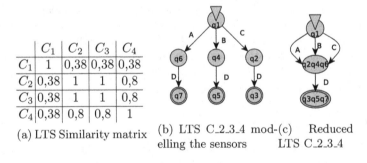

	C_1	C_2	C_3	C_4
C_1	1	0,38	0,38	0,38
C_2	0,38	1	1	0,8
C_3	0,38	1	1	0,8
C_4	0,38	0,8	0,8	1

(a) LTS Similarity matrix

(b) LTS C_2_3_4 modelling the sensors

(c) Reduced LTS C_2_3_4

Fig. 4. LTS results.

From the trace sets of Fig. 3, we obtain the two LTS clusters: (C_1) and (C_2, C_3, C_4), the first one expressing the behaviour of the Web interface, and the other one, the component that sends data. Figure 4b depicts the LTS C_{234} derived from the second cluster. The LTS C_{234} holds two equivalent state classes $(q2, q4, q6)$ and $(q3, q5, q7)$. kTail merges them and returns the LTS of Fig. 4c.

3   Preliminary Evaluation

We have implemented COnfECt in a prototype tool on which we conducted several experiments. We initially collected traces from an IOT device, a smart connected thermostat. It integrates 3 components providing HTTP traces. Several experiences have been performed, only five of them are provided in Tables 1 and 2: exp 1 and 2, traces of only one component is recovered, exp 3 and 4, traces of 2 components, and the last one with all the components.

Firstly, we evaluated the capability of COnfECt to recover the correct number of components, and then we compared the number of states and transitions with kTail. The tool, the trace sets and results are available here[1]. In Table 1, for exp. 1 to 5, the number of LTSs is equal to the number of real components with the Weak and Strong strategies, but not with the Strict strategy. This strategy segments traces, which are lifted to the level of LTS, but these are not merged.

Table 1. Number of components detected by COnfECt.

Exp.	# real components	Strict	Weak	Strong
Exp. 1	1	10	1	1
Exp. 2	1	1	1	1
Exp. 3	2	85	2	2
Exp. 4	2	67	2	2
Exp. 5	3	173	3	3

Table 2 gives the number of states and transitions of all the LTSs generated by COnfECt in Exp. 1 to 5. We also provide the number of states and transitions of these LTSs after removing the transitions labelled by the synchronisation actions in the last three columns. For comparison purposes, we applied kTail on the same trace sets. As expected, we obtain bigger LTSs with COnfECt than the ones achieved by kTail (excepted with Exp. 2 since there is no trace

Table 2. Size of the LTSs obtained with kTail and the three strategies of COnfECt. The label "hide" refers to the removal of the LTS transitions labelled by synchronisation actions.

Exp.	kTail		Strict		Weak		Strong		Strict + hide		Weak + hide		Strong + hide	
	#states	#trans	#states	#trans	#states	#trans	#states	#trans	#states	#trans	#states	#trans	#states	#trans
Exp 1	40	66	152	169	46	78	60	150	120	137	39	70	36	67
Exp 2	6	8	6	8	6	8	6	8	6	8	6	8	6	8
Exp 3	60	115	731	691	104	188	72	183	399	359	71	124	36	85
Exp 4	22	47	496	470	41	81	25	57	236	210	24	55	10	23
Exp 5	85	175	1307	1185	158	286	82	197	627	505	96	169	36	87

---

[1] https://github.com/Elblot/COnfECt.

segmentation). This result comes from the functioning of our method since the LTSs are completed with transitions labelled by synchronisation actions.

The transitions labelled by synchronisation actions help interpret the components combination and are required to compose LTSs, but are not relevant if one want to focus on the component behaviours only. If we remove them, the models achieved by COnfECt become more concise than those obtained with kTail.

4   Conclusion

We have introduced COnfECt, a passive model learning method that generates systems of LTSs from execution traces. A system of LTSs captures the behaviours of components and their synchronisations. COnfECt detects component behaviours by analysing traces with a Correlation coefficient and Similarity coefficients. It proposes different LTS synchronisation strategies, which help manage the model generalisation. With this hierarchic component organisation, we believe it offers better readability and comprehensibility than classical learned models, and consequently can be easily used for testing. In future work, we plan to perform more evaluations of COnfECt on several kinds of systems. We also plan to use the models for security testing.

References

1. van der Bijl, M., Rensink, A., Tretmans, J.: Compositional testing with IOCO. In: Petrenko, A., Ulrich, A. (eds.) FATES 2003. LNCS, vol. 2931, pp. 86–100. Springer, Heidelberg (2004). https://doi.org/10.1007/978-3-540-24617-6_7
2. Salva, S., Blot, E., Laurençot, P.: Combining model learning and data analysis to generate models of component-based systems. Limos research report, May 2018. http://sebastien.salva.free.fr/RR-18-05.pdf
3. Yoon, K.P., Hwang, C.L.: Multiple Attribute Decision Making: An Introduction. Quantitative Applications in the Social Sciences. SAGE Publications, Thousand Oaks (1995)

Deriving Tests with Guaranteed Fault Coverage for Finite State Machines with Timeouts

Aleksandr Tvardovskii[1], Khaled El-Fakih[2(✉)],
and Nina Yevtushenko[3]

[1] Tomsk State University, Tomsk, Russia
tvardal@mail.ru
[2] American University of Sharjah, Sharjah, UAE
kelfakih@aus.edu
[3] Ivannikov Institute for System Programming of the RAS, Moscow, Russia
evtushenko@ispras.ru

Abstract. In contrast to untimed FSMs, two minimal initialized FSMs with timeouts can be equivalent but not isomorphic. Accordingly, we propose an appropriate fault model and a method for complete test derivation for initialized deterministic FSMs with timeouts based on an appropriate FSM abstraction of the timed FSM specification. We also show how the same approach can be used for deriving tests for FSMs with both time guards and timeouts.

Keywords: Conformance testing · Timed finite state machines

1 Introduction

A multitude of approaches are given for test derivation from formal specifications modeled as Finite State Machines (FSMs). The W method [1] paved the way for many derivatives to work on the test derivation considering various classes of FSM specifications and Implementations Under Test (IUT). For related summary and experiments the reader may refer to [2, 3]. Extensions to the W-based methods are also considered in the context of systems with timed constraints [4, 5]. Merayo et al. [6] establish a number of conformance relations for possibly non-deterministic FSM with input and output timeouts; however, test derivation is not considered in [6]. El-Fakih et al. [7] consider test derivation and assessment for timed FSMs with timed guards and single clock that is reset at every transition. Zhigulin et al. [8] presented a method for deriving complete test suites for FSMs with timeouts considering a traditional fault domain assuming that the number of states of an implementation TFSM does not exceed that of the reduced specification TFSM as well as the maximal finite timeout of the IUT does not exceed this of the specification. Recently, Bersolin et al. [9] investigated many timed FSM models with a single clock.

In this paper, we consider complete test derivation against FSMs with timeouts, hereafter denoted as TFSMs. In contrast to untimed FSMs, we show that two minimal initialized TFSMs can be equivalent but not isomorphic; moreover, we show that these

© IFIP International Federation for Information Processing 2018
Published by Springer Nature Switzerland AG 2018. All Rights Reserved
I. Medina-Bulo et al. (Eds.): ICTSS 2018, LNCS 11146, pp. 149–154, 2018.
https://doi.org/10.1007/978-3-319-99927-2_13

TFSMs can have different number of states. According to [9], the behavior of a TFSM can be completely described by its corresponding (untimed) FSM abstraction and the reduced initially connected forms of corresponding FSM abstractions of two initialized equivalent TFSMs are isomorphic. This hints that the fault model and complete test derivation can be developed based on the reduced form of the FSM abstraction of a given TFSM specification. We consider complete test derivation with respect to an appropriate fault domain that contains every TFSM over the same input alphabet as the specification such that the reduced form of the FSM abstraction of an IUT has at most $m > 1$ states, and thus, the proposed approach is easily extended to FSMs with timeouts and timed guards.

2 Preliminaries

An initialized FSM is a 5-tuple $S = (S, I, O, h_S, s_0)$ where I and O are input and output alphabets, S is a finite non-empty set of states with the designated initial state s_0, and $h_S \subseteq (S \times I \times O \times S)$ is the transition relation. We consider complete and deterministic FSMs, i.e., for each pair $(s, i) \in S \times I$ there exists exactly one transition $(s, i, o, s') \in h_S$. The equivalence and distinguishability relations between different states of FSMs are defined in a usual way [3]. It is known that given a complete deterministic initialized initially connected FSM, any two reduced initially connected forms of this FSM are isomorphic.

An *FSM with timeouts*, a TFSM for short, is an FSM annotated with a *clock* that is reset to zero at the execution of any transition. In addition, such a TFSM has input timeout transitions. When an input timeout expires at a state, the TFSM can sponta-neously move to the destination state of the timeout transition while resetting the time to zero. An initialized TFSM is a 6-tuple $S = (I, S, O, h_S, \Delta_S, s_1)$ where I and O are input and output alphabets, S is the finite non-empty set of states, $h_S \subseteq S \times I \times O \times S$ is the *transition relation* and Δ_S: $\Delta_S : S \rightarrow S \times (N \cup \{\infty\})$ is the timeout function, where N is the set of positive integers: for each state, this function specifies the maximum time for waiting for an input. Given state s of TFSM S such that $\Delta_S(s) = (s', T)$, if no input is applied before the timeout T expires, S moves to state s' and the clock is set to zero. If $s = s'$ then the clock is set to zero when timeout is expired. The transition $(s, i, o, s') \in S \times I \times O \times S$ means that S being at state s accepts an input i applied at time $t < T$ measured from the moment when the clock was reset at state s of S; the clock then is set to zero and S produces o. Hereafter, the timeout at state s can be written as T_s or T when s is known from the context, for short.

TFSM S is a *deterministic complete* TFSM if for each pair $(s, i) \in S \times I$, there is exactly one transition $(s, i, o', s') \in h_S$. In this paper, we consider only deterministic complete TFSMs. TFSM is (initially) connected if each state is reachable from the initial state. Given a TFSM S, a *timed input* is a pair (i, t) where $i \in I$ and t is a real; a timed input (i, t) means that input i is applied to the TFSM at time instance t where t is a local time. A sequence of timed inputs $\alpha = (i_1, t_1) \ldots (i_n, t_n)$ is a *timed input sequence*. A sequence $\alpha/\gamma = (i_1, t_1)/o_1 \ldots (i_n, t_n)/o_n$ of consecutive pairs of timed inputs and outputs starting at the state s is a *timed trace* of TFSM S at state s. Given complete deterministic TFSMs S and P, states s of S and p of P are *equivalent* if output responses at these states coincide for each timed input sequence; otherwise, s and p are *distinguishable*. Two initialized TFSMs S and P are *equivalent* if their initial states are equivalent. If any two different states of TFSM S are distinguishable then S is (*state*) *reduced* or *minimal*.

Consider two complete deterministic TFSMs in Fig. 1 which are equivalent. Each state in S_1 (a) and S_2 (b) is reachable from the initial state and both machines are reduced. However, these two equivalent machines are not isomorphic; moreover, they have different number of states.

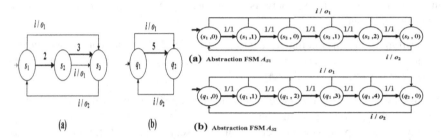

Fig. 1. Two equivalent yet not isomorphic TFSMs S_1 (a) and S_2 (b) and their FSM abstractions.

In order to calculate an output for a timed input (i, t) for each state s of TFSM S we consider the function $time(s, t) = s'$ that determines state s' that will be reached by S through timeouts if no input was applied during t time units. The output response β of S to a sequence $\alpha = (i_1, t_1)(i_2, t_2)\ldots(i_n, t_n)$ at state s is iteratively determined starting from state s.

Determining if two states of a TFSM S are equivalent or distinguishable can be done using the (untimed) FSM-abstraction A_S of S defined in [9].

FSM Abstraction: Given a complete deterministic TFSM $S = (S, I, O, h_S, \Delta_S, s_0)$, we derive the FSM abstraction of S as the FSM $A_S = (S_A, I_A, O_A, \lambda_{AS}, (s_0, 0))$, where $I_A = I \cup \{1\}, O_A = O \cup \{1\}$. The input (output) 1 is a special input (output) of the FSM abstraction denoting the time duration. For each state s, the set S_A has a state $(s, 0)$. Moreover, for each state s where the timeout T_s is finite, the set S_A has the states $\{(s, 1), .., (s, T_s-1)\}$. Given state $(s, t_j) \in S_A$ of A_S and input i, a transition $((s, t_j), i, o, (s', 0))$ is a transition of the abstraction A_S iff there exists a transition $(s, i, o, s') \in h_S$. Transitions under the input 1 correspond to timeout transition between states. Given state s such that $\Delta_S(s) = (s', T_s)$ where $1 < T_s < \infty$, there are transitions $((s, 0), 1, 1, (s, 1)), \ldots, ((s, T_s - 2), 1, 1, (s, T_s - 1)), ((s, T_s - 1))$, in λ_{AS}. If $\Delta_S(s) = (s', T_s)$ then there is a transition $((s, T_s - 1), 1, 1, (s', 0))$ while there is a transition $((s, 0), 1, 1, (s, 0)) \in \lambda_{AS}$ iff $T_s = \infty$. In [9], it is shown that the FSM abstraction of a complete and deterministic TFSM S is also complete and deterministic. As an example, consider the FSMs S_1 and S_2 in Fig. 1(a) and (b), their corresponding isomorphic FSM abstractions A_{S1} and A_{S2} are also shown in Fig. 1.

By definition, given an FSM with timeouts with n states and k inputs, the corresponding FSM abstraction has $(k+1)$ inputs and the number of states of the FSM abstraction equals $\sum_{s \in S'} (T_s + |S \backslash S'|)$ where S' is the subset of all FSM states for which the timeout T_s is finite.

A timed input sequence α of TFSM S can be transformed into a corresponding input sequence α_{FSM} of the FSM abstraction A_S. In this case, each timed input (i, t) is replaced by sequence $1.1 \ldots 1. i$ of inputs of the FSM abstraction where the number of inputs 1 equals t. At the same time the response of the FSM abstraction to sequence $1.1 \ldots 1. i$ is the sequence $1.1 \ldots 1. o$ where the number of outputs 1 is the same as for the timed input (i, t) and o is the response of the TFSM to timed input (i, t). Thus, the output sequence of the FSM abstraction γ_{FSM} is exactly the output sequence γ after removing all outputs 1. As there is no ambiguity, we further do not distinguish sequences γ_{FSM} and γ.

Proposition 1. Given a complete deterministic TFSM S and its corresponding FSM abstraction A_S, a timed trace α/γ exists for TFSM S if and only if there exists a trace α_{FSM}/γ for the FSM abstraction A_S.

Proposition 2 [9]. Two complete deterministic TFSMs are equivalent if and only if their FSM abstractions are equivalent.

The following proposition describes an input sequence that distinguishes two non-equivalent TFSMs.

Proposition 3. Given two non-equivalent complete deterministic TFSMs S and P over the same input and output alphabets, let A_S and A_P be their FSM abstractions. If an input sequence $\alpha_{FSM} = 1.1 \ldots 1. i_1 \ldots 1.1 \ldots 1. i_k$ distinguishes FSM abstractions A_S and A_P, then the timed input sequence $(i_1, t_1) \ldots (i_k, t_k)$ where t_j is the number of inputs before the input i_j, $1 \leq j \leq k$, distinguishes machines S and P.

An FSM abstraction of a TFSM can be reduced using a traditional way. Then the FSM abstraction of a TFSM implementation can be compared with the FSM abstraction of the specification TFSM and if they are not equivalent then corresponding TFSMs can be distinguished by some input sequence α_{FSM}. Moreover, a corresponding timed input sequence α will distinguish the TFSM implementation from the specification TFSM (Proposition 3). Correspondingly, a complete test suite can be derived based on the minimal form of the FSM abstraction of the specification TFSM. Such a test suite is derived for timed sequences over local time and later we discuss how the test cases can be written over global time. We also note that when distinguishing two initialized deterministic complete FSMs A_S and A_P, a distinguishing input can be only $i \in I$, as input 1 is defined at each state with the output 1. The sequence $\alpha_{FSM}. i$ distinguishes FSMs A_S and A_P and based on it a corresponding distinguishing sequence for TFSMs S and P can be constructed (Proposition 3).

When applying test cases to an IUT, we reasonably assume that each transition is performed with some small output delay θ such that the sum of all delays during a test case application is less than 1 and since timeouts are integers and these delays are very small they do not effect a proposed fault model.

3   Fault Models and Test Derivation

Given a specification TFSM S, we consider the fault model $<S, \cong, FD_m>$, where FD_m contains every TFSM P over the same input alphabet as S such that the reduced form of the FSM abstraction of P has at most $m > 1$ states. We note that it can well happen that some timed FSMs with less states than the specification TFSM are not included into the fault domain and vice versa a number of timed FSMs with more states than the specification TFSM are included into the fault domain.

Algorithm 1: Test Derivation Algorithm
Input : The deterministic complete specification FSM S with timeouts
Output: A complete test suite w.r.t. the fault model $<S, \cong, FD_m>$
Step 1. Derive the reduced form of the FSM abstraction A_S of S
Step 2. Derive using the W-method (or any of its derivatives) a complete test suite TS^{A_S} for the fault model $<A_S, \cong, \Omega_m>$ where Ω_m contains every minimal FSM with up to m states.
Step 3. Transform test cases of the test suite TS^{A_S} into corresponding timed sequences over the TFSM S (according to Proposition 1) and obtain TS^S. Transform the sequences of TS^S into timed input sequences over global time (by adding a negligible output delay θ) and obtain the test suite TS.

Theorem 1. The test suite TS obtained by Algorithm 1 is complete with respect to the fault model $<S, \cong, FD_m>$.

4   Deriving Tests for FSMs with Timed Guards and Timeouts

In [9], FSMs with timed guards and timeouts are considered. Input timed guards describe the behavior at a given state for inputs, which arrive at different time instances. Formally, an initialized TFSM is a 6-tuple $S = (I, S, O, h_S, \Delta_S, s_0)$ where I and O are input and output alphabets, S is the finite non-empty set of states, $h_S \subseteq S \times I \times O \times S \times \Pi$ is the *transition relation* and Δ_S is the timeout function. The set Π is a set of *input timed guards*. An input timed guard $g \in \Pi$ describes the time domain when a transition can be executed and is given in the form of interval $\lceil min, max \rceil$ from $[0; T)$, where $\lceil \in \{(, [\},\rceil \in \},),]\}$ and T is the value of the (input) timeout at the current state. The transition $(s, i, o, s', g) \in S \times I \times O \times S \times \Pi$ means that TFSM S being at state s accepts an input i applied at time $t \in g$ measured from the moment when S entered state s; the clock then is set to zero and S produces output o. TFSM S is a *deterministic complete* TFSM if for each two transitions $(s, i, o_1, s_1, g_1), (s, i, o_2, s_2, g_2) \in h_s$ it holds that $g_1 \cap g_2 = \emptyset$ and the union of all input timed guards at state s under input i equals $[0; T)$ when $\Delta_S(s) = (s', T)$. Given a complete deterministic TFSM S, the largest finite boundary B_S of input timed guards and timeouts, we derive the FSM abstraction of S as the FSM $A_S(B) = (S_A, I \cup \{1\}, O \cup \{1\}, \lambda_{AS}, (s_0, 0)), B \geq B_S$, where $S_A = \{(s, 0), (s, (0, 1)), \ldots, (s, (B-1, B)), (s, B), (s, (B, \infty)) : s \in S\}$. In [9], it is shown that such an FSM abstraction of a complete and deterministic TFSM S is also complete and deterministic and a timed input sequence α of TFSM S can be transformed into a corresponding input sequence α_{FSM} of the FSM abstraction $A_S(B)$ similar to an FSM with timeouts. We then consider the fault model $<S, \cong, FD_m(B)>$, where $FD_m(B)$ contains every TFSM P over the same input alphabet as S such that the reduced form of the FSM abstraction of P has at most $m > 1$ states and the largest finite boundary of input timed guards and timeouts is $B \geq B_S$. In our case, the test derivation technique completely coincides with Algorithm 1 where the FSM abstraction A_S is considered and the test suite TS obtained by Algorithm 1 is complete w.r.t. the fault model $<S, \cong, FD_m(B)>$.

5 Conclusion

A proper fault domain is considered for complete test derivation against timed FSMs. The fault domain takes into account the fact that a reduced TFSM specification and a reduced TFSM implementation with timeouts can be equivalent yet not isomorphic. A proper characterization of the fault domain is then considered using the unique reduced form of the FSM abstraction of the given timed FSM specification. The fault domain is extended to consider FSMs with timeouts and timed guards.

Acknowledgement. This work is partly supported by Russian Science Foundation (RSF), Project No. 16-49-03012.

References

1. Chow, T.S.: Testing software design modeled by finite-state machines. IEEE TSE **4**(3), 178–187 (1978)
2. Simao, A., Petrenko, A., Maldonado, J.C.: Comparing finite state machine test coverage criteria. IET Softw. **3**(2), 91–105 (2009)
3. Dorofeeva, R., El-Fakih, K., Maag, S., Cavalli, A.R., Yevtushenko, N.: FSM-based conformance testing methods: a survey annotated with experimental evaluation. Inf. Softw. Technol. **52**, 1286–1297 (2010)
4. Springintveld, J., Vaandrager, F., D'Argenio, P.: Testing timed automata. Theor. Comput. Sci. **254**(1–2), 225–257 (2001)
5. En-Nouaary, A., Dssouli, R., Khendek, F.: Timed Wp-method: testing real-time systems. IEEE TSE **28**(11), 1023–1038 (2002)
6. Merayo, M.G., Nunez, M., Rodriguez, I.: Formal testing from timed finite state machines. Comput. Netw. **52**(2), 432–460 (2008)
7. El-Fakih, K., Yevtushenko, N., Simao, A.: A practical approach for testing timed deterministic finite state machines with single clock. Sci. Comput. Program. **80**(1), 343–355 (2014)
8. Zhigulin, M., Yevtushenko, N., Maag, S., Cavalli, A.: FSM-based test derivation strategies for systems with time-outs. In: International Conference on Quality Software, pp. 141–150 (2011)
9. Bersolin, D., El-Fakih, K., Villa, T., Yevtushenko, N.: Timed finite state machines: equivalence checking and expressive. In: International Symposium on Games, Automata, Logic and Formal Verification, pp. 203–216 (2014)

From Ontologies to Input Models for Combinatorial Testing

Franz Wotawa$^{(\boxtimes)}$ (ID) and Yihao Li (ID)

Institute for Software Technology, Technische Universität Graz, Inffeldgasse 16b/2,
8010 Graz, Austria
{wotawa,yihao.li}@ist.tugraz.at

Abstract. Ordinary tools for computing combinatorial test suites rely on simple input models comprising variables together with their domains and constraints limiting possible combinations. Modeling for combinatorial testing requires to represent the input domain of the application in a way such that it fits to the combinatorial testing input model. Depending on the application's domain this mapping ranges from trivial to more complicated. In this paper, we focus on modeling for combinatorial testing in cases the application's domain can be represented in form of an ontology, i.e., concepts and their relationships. We formally introduce the notation of ontology we rely on in this paper, and show how such ontologies can be automatically mapped to a combinatorial testing input model. We discuss the algorithm and show its properties.

Keywords: Combinatorial testing · Ontologies · Combinatorial testing input models

1 Introduction

System development more and more rely on models describing the system's environment, potential interaction as well as its intended behavior. Such models often conceptualize the application domain and are often available in a formal form that can be used for various purposes. Ontologies, which are a formal conceptualization of entities, their interfaces and behaviors, and relationships, describe the knowledge behind such an application domain are more often used for various purposes. For example, in the context of autonomous driving such ontologies have been used for decision making [17], describing traffic situations [4], and navigation [21].

In the context of testing and in particular test suite generation, ontologies provide information about certain entities and their relationships from which we might extract test cases. Let us have a look at simplified text ontology comprising the concepts of *Text*, *Sentence*, *Delimiter* and *Word*. An instance of a *Text*

© IFIP International Federation for Information Processing 2018
Published by Springer Nature Switzerland AG 2018. All Rights Reserved
I. Medina-Bulo et al. (Eds.): ICTSS 2018, LNCS 11146, pp. 155–170, 2018.
https://doi.org/10.1007/978-3-319-99927-2_14

is a sequence of sentences, i.e., instances of *Sentence* followed by a instance of *Delimiter*. A particular sentence comprises words, which are instances of the concept *Word*. We depict the relationships between these concepts in Fig. 1. A test case would be a certain instance of *Text* comprising its parts specified in the ontology. If we want to use such tests for verifying a program like a text processor, we would be interested in obtaining certain combinations of words and delimiters that form a sentence.

One possible way of coming up with such combinations would be the use of combinatorial testing [8] that has been successfully applied for verifying different software applications. Combinatorial testing in its simplest form takes a set of variables representing inputs and parameters together with their domains as input model and generates test cases including certain combinations of variable values. In particular, in combinatorial testing we search for all tests that cover all combinations for any subset of size k of the variables, where k is called the strength of the generated test suite.

Unfortunately, there has been no algorithm reported that takes an ontology as input and which returns a combinatorial test input model (or a combinatorial test suite of strength k) as output. In this paper, we focus on this open challenge and present an algorithm that allows using ontologies as input for the generation of combinatorial test suites. For this purpose, we formalize ontologies and discuss an algorithm that maps those ontologies to combinatorial input models. In addition, we show the underlying functionality of the algorithm using the text ontology as a case study.

The intention behind this work is to use it for test suite generation of ontologies for autonomous driving, which are currently under development. There the focus is on tests that reveal situations an autonomous vehicle has to deal with under which it might fail. A first ontology comprises more than 200 concepts from which we want to generate test suites used to verify the correct functionality of an autonomous vehicle even in critical situations comprising different combinations of static elements like roads or dynamic elements like other cars of pedestrians.

We structure this paper as follows: First, we discuss related research including mappings of UML diagrams to combinatorial test suites. Afterwards, we formally introduce the concept of ontologies and in order to be self-contained discuss the foundations of combinatorial testing. We further introduce the algorithm for converting ontologies into combinatorial test suites followed by a section where we apply this algorithm on our text ontology. Finally, we conclude the paper.

2   Related Research

Software testing is tedious and expensive yet critical to quality assurance. Designing suitable test cases requires that programmers possess a certain amount of domain knowledge. Therefore, ontology can aid in software testing as they encode domain knowledge in a machine processable format. It provides people and software systems a common shared understanding of knowledge which is easy to

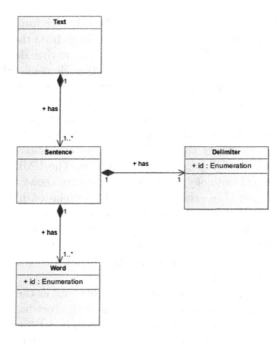

Fig. 1. A simplified textual input ontology depicted using UML comprising sentences, which themselves have words and one delimiters.

organize, maintain and update [13]. Although the study of ontology has become active since the last decade, few works have been done regarding the ontology-based software testing, especially in the field of combinatorial testing (CT). Li et al. [10] developed an ontology to generate user-centric GUI test cases. First, GUI and non-GUI components are captured by reverse engineering techniques. Relations among GUI components are then analyzed to create a GUI ontology and rules for test case generation.

Nguyen et al. [15] proposed an ontology-based test generation framework for multi-agent systems. An ontology that defines content semantics of agent interactions is developed to generate test inputs, guide the input space exploration, and verify messages exchanged between agents. Li and Ma [11] discussed how to generate the parameter setting interface for test atom in spacecraft automatic test based on an ontology knowledge base. The knowledge base represents the information extracted from the test atom and user interface and the rules predefined to the mapping relationship between test atom attributes and interface elements.

Satish et al. [18] proposed a rule-based approach to derive CT parameters and values from use case specification (UCS) and UML use case diagrams (UCD). The UCS specifies the requirements in a predefined structure such as the precondition, normal-flow, alternative-flow, and postconditions. The UCD depicts the software under test (SUT) from functionality point of view, and the function is encompassed within a use case in a UCD. The rules are formulated to derive the combinatorial test design model (CTDM) elements from the UCS and UCD parsers. A set combined set of parameters and values are then derived from these rules to provide suggestions to the testers for further elements selection. Before this work, Satish's team had applied similar strategy to derive CT parameters and values from UML activity diagrams [20] and sequence diagrams [19].

Use case diagrams focus on the system's functional usage and their interrelationships, dependencies, etc. They are useful for understanding how a feature is used. However, they isolate the details of the system. These details provides information for deriving CT parameters and values. The UML class diagrams, which we use to depict ontology in this paper, directly shows the reflections of the real world as objects (i.e., classes) and their interrelationships. Different use cases identified in use case diagram can turn into classes. In addition, the ontology depicted by UML class diagrams can be represented in hierarchical style which is perfect for generating the target CT model. Therefore, using ontology depicted by class diagrams is more straight forward to structure the entire system in a CT-oriented way.

Moser et al. [12] argued that measurable benefits such as the feasibility of the ontology-based test case generation approach and the cost-benefit potential of ontology-based test case generation approaches (e.g., cost-benefit for a constant number of parameters and for expanding the number of parameters) are essential to decide whether an ontology-based approach and the change costs is acceptable or not. Studies in [1, 14, 22, 23, 25] designed ontologies that focus on the software testing process and the corresponding activities and artifacts. The aim is to manage software testing knowledge so that different knowledge items in software testing are collected, shared, reused and organized.

3   Basic Definitions

In this section, we briefly outline the basic foundations of ontologies used for providing input models, and combinatorial testing used for generating test cases from the given model. In contrast, to ordinary combinatorial input models, the ontology-based models provide more details about relationships between different conceptual entities.

3.1   Ontology

Feilmayr and Wöß [3] stated that *"an ontology is a formal, explicit specification of a shared conceptualization that is characterized by high semantic expressiveness required for increased complexity "*. From this informal definition we are able to deduce that ontologies need to describe concepts in a formal way as well as knowledge about these concepts including their relationships. In the following, we introduce a very much simplified definition of ontologies based on concepts restricting relations to composition and inheritance. We use the former relations to formalize knowledge that one concept comprises some other concepts and the latter for stating that one concept is more general than another concept. A concept itself describes an entity either from the real world, e.g., a car, or from nonmaterial descriptions, e.g., a sentence or a (physical) force.

Concepts form the basic building blocks of ontologies. In the context of this paper, concepts shall describe the basic entities of the input model. For example, in our running example depicted in Fig. 1 we use the concepts of Text, Sentence, Word, and Delimiter to construct an ontology for textual input. Concepts are also allowed to have attributes, i.e., properties that characterize concepts. For example, a person has a name, a birth day, and other specific properties that distinguishes one person from another. An attribute itself has a certain type like a string or a date. Note that for providing input models for test case generation, we only rely on enumeration types as basic type where someone has to specify the elements of the enumeration that corresponds to an attribute.

Definition 1 (Ontology). *An* ontology *is a tuple* $(C, A, D, \omega, R, \tau, \psi)$ *where* C *is a finite set of concepts,* A *is a finite set of attributes,* D *is a finite set of domain elements,* $\omega : C \mapsto 2^{A \times 2^{D}}$ *is a function mapping concepts to a set of tuples specifying the attribute and its domain elements, and* R *is a finite set of tuples from* $C \times C$ *stating that two concepts are related. The function* $\tau : R \times R \mapsto \{\mathtt{c}, \mathtt{i}\}$ *assigns a type to each relation using* $\mathtt{i}$ *for inheritance and* $\mathtt{c}$ *for composition. Furthermore,* $\psi : R \times R \mapsto \mathbb{N}_0 \times \mathbb{N}_0$ *is a function mapping relationships solely of type* $\mathtt{c}$ *to its minimum and maximum arity. The arity is for specifying how many concepts a particular concept may comprise and ranges from 0 to any arbitrary natural number.*

Note that this definition of ontologies assures that there is at the maximum one relation between two concepts. Hence, it is not possible to state that one concept is a sub-concept of another concept and that there is a compositional relationship between them as well. For simplicity, we further introduce the function $dom : C \times A \mapsto 2^{D}$ that we will use later in this paper. The function dom returns the domain for an attribute of a given concept.

Obviously ontologies can also be represented in a graphical form. In Fig. 2, we depict the graphical representation of concepts and their relations using UML2 syntax[1]. Note that in the graphical representation the arity of the concept $C1$ of the composition relation is always 1. The minimum and maximum arity of concept $C2$ is given as follows: In case of * the minimum arity is 0 and the maximum arity is any value. Otherwise, we have a 1..* indicating a minimum arity of 1.

Example 1. Using the graphical representation of the text ontology from Fig. 1, we can easily obtain a formal description of the ontology accordingly to Definition 1. The text ontology comprises four concepts, i.e., $C = \{$Text, Sentence, Word, Delimiter$\}$, and one attribute leading to: $A = \{$id$\}$. We further assume that we have three different words and only a period and a

---

[1] For the UML language specification have a look at https://www.omg.org/spec/ UML/2.5.1/ (last visited March 3rd, 2018).

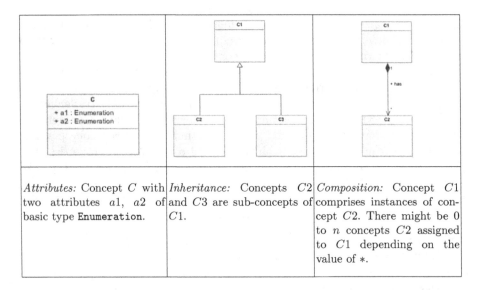

Attributes: Concept C with two attributes $a1$, $a2$ of basic type Enumeration.	Inheritance: Concepts $C2$ and $C3$ are sub-concepts of $C1$.	Composition: Concept $C1$ comprises instances of concept $C2$. There might be 0 to n concepts $C2$ assigned to $C1$ depending on the value of $*$.

Fig. 2. Basic concepts, their attributes, and relationships considered for coming up with an ontology for a particular application domain.

questionmark as delimiters. Hence, the domain comprises five elements, i.e.: $D = \{\text{'word1'}, \text{'word2'}, \text{'word3'}, \text{'.'}, \text{'?'}\}$.

Only delimiters and words have attributes. Hence, ω can be defined as follows: $\omega(\text{Text}) = \{\}$, $\omega(\text{Sentence}) = \{\}$, $\omega(\text{Delimiter}) = \{(\text{id}, \{\text{'?'}, \text{'.'}\})\}$, and $\omega(\text{Word}) = \{(\text{id}, \{\text{'word1'}, \text{'word2'}, \text{'word3'}\})\}$. Finally, we only need to specify the relationships between concepts and the function ψ. R can be easily obtained from Fig. 1: $R = \{(\text{Text}, \text{Sentence}), (\text{Sentence}, \text{Delimiter}), (\text{Sentence}, \text{Word})\}$. For these relations, we further specify their types: $\tau(\text{Text}, \text{Sentence}) = \text{c}$, $\tau(\text{Sentence}, \text{Delimiter}) = \text{c}$, and $\tau(\text{Sentence}, \text{Word}) = \text{c}$. For ψ we have to take the numbers from the figure, where we assume $*$ to be 2 leading to: $\psi(\text{Text}, \text{Sentence}) = (1, 2)$, $\psi(\text{Sentence}, \text{Delimiter}) = (1, 1)$, and $\psi(\text{Sentence}, \text{Word}) = (1, 2)$. It is worth noting that we can assume any arbitrary value of the arity for each relationship in case of $*$. However, it is not recommended to choose too high values, because - as we will see later - this increases the number of test cases to be generated.

When having a look at the graph representation of ontologies, we can obviously add structural means for characterizing ontologies. Concepts correspond to graph vertices, and relations to the edges of a graph. Considering the definition of ontologies, the relations are tuples comprising two concepts and a type and can be interpreted as directed edges. Hence, we can easily find a mapping from constraints to directed graphs and define the corresponding means for root vertices, leaf vertices, and cycles.

Definition 2 (Root concept; leaf concept). *Given an ontology* $(C, A, D, \omega, R, \psi)$. *A concept* $c \in C$ *is a* root concept *if and only if there exists no relation*

$(c', c, x) \in R$ for $c' \in C$, $x \in \{i, c\}$. A concept $c \in C$ is a leaf concept *if and only if there is no relation* $(c, c', x) \in R$ for $c' \in C$, $x \in \{i, c\}$.

Accordingly to this definition, there is one root vertex `Text` and two leaf vertices `Delimiter` and `Word` in the text ontology.

Definition 3 (Cyclic ontology). *An ontology* $(C, A, D, \omega, R, \psi)$ *is called a cyclic ontology if and only if (i) there is a relation* $(c, c, x) \in R$ *for a concept* $c \in C$ *and* $x \in \{i, c\}$*, or (ii) there are relations* $(c_0, c_1, x_0), \ldots, (c_i, c_0, x_i)$ *in* R *for* $i > 0$*, concepts* $c_0, \ldots, c_i in C$ *and* $x_0, \ldots, x_i \in \{i, c\}$*. In this case the sequence of relations is called a cycle. If an ontology is not cyclic, it is called acyclic ontology.*

Obviously the ontology for texts is an acyclic ontology. Note that for generating an input model for combinatorial testing, we rely on acyclic ontologies comprising exactly one root concept. We call such an ontology a well-formed ontology.

Definition 4 (Well-formed ontology). *An ontology* $(C, A, D, \omega, R, \psi)$ *is a well-formed ontology if and only if (i) it comprises exactly one root concept, (ii) it is acyclic, and (iii) where all its leaf concepts have attributes.*

It is worth noting that rule (iii) in the definition of well-formed ontologies assures that we are able to construct test cases from ontologies.

In order to model the input for a particular application, we have to first come up with concepts that are used for describing that input. For each of these concepts, we further on define the attributes and finally the relations capturing the relationship between two concepts. For inheritance, we have to show that one concept is a generalization of the other or vice versa a specialization. For example, in the case of the automotive domain, we have the concepts of `vehicle`, `car`, and `truck`, where both `truck` and `car` are a specialization of the more general concept of `vehicle`. In case of composition, we have to ask whether one concept can be part of the description of another concept. In the text ontology, we know that a sentence has parts, i.e., its words, and also delimiters at the end. Hence, the concepts of `word` and `delimiter` have to be in compositional relation with `sentence`. As already mentioned, we also want to have exactly one root concept in the resulting ontology and no cycles.

3.2   Combinatorial Testing

Combinatorial testing (CT) is a method that aims to improve the effectiveness of software testing while lowering its cost at the same time. The essence of CT is that not all parameters contribute to failures but by interactions between relatively few parameters [6].

CT is rooted in the mathematical concept of combinatorics, which is used for the construction of combinatorial objects called Covering Arrays (CA). A fixed-value covering array denoted by $CA(N, v^k, t)$ or $CA(N, k, v, t)$ is an $N \times k$

matrix of elements from a set of v symbols $\{0, \ldots, (v-1)\}$ such that every set of t columns contains each possible t-tuple of elements at least once where t is the strength of the covering array. A mixed-value covering array is an extension of fixed value CA where $k = k_1 + \ldots + k_n$ meaning that for each column k_1 ($i = 1$ to n) it has v_1 ($i = 1$ to n)different elements, respectively [7].

Hence, the input model required for combinatorial testing has to have variables and their domains. In addition, there might be constraints that restrict the number of valid value combinations. Formally, we are able to define combinatorial testing input models as follows:

Definition 5 (Combinatorial testing input model). *A combinatorial testing input model is a tuple $(V, DOM, CONS)$ where V is a set of variables, DOM is a function mapping variables from V to a set of values, i.e., the variables' domains, and $CONS$ is a set of constraints over variables that have to be fulfilled for each test case.*

Table 1. A 2-way test suite for platform configuration

Test	OS	Browser	Protocol	CPU	DBMS
1	XP	IE	IPv4	Intel	MySQL
2	XP	Firefox	IPv6	AMD	Sybase
3	XP	IE	IPv6	Intel	Oracle
4	OS X	Firefox	IPv4	AMD	MySQL
5	OS X	IE	IPv4	Intel	Sybase
6	OS X	Firefox	IPv4	Intel	Oracle
7	RHEL	IE	IPv6	AMD	MySQL
8	RHEL	Firefox	IPv4	Intel	Sybase
9	RHEL	Firefox	IPv4	AMD	Oracle
10	OS X	Firefox	IPv6	AMD	Oracle

Testing with a test suite of t-way covering array is called t-way testing [7]. It requires that every combination of any t parameter values in the software must be tested at least once. When $t = 1$, it is called the Each Choice (EC) combination strategy. It becomes Pairwise Testing (PW) when $t = 2$. When $t = n$, it is called the All Combination (AC) strategy meaning that every combination of all n parameter values must be tested at least once. The input model for CT includes the number of parameters, the value range for each parameter, and any constraints among these parameters. For example [9], assume that there is an application which needs to be run on different platforms consisting of five components (or parameters): OS (Windows XP, Apple OS X, Red Hat Enterprise Linux), browser (Internet Explorer, Firefox), protocol (IPv4, IPv6), CPU (Intel, AMD), and database (MySQL, Sybase, Oracle). There is a total of 72 (i.e.,

$3 \times 2 \times 2 \times 2 \times 3$) possible platforms (or combinations). However, as shown in Table 1, it only requires 10 tests for conducting a 2-way or pairwise testing to cover all possible pairs of platform components.

According to Nie and Leung [16], CT has the following characteristics: (1) CT generates test cases by selecting values for parameters and by combining these values to form a CA. These test cases cover all t-way combinations of parameter values, where t is the strength specifying the number of parameters in combination; (2) CT uses a CA as the test suite. The CA aims to test as many parameter value combinations as possible to detect failures triggered by these interactions; (3) Not every parameter contributes to a fault, and some faults can only be triggered by a small number of parameters; (4) CT does not require knowledge about the implementation of SUT; and (5) Test generation for CT can be automated.

In addition, to conduct a CT-based test generation strategy, four aspects need to be considered [16]: (1) specifying the strength for CT as the corresponding CAs have different failure detection abilities with different cost. Two of the most widely used covering array generators are ACTS [26] and PICT [5]; (2) assign some specific test cases in advance; (3) considering constraints can increase the difficulty in applying CT; and (4) method to be used to generate test cases. In general, the methods can be categorized into four groups: greedy algorithm (e.g., AETG [2] and IPO [24]), heuristic search algorithm, mathematical method, and random method.

4   Ontology Conversion

Before introducing the ontology conversion formally, we first illustrate the underlying ideas using our text ontology.

Example 2. Let us explain our approach using the text ontology formally introduced in Example 1. First, have a look at the concept Sentence composed from Word and Delimiter. A test case capturing one particular Sentence can be considered as an instance or individual of Sentence. Each instance of Sentence, therefore, comprises 1 to n instances of Word, i.e., $w_1, \ldots, w_n$, and one instance of Delimiter, i.e., d. Note that each instance of the leaf concepts Word and Delimiter comprises a particular value of their attributes, which can be obtained from their domains.

An instance of a concept that is not a leaf concept now comprise the instances of the concepts staying in relation. Hence, one instance of Sentence is $w_1 \ldots w_n$ d. This is exactly what we need for combinatorial testing. The w_i's and d represent the variables of the input model and their domains come from leaf concepts, i.e., defined using the attributes and their domains that can be accessed using the *dom* function. For this example, instances of Word can be represented as a variable Word_id with a domain $dom(\text{Word}, \text{id}) = \{\text{'word1', 'word2', 'word3'}\}$. Using the same idea for the delimiter concept, we finally obtain a combinatorial input model for Sentence comprising the variables Word_id_1, ..., Word_id_n, Delimiter_id, which represent the words $w_1, \ldots, w_n$

and the delimiter d, and their corresponding domains given when using the dom function.

In the following, we formally introduce the conversion of ontologies into an input model for combinatorial testing. Given an ontology $(C, A, D, \omega, R, \tau, \psi)$, we describe the conversion for the three cases, i.e., concepts with attributes, inheritance relations, and compositional relations. For each case, we compute the combinatorial testing input model M^{CT} comprising its variables, their domains, and constraints denoted by V^{CT}, DOM^{CT}, and $CONS^{CT}$ respectively, i.e., $M^{CT} = (V^{CT}, DOM^{CT}, CONS^{CT})$. Whenever needed we use a combinatorial testing algorithm $CT(M, t)$ where M is a combinatorial testing input model and t the combinatorial strength, returning a test suite.

Concepts with attributes. Let us assume a concept $c \in C$ with attributes $a_1, \ldots, a_n \in A$, $n \geq 1$. This is the simplest case where we only have to construct input variables for combinatorial testing for each attribute of the concept. The domain of each combinatorial testing input variable is equivalent to the domain of its corresponding attribute, and there are no further constraints to add. I.e.: $V^{CT} = \{c\_a_1, \ldots, c\_a_n\}$, $\forall_{i=1}^n : DOM^{CT}(c\_a_i) = dom(c, a_i)$, and $CONS^{CT} = \{\}$.

Concepts and inheritance. Let us assume a concept $c \in C$ having $n \geq 1$ subconcepts $c_1, \ldots, c_n \in C$ such that $\forall_{i=1}^n : (c, c_i) \in R$. In this case, for c we have only one variable on side of combinatorial testing, and all its values come from the different values obtained when using the models from its sub-concepts and generating their combinatorial test suites. Let us assume M_i^{CT} be the combinatorial testing model of sub-concept c_i, then M^{CT} of c is given as follows: $V^{CT} = \{c\}$, $DOM^{CT}(c) = \bigcup_{i=1}^n CT(M_i^{CT}, t)$, and $CONS^{CT} = \{\}$, where CT is an algorithm computing a combinatorial test suite of strength t.

Concepts and composition. Assume the case of two concepts c_1 and c_2 from C and a relation $(c_1, c_2) \in R$ of type $\tau(c_1, c_2) = c$ in our ontology. This is the case we already discussed at the beginning of this section in Example 2. Depending on the minimum arity of the relation we have to consider two cases. If the minimum arity is zero, then there need not to be any instance of c_2 attached to c_1. In case the minimum arity is one, we have at least one individual of c_2. We distinguish these two cases using a constraint. Before, we discuss how to handle the different instances of c_2, i.e., $c_2^1, \ldots, c_2^m$. For a fixed m, we are able to construct a combinatorial testing input model. We only need to say that each instance is itself a variable and its domain is given from all values computed when using the combinatorial testing model of c_2, i.e., $M^{CT}(c_2)$. $V^{CT} = \{c_2^1, \ldots, c_2^m\}$ and $\forall_{i=1}^m : DOM^C T(c_2^i) = CT(M^{CT}(c_2), t) \cup \{\epsilon\}$ where CT is an algorithm computing a combinatorial test suite of strength t.

Note that ϵ represents the empty value allowing a certain instance of c_2 not to be relevant. We decided to use this, in order to finally come up with compositions of arbitrary length less than or equal to m. Because there might be the case that all instances of c_2 have a value of ϵ, we have to consider two cases depending on the minimum arity of the relation. In case there need to be no instance of c_2, i.e., when the minimum arity is zero, there is no need for a constraint, i.e., $CONS^{CT} = \{\}$. Otherwise, $CONS^{CT} = \{\exists_i : 1 < i \leq m \wedge c_2^i \neq \epsilon\}$ stating that at least one individual of c_2 has to have a non empty value when computing the combinatorial test suite.

For general well-formed ontologies there might be cases where we have to combine the different rules described for computing a combinatorial test suite. For example, there might be a concept that has itself attributes and relations with other concepts. In such cases, we have to combine the variable, domains and constraints in order to compute the summary model of this concept for generating combinatorial test suites.

Algorithm 1 TC_GEN (O,t)

Require: *A well-formed ontology O and a combinatorial strength t.*
Ensure: *A combinatorial test suite for the root concept of the ontology O.*
 1: Let r be the root concept of ontology O.
 2: Call **CT_ONT**(r, O, t) and store the result in $(V^{CT}, DOM^{CT}, CONS^{CT})$.
 3: **return** $CT((V^{CT}, DOM^{CT}, CONS^{CT}), t)$

Algorithm 1 **TC_GEN** computes combinatorial test suites for the root concept of given ontology, and makes use of Algorithm 2 **CT_ONT** that recursively computes the combinatorial input models for the different concepts starting with the root node down to the leafs. In this algorithm the different cases are directly implemented. In the algorithm description we assume that the global variable m stores the number of instances that should be generated for compositional relations. The algorithm can be easily adapted in order to cope with a value of m to adapted for each concept. We only need to introduce a function that maps a concept to its maximum value of instances to be considered.

Obviously, **CT_ONT** terminates because we only consider finite and well-formed ontologies where there are no cycles and a finite number of concepts and relations. The algorithm traverses the whole graph and has therefore a computational complexity in the size of the graph when ignoring the computational complexity of combinatorial test suites during the traversal. The algorithm can be optimized to avoid multiple computations of input models, which may occur. The drawback of **CT_ONT** is that the number of computed test cases can be high. For example, let us consider the simplest case assuming a combinatorial strength of 2 and only 2 instances to be generated for every relation. If we consider the first relation with one leaf concept having one attribute with n elements in its domain, the number of generated tests is bound by n. If we use this result in a further step with 2 instances, we get n^2 combinations because we have to combine all elements in the domain of the instances, which are n elements. In the next levels we obtain $n^4, n^{16}, \ldots, n^{2^m}$ test cases where m is the depth of the concept hierarchy. Hence, the depth of the ontology has to be small in order to be still feasible.

Algorithm 2 CT_ONT (c, O, t)

Require: *A concept c of a well-formed ontology O, and a combinatorial strength k.*
Ensure: *A combinatorial input model for n.*
1: Let V^{CT} and $CONS^{CT}$ be empty sets.
2: **for all** attributes $a \in \omega(c)$ **do**
3:     Add c_a to V^{CT}.
4:     Let $DOM^{CT}(c\_a)$ be $dom(c, a)$.
5: **end for**
6: **if** c is not a leaf concept **then**
7:     Let tmp be the empty set.
8:     **for all** relations $(c, c') \in R$ with type $\tau(c, c') = $ i **do**
9:         Add $CT(\textbf{CT\_ONT}(c', O, t), t)$ to tmp
10:     **end for**
11:     **if** tmp is not empty **then**
12:         Add c to V^{CT}.
13:         Let $DOM^{CT}(c)$ be tmp.
14:     **end if**
15:     **for all** relations $(c, c') \in R$ with type $\tau(c, c') = $ c **do**
16:         Add variables c'_1 to c'_m to V^{CT}.
17:         Let d be $CT(\textbf{CT\_ONT}(c', O, t), t) \cup \{\epsilon\}$
18:         **for** $i = 1$ to m **do**
19:             Let $DOM^{CT}(c'\_i)$ be d.
20:         **end for**
21:         **if** $\psi(c, c') = (1, x)$ **then**
22:             Add $\bigvee_{i \in \{1, \ldots, m\}} c'\_i \neq \epsilon$ to $CONS^{CT}$.
23:         **end if**
24:     **end for**
25: **end if**
26: **return** $(V^{CT}, DOM^{CT}, CONS^{CT})$

---

5   Case Study

For the case study, we use the Text ontology mentioned in previous sections for demonstration. In the following, we provide a step-by-step instruction for elaborating the process of applying the proposed algorithm **TC_GEN** to convert a given ontology to a CT-based input model.

Using the text ontology O, we invoke the function **TC_GEN**(O, t) at the beginning, which internally calls the function **CT_ONT**$(Text, O, t)$, where $Text$ is the root concept of our ontology O is (Algorithm 1, Line 2). In this step $\omega(Text) = \{\}$ meaning that $Text$ currently does not have any attributes. Therefore, the corresponding $V^{CT}(Text)$ is empty and DOM^{CT} of $Text$ is also empty (see Algorithm 2, Lines 1 to 6).

Since $Text$ is not a leaf concept and there is one compositional relation between the concepts $Text$ and $Sentence$, $\tau(Text, Sentence) = $ c with $\psi(Text, Sentence) = (1, 2)$. Then for the relation $(Text, Sentence)$, we add two variables $s1$ and $s2$ to $V^{CT}(Text)$. For each of these variables, $DOM^{CT}(s\_i)$ is defined calling the combinatorial testing algorithm CT using the recursive call to **CT_ONT**, i.e., $CT(\textbf{CT\_ONT}(Sentence, O, t), t) \cup \{\epsilon\}$ (Algorithm 2, Lines 18 to 20). Because $\psi(Text, Sentence) = (1, 2)$, we add the constraint $s1 \neq \epsilon \vee s2 \neq \epsilon$ to $CONS^{CT}$ for concept $Text$ (Algorithm 2, Lines 21 to 23).

In order to determine the CT input model for $Text$, we first have to have the input model for concept $Sentence$. Obviously, $DOM^{CT}(s1) = DOM^{CT}(s2)$ we obtain calling $CT(\textbf{CT\_ONT}(Sentence, O, t), t) \cup \{\epsilon\}$. When invoking **CT_ONT** $(Sentence, O, t)$, we see that $Sentence$ is not a leaf concept because it has two compositional relations with $\tau(Sentence, Delimiter) = \text{c}$, and $\psi(Sentence, Delimiter) = (1, 1)$ and $\tau(Sentence, Word) = \text{c}$ and $\psi(Sentence, Word) = (1, 2)$, respectively. As a result, for $(Sentence, Delimiter)$ we add one variable d to $V^{CT}(Sentence)$ and let $DOM^{CT}(d) = CT(\textbf{CT\_ONT}(Delimiter, O, t), t) \cup \{\epsilon\}$. For $(Sentence, Word)$ we add two variables $w1$ and $w2$ to $V^{CT}(Sentence)$ and let $DOM^{CT}(wi) = CT(\textbf{CT\_ONT}(Word, O, k), k) \cup \{\epsilon\}$ for $i = 1, 2$. In addition, we also add the two constraints $d \neq \epsilon$ and $w1 \neq \epsilon \vee w2 \neq \epsilon$ to $CONS^{CT}$ for $Sentence$. For the recursive function call **CT_ONT**$(Delimiter, O, k)$, and because $Delimiter$ is a leaf concept we set $V^{CT}(Delimiter) = \{id\}$, $DOM^{CT}(id) = \{\text{`.'}, \text{`?'}\}$, and $CONS^{CT}(Delimiter) = \{\}$, Therefore, the domain $DOM^{CT}(d) = \{\text{`.'}, \text{`?'}, \epsilon\}$.

Regarding $DOM^{CT}(wi) = CT(\textbf{CT\_ONT}(Word, O, t), t) \cup \{\epsilon\}$, let us again only   focus on $DOM^{CT}(w1) = CT(\textbf{CT\_ONT}(Word, O, t), t) \cup \{\epsilon\}$ in this example, because the same applies for computing $DOM^{CT}(w2)$. For **CT_ONT**$(Word, O, t)$, since $Word$ is a leaf concept and $\omega(Word) = \{(id, \{\text{`word1'}, \text{`word2'}, \text{`word3'}\})\}$, we obtain $DOM^{CT}(w1) = \{\text{`word1'}, \text{`word2'}, \text{`word3'}, \epsilon\}$ which is the same for $DOM^{CT}(w2)$.

When taking this together, we are now able to come up with a CT input model M^{CT} for $Sentence$: $V^{CT}(Sentence) = \{w1, w2, d\}$, with $DOM^{CT}(w1) = DOM^{CT}(w2) = \{\text{`word1'}, \text{`word2'}, \text{`word3'}, \epsilon\}$, $DOM^{CT}(d) = \{\text{`.'}, \text{`?'}, \epsilon\}$, and $CONS^{CT}(Sentence) = \{w1 \neq \epsilon \vee w2 \neq \epsilon, d \neq \epsilon\}$.

Now we use ACTS 3.1 and IPOG to generate a 2-way (i.e., $t = 2$) CT-based test suite for the instances of $Sentence$, i.e., $s1$ and $s2$. The hardware environment used to carry all experiments is a Dell XPS Laptop with 2.6 GHz, Intel Core i7, 16 GB memory using Windows 10. In Table 2 we see the obtained 15 test cases, which is far less compared to a total of 48 $(= 4 \times 4 \times 3)$ possible test cases given the corresponding input model extracted from the ontology and assuming strength 2.

Note that the test suite in Table 2 forms the domain for variables $s1$ and $s2$ of the $Word$ concept. Hence, we obtain the following CT input model M^{CT} for $Word$: $V^{CT}(Text) = \{s1, s2\}$, with $DOM^{CT}(s1) = DOM^{CT}(s2) = \{(\text{`word1'}, \text{`word2'}, \text{`?'}), (\text{`word1'}, \text{`word2'}, \text{`.'}), \ldots, (\epsilon, \text{`word3'}, \text{`?'}), \epsilon\}$ having 15 items from the test suite of $Sentence$ and additionally ϵ, and, $CONS^{CT}(Text) = \{s1 \neq \epsilon \vee s2 \neq \epsilon\}$. When using ACTS 3.1 and IPOG, we obtain 255 test cases for the concept $Text$ from this input model and combinatorial strength 2. Obviously, with the exception of one test case that would capture the case where both sentences are empty, this test suite comprises all possible elements. If we

Table 2. 2-way test suite for the instances $s1$, and $s2$ of concept *Sentence*

	$w1$	$w2$	d
1	'word1'	'word1'	'?'
2	'word1'	'word2'	'.'
3	'word1'	'word3'	'?'
4	'word1'	ϵ	'.'
5	'word2'	'word1'	'.'
6	'word2'	'word2'	'?'
7	'word2'	'word3'	'.'
8	'word2'	ϵ	'?'
9	'word3'	'word1'	'.'
10	'word3'	'word2'	'?'
11	'word3'	'word3'	'.'
12	'word3'	ϵ	'?'
13	ϵ	'word1'	'.'
14	ϵ	'word2'	'?'
15	ϵ	'word3'	'?'

would not restrict the number of instances for sentence to 2, we would be able to obtain fewer tests if the strength is less than the number of sentences.

From this case study we see that the proposed algorithm **TC_GEN** allows for obtaining combinatorial test suites from specified ontologies. It is obvious that the proposed algorithm can be easily improved avoiding unnecessary recursive calls. For this purpose, we need only to store the outcome of combinatorial testing for one concept whenever available and re-use it during the process. It is also worth mentioning that in the algorithm and the explanations we assume a certain amount of instances to be generated. This information might be given for each concept in the ontology. In addition, the algorithm does not specify any order in the sequence of attributes or instances. For example, in Table 2 we stated the order $w1$, $w2$ followed by d. Hence, for coming up with concrete test cases, we have to make use of such an order to obtain meaningful information to be used to stimulate the system under test.

6   Conclusions

In this paper, we introduced an algorithm that is able to obtain a combinatorial test suite for a given ontology. We discussed the basic foundations and outlined the basic principles behind the algorithm. In addition, we elaborate on a case study showing that the algorithm can be applied delivering combinatorial test suites. Furthermore, we discussed additional assumptions used in the case study and potential improvements of the algorithm, e.g., for avoiding the re-computation of test input models in a recursive algorithm call.

To the best of our knowledge the proposed algorithm is the first one allowing to obtain combinatorial test suites from ontologies that can also be applied to UML class diagrams. Previous research has mainly focused on obtaining combinatorial test suites from use cases, activity or sequence diagrams. Improvements might consider generating a CT input model for the root concept of an ontology via collecting all variables from their related concepts instead of obtaining domain information from those concepts. In future research, we will investigate in this direction and also provide an empirical evaluation with the purpose of showing the practicability of the proposed approach for practical applications and comparing different versions of test suite generation using ontologies and combinatorial testing. In particular, we will focus on the automated and autonomous driving domain where practitioners and researchers are currently working on ontologies describing driving scenarios.

Acknowledgment. The research was supported by ECSEL JU under the project H2020 737469 AutoDrive - Advancing fail-aware, fail-safe, and fail-operational electronic components, systems, and architectures for fully automated driving to make future mobility safer, affordable, and end-user acceptable. AutoDrive is funded by the Austrian Federal Ministry of Transport, Innovation and Technology (BMVIT) under the program "ICT of the Future" between May 2017 and April 2020. More information https://iktderzukunft.at/en/ bm◐ f .

References

1. Blomqvist, E., Seil Sepour, A., Presutti, V.: Ontology testing - methodology and tool. In: ten Teije, A. (ed.) EKAW 2012. LNCS (LNAI), vol. 7603, pp. 216–226. Springer, Heidelberg (2012). https://doi.org/10.1007/978-3-642-33876-2_20
2. Cohen, D.M., Dalal, S.R., Fredman, M.L., Patton, G.C.: The AETG system: an approach to testing based on combinatorial design. IEEE Trans. Softw. Eng. **23**(7), 437–444 (1997)
3. Feilmayr, C., Wöß, W.: An analysis of ontologies and their success factors for application to business. Data Knowl. Eng. **101**, 1–23 (2016). https://doi.org/10.1016/j.datak.2015.11.003
4. Hülsen, M., Zöllner, J.M., Weiss, C.: Traffic intersection situation description ontology for advanced driver assistance. In: 2011 IEEE Intelligent Vehicles Symposium (IV), pp. 993–999, June 2011. https://doi.org/10.1109/IVS.2011.5940415
5. Khalsa, S.K., Labiche, Y.: An orchestrated survey of available algorithms and tools for combinatorial testing. In: 25th International Symposium on Software Reliability Engineering, pp. 323–334 (2015)
6. Kuhn, D.R., Kacker, R.N., Lei, Y.: Combinatorial testing. In: Laplante, P.A. (ed.) Encyclopedia of Software Engineering. Taylor & Francis, Abingdon (2012)
7. Kuhn, D.R., Bryce, R., Duan, F., Ghandehari, L.S., Lei, Y., Kacker, R.N.: Combinatorial testing: theory and practice. Adv. Comput. **99**, 1–66 (2015)
8. Kuhn, R., Kacker, R., Lei, Y., Hunter, J.: Combinatorial software testing. Computer **42**, 94–96 (2009)
9. Kuhn, R., Kacker, R., Lei, Y.: Practical combinatorial testing. Technical report 800–142, NIST Special Publication (NIST SP), 100 Bureau Drive, Gaithersburg, MD 20899, USA, October 2010

10. Li, H., Guo, H., Chen, F., Yang, H., Yang, Y.: Using ontology to generate test cases for GUI testing. Int. J. Comput. Appl. Technol. **42**(2/3), 213–224 (2011)
11. Li, R., Ma, S.: The implementation of user interface autogenerate for spacecraft automatic tests based on ontology. In: 12th International Conference on Fuzzy Systems and Knowledge Discovery, pp. 2676–2681 (2015)
12. Moser, T., Dürr, G., Biffl, S.: Ontology-based test case generation for simulating complex production automation systems. In: 22nd International Conference on Software Engineering and Knowledge Engineering, pp. 478–483 (2010)
13. Naseer, H., Rauf, A.: Validation of ontology based test case generation for graphical user interface. In: 15th International Multitopic Conference (2012)
14. Nasser, V.H.: Ontology-based unit test generation. Master's thesis, Amirkabir University of Technology (2007)
15. Nguyen, C.D., Perini, A., Tonella, P.: Ontology-based test generation for multiagent systems. In: 7th International Conference on Autonomous Agents and Multi-agent Systems, pp. 1315–1318, May 2008
16. Nie, C., Leung, H.: A survey of combinatorial testing. ACM Comput. Surv. **43**(2), 11 (2011)
17. Regele, R.: Using ontology-based traffic models for more efficient decision making of autonomous vehicles. In: Fourth International Conference on Autonomic and Autonomous Systems (ICAS 2008), pp. 94–99, March 2008. https://doi.org/10.1109/ICAS.2008.10
18. Satish, P., Basavaraja, M., Narayan, M.S., Rangarajan, K.: Building combinatorial test input model from use case artefacts. In: 10th IEEE International Conference on Software Testing, Verification and Validation Workshops, pp. 220–228 (2017)
19. Satish, P., Paul, A., Rangarajan, K.: Extracting the combinatorial test parameters and values from UML sequence diagrams. In: 7th IEEE International Conference on Software Testing, Verification, and Validation Workshops, pp. 88–97 (2014)
20. Satish, P., Sheeba, K., Rangarajan, K.: Deriving combinatorial test design model from UML activity diagram. In: 6th IEEE International Conference on Software Testing, Verification and Validation Workshops, pp. 331–337 (2013)
21. Schlenoff, C., Balakirsky, S., Uschold, M., Provine, R., Smith, S.: Using ontologies to aid navigation planning in autonomous vehicles. Knowl. Eng. Rev. **18**(3), 243–255 (2003). https://doi.org/10.1017/S0269888904000050
22. Souza, E.F., Falbo, R.A., Vijaykumar, N.L.: Using ontology patterns for building a reference software testing ontology. In: 17th IEEE International Enterprise Distributed Object Computing Conference Workshops, pp. 21–30 (2013)
23. de Souza, E.F.: Knowledge management applied to software testing: an ontology based framework. Ph.D. thesis, National Institute for Space Research (2014)
24. Tai, K., Lei, Y.: A test generation strategy for pairwise testing. IEEE Trans. Softw. Eng. **28**(1), 109–111 (2002)
25. Vasanthapriyan, S., Tian, J., Zhao, D., Xiong, S., Xiang, J.: An ontology-based knowledge sharing portal for software testing. In: 17th IEEE International Conference on Software Quality, Reliability and Security (Companion Volume), pp. 472–479 (2017)
26. Yu, L., Lei, Y., Kacker, R., Kuhn, D.: ACTS: a combinatorial test generation tool. In: 2013 IEEE Sixth International Conference on Software Testing, Verification and Validation (ICST), pp. 370–375 (2013)

Author Index

Arcaini, Paolo   1
Avellaneda, Florent   119

Berriri, Asma   69
Blot, Elliott   142
Bonfanti, Silvia   17
Börding, Paul   39
Bozic, Josip   33

Cárdenas, Marlon   56

De Busser, Seph   102
Demeyer, Serge   102
Desai, Nisha   62

El-Fakih, Khaled   85, 149

Gargantini, Angelo   1, 17
Gogolla, Martin   62

Haltermann, Jan   39
Higashino, Teruo   85

Jakobs, Marie-Christine   39

Kushik, Natalia   69

Laurencot, Patrice   142
Li, Yihao   155
López, Jorge   69

Mashkoor, Atif   17
Mizumoto, Teruhiro   85

Parsai, Ali   102
Pavón, Juan   56
Petrenko, Alexandre   119
Prasetya, I. S. Wishnu B.   135

Riccobene, Elvinia   1

Salva, Sébastien   142
Sanz, Jorge Gómez   56

Tran, Minh An   135
Tvardovskii, Aleksandr   149

Wehrheim, Heike   39
Wotawa, Franz   33, 155

Yasumoto, Keiichi   85
Yevtushenko, Nina   69, 149

Zeghlache, Djamal   69

Printed in the United States
By Bookmasters